beautiful
ashes

Lauralee —
Thank you for your
support! Shelly

A True Story of Murder, Betrayal,
and One Woman's Search for Peace

beautiful
ashes

shelly edwards jorgensen

Cover design by MiblArt
Author bio photo by Hannah Shurtleff
Interior print design and layout by Sydnee Hyer
Ebook design and layout by Sydnee Hyer

Published by The Edgeworth Group LLC

Paperback ISBN: 979-8-9850120-0-2
eBook ISBN: 979-8-9850120-1-9

To my amazing and loving mother, who sacrificed all she had to support me in my life goals. Mom, you inspired me to write this book to help others overcome the adversity in their lives. I love and miss you more than words can even describe!

Chapter One

October 14, 1985

I'd pretended to be an ordinary girl for as long as I could remember, and no one knew the truth. They assumed a fifteen-year-old knew nothing helpful and had detained me in a neighboring home—out of their way and safe from the fire raging through my family's estate. Though I hadn't seen the flames, smoke lingered on the cops and neighbors who'd come inside from the cold. That odor fed the smoldering doubt churning in my chest and made breathing difficult.

I tried to extinguish my suffocating anxiety, but my suspicions of my father's involvement and my concern for my missing mother only grew during the four hours they fought the fire. Shortly before nine that evening, a heavy-coated policeman came bustling in to tell Dad that the flames had at last been extinguished. The cop said nothing of finding Mom. So, terrified of being right, I decided to find her myself.

I'd played for hours as a child in the Zajdel's house, the same house that now confined me, and I remembered that the home's main-floor bathroom occupied the same hallway as the door to their garage. No one guarded the bathroom, or the garage, as everyone was in and out the front door.

The middle-aged cop assigned to secure my father's and my whereabouts had been perched at the kitchen bar overlooking the family room for as long as I had sat in my corner. Bright-eyed and talkative at first, his chin now rested in his hand. His half-closed eyes were weary with waiting. My escape plan was so simple it was irresistible.

He watched my slight form stand and draw near.

"Uh, hey. Can I use the bathroom?" I said, making a face. I placed a hand over my stomach.

The aching in my bowels was real enough—it just had nothing to do with digestion. A typical teenage girl would have become hysterical at finding her mother missing during a house fire and made herself the center of attention. But I'd been a quiet and ideal inmate, and if I'd learned anything in my turbulent, short life, it was that most adults failed to suspect well-behaved kids of deceit.

I banked on this cop having no problem with my request.

My question roused the drowsy detective, who yawned and stretched before studying my face. A spark of fear struck my heart that he would discern my real intentions. My face tightened at the sight of the hallway entrance beyond him. Luckily, the subtle betrayal of my emotions seemed to enhance my deception despite the real source. The cop nodded and looked around, waving me past. His bored expression returned.

My heart raced as the second phase of my plan unfolded. Unobserved in the hallway, I reached inside the bathroom and turned on its fan and lights. Closing the door with a soft click and a glance over my shoulder, I prayed the ruse would last long enough. I slipped unseen out the garage entry door at the end of the short hall. The buzz of voices from inside hushed with the sweep of the heavy door's closing.

The smell of leaked oil, bagged leaves, and musty grass clippings floated on the stale, cool air. Directly across the dark space, feeble light filtered through dusty curtains covering a small-paned window in the garage's side door. Not knowing how long I had, I didn't wait for my eyes to adjust.

Hands out, I felt my way past car bumpers and bikes—silently cursing when my shin hit a pedal.

Having crossed the garage, I found the doorknob and twisted. The wood door swung inward with a click. A sharp Michigan gale whipped my short brown locks as I stood on the threshold of freedom. I shivered in my thin polyester basketball jersey and shorts and realized my one miscalculation: night had fallen, and with it, the temperature.

I crossed my arms tightly against my chest and half turned in debate. I could have returned to snatch a warm coat from the hall closet, but voices on the cold wind caught my ear and spurred my decision to plunge into the frosty night without delay. Arms pumping, I fell into a headlong sprint toward the muffled shouts.

Moonlight lit the lot immediately adjacent to my family's estate—the lot between the Zajdel's home and ours. We'd lived beside the Owens for a dozen years, but their heavily wooded two-hundred-foot frontage had never seemed so expansive and hazardous. I avoided the small patches of illuminated ground, sticking to the shadows provided by a rippling canopy of dry leaves above me. In weeks, those same leaves would carpet the sweeping paths I now made beneath the maple and birch.

The border between the Owens' home and ours was marked by a row of towering pines. As I approached the group of dense giants, I was so preoccupied with remaining unseen that I didn't realize until I reached them that I could go no further. The twenty yards between me and my home teemed with movement.

I hid beneath a particularly thick white pine immediately to my left with a sweeping skirt of boughs that touched the ground. The conifer's lowest branches had been trimmed, creating a small space about a meter high surrounding the trunk. Water had beaded on its needles, a byproduct of the thousands of gallons of water being sprayed just feet away. Drops covered me from head to toe as I fell to my knees and crawled inside the pine's girth.

Though the branches buffered the wind a bit, I now felt a thousand times colder concealed beneath the damp tree. I sat and pulled my legs in for warmth, rubbing hard at the goose bumps on my arms. I regretted not returning for a coat but remained to survey the scene before me.

Huge spotlights infused the air with thrumming light. Washed out by thousands of watts, our house shone in stark relief against an acre of dark lawn and black sky. Its windows gaped with broken shards. Stain-soaked drapes hung halfway out. Upended, dripping furniture covered the sloping yard, which stretched to our meandering stream in back. Steel-and-spring skeletons bobbed on the backs of yellow-clad firefighters carting more things outside. Flattened hoses snaked across a field of charred and wet possessions.

I recognized the table I had set my geometry book on after school. It lay upside down in the flower bed outside the front door. Its black wrought-iron legs stuck out at odd angles in the air. I closed my eyes, remembering Mom's face above mine at the table that afternoon as she took a drag from her cigarette. She had been helping me study before I left for basketball. How had everything gone to hell in mere minutes?

I had been at practice for less than an hour when my coach called for a water break. Heading to the water fountain in the hallway outside Farmington High School's gym, I had rounded a blind corner and almost been clotheslined by someone running the opposite way. I'd stumbled back and begun to apologize before I realized that my unintentional assailant was my neighborhood friend Carolyn Zajdel. My smile of recognition had faded at the horror in her eyes.

"Your house—it's on fire."

Her words had been incomprehensible. I'd repeated what she'd said.

"My house is on fire?"

Several teammates running past had gasped, but Carolyn ignored them and nodded.

Then I understood, and a terrible foreboding had lodged in my chest and not left since.

Carolyn had waited while I ran back to the gymnasium to get my sister, Lisa. But she and Lisa had struggled to catch up with me as I sprinted down the tiled hallway in the direction Carolyn had come from. My heart rate had outpaced their pounding feet.

Carolyn's mother, Mrs. Zajdel, had her station wagon rolling backward before we were entirely inside. We had shut our doors while she shifted into drive and then listened to her describe the chaos at home as she ripped out of the parking lot, tires squealing.

Even with her report, the scene before me was worse than I'd imagined.

I surveyed the fire's handiwork. There were numerous entry points. Every window on the first floor was smashed. Judging from the blackened window frames and charred remains of furniture, the interior had been devoured.

The flames had been doused, but the air remained hazy. Local news vans parked beyond flashing police cruisers on the other side of the house. Two reporters still rolled tape, interviewing onlookers. Detectives wearing bright police vests over navy suits splashed through puddles. I realized with a rising sense of panic that the whole area was under heavy surveillance.

I lacked my sister's intuition for precarious situations. Lisa had always known what to do in a crisis. God knows we'd had plenty enough to make her adept—though nothing this bad. But our current separation left me disadvantaged.

I swore silently at the crowd milling around the house. I'd thought that with the fire out, it'd be quieter. All day, I'd been a step too slow, and events had overtaken me.

I had no idea what to do next, and even fleeing my captors was merely copying my sister. Lisa had escaped before I even realized we needed to.

When Mrs. Zajdel had turned her car into their driveway that afternoon, my sister had been way ahead of me. While I'd merely gaped at the billowing smoke filling the skyline above the trees and wondered for the first time if I'd be able to get inside the house, Lisa had bolted from the back seat before the car stopped rolling.

At first, everyone had been too stunned to react. We'd all stared as her flying form made a beeline toward our property.

"Dear God!" Mrs. Zajdel had exclaimed, stomping on the brakes.

Eyes on my sister, I'd recognized her brilliance. I had opened my door as Lisa sprinted past police cars blocking the road. Beyond them were fire trucks and trees and smoke. I hadn't been able to see the house or flames.

She passed the trucks. Others had moved to intercept her then, but Lisa smacked away their outreached hands. Watching the adults' determined faces, I'd understood that my sister had the right idea. I'd slammed my own door and circled the car.

Lisa had made it several hundred feet from me and onto the front lawn of our estate.

I had just tensed to spring forward when someone caught hold of my basketball jersey from behind. I'd not made it past the edge of the concrete driveway.

"No!" I cried in frustration.

I turned to discover Carolyn's mother.

"But my mom!" I cried.

Mrs. Zajdel maintained her iron grip but failed to meet my eyes.

"You can't go. It's not safe," she said.

She swung me around and pushed me toward their house as if it were for my own good. I cussed but didn't fight. Carolyn silently followed us.

Looking over my shoulder, I'd strained to see between the trees as Mrs. Zajdel dragged me inside. I'd caught glimpses of Lisa's desperate attempts to break past a wall of uniforms that had suddenly formed in her path. Her blue Farmington Falcons jersey had bounced off the yellow-and-blue uniforms in a merciless version of Red Rover. Before I could see who won, Mrs. Zajdel had shut the door.

They'd separated us. From what I'd heard, Lisa had to be forcibly restrained at the Owens' home.

I turned my head and studied the house whose shadowed yard I'd just run through. No one appeared to be in the front rooms, but soft light filtered into the front entry. They'd probably kept her in the back of the house, so she couldn't see our home—like how I'd been held at the Zajdel's.

To a degree, the grownups were correct—we were more formidable together.

Their mistake was underestimating how desperate I'd become when Lisa's preemptive tactics had spectacularly failed and I realized they had no intention of letting me out to help find Mom. I was quieter than my sister but no less determined.

I squinted past the glaring lights and into the yards behind and beyond my house. Maybe if I circled our estate boundaries, I could find a better angle to approach. There had to be a way inside our house. It would just take me longer than my sister to find it. I got onto my hands and feet, anxious to move once more.

Just then, a firefighter headed in my direction, pulling hose. Startled, I backed up until the pine trunk's rough, knobby bark stopped my retreat. Its solid mass anchored my thoughts. Patience had given me my first opening. I had to be patient still. If I held it together long enough, an opening would appear. Long minutes passed. I shivered. The chilly air numbed my extremities by degrees. Flexing my fingers, I shifted in my crouch and watched. I mentally rehearsed what I knew.

Though my father had asked Mrs. Zajdel to pick up my sister and me from basketball practice, he ignored us after we arrived. I had heard his story through eavesdropping, which wasn't difficult considering Dad's volume.

My father had gone shopping. At least, that is what he repeated to cops with Steno pads and the neighbors who filled the Zajdel's house. I had watched from across the Zajdel's family room while he explained how he'd found our sprawling home in flames upon returning from the hardware store. He said he'd tried to extinguish the fire with a garden hose. Through narrowed eyes, I'd studied him. His khaki pants were pressed but smudged, and his dark, unbuttoned polo had come untucked as he pantomimed his attempts to enter the house.

I observed that despite Mom's continued absence, only once did I hear him mention her, and only in passing to Mrs. Zajdel's cautious inquiry: "Have you heard from Marlene?"

"She probably went to Joan's," Dad had replied.

Mrs. Zajdel had pressed her lips together and nodded before glancing at me.

Everyone knew Mom and Joan were best friends, and Joan lived the next street over. But I had looked out the window and clenched my hands at my sides. I knew in a crisis like this, my mother would have moved heaven and earth to find us if she could.

My heart had raced with the need to find her. I knew Mom had been home before basketball practice. I had left her alone—with Dad.

Mary, Holy Mother of Jesus, let her be safe. I lacked a rosary, but my fingers had worked against my palms, needing something to do. I had lost count of the repetitions.

When Joan had shown up looking for Mom, Dad's shrug filled my soul with terror.

Now, freezing under the tree, I was suddenly snapped to the present. The pandemonium and movement had ceased. In the space of one breath, a hundred unblinking eyes turned and regarded the front door. I saw faces go slack in shock, but a fire engine in the driveway blocked my view. I was forced to crawl forward on all fours, almost breaching the needled skirt to see past the truck.

From my new vantage point, I saw sooty firefighters shuffle down the porch steps, a stretcher between them. They set it down, then turned it to roll across the driveway. They moved as a group, trying to give whoever occupied the stretcher some privacy, but it could only be my mother. A chance glimpse checked my instinct to run to her.

The sight of the black body bag on the stretcher struck me with physical force, and I froze in disbelief. My eyes saw everything, but my mind grasped at trivial details to avoid facing the reality of the stretcher's cargo. I heard the crunch of the stretcher's wheels on the gravel and then a police dispatcher on a nearby squad car's radio, though the urgent message was lost on me. I wondered why the owner had left his windows rolled down on such a cold night.

The smack of the stretcher's frame as it hit the ambulance deck startled me. I looked back to the yellow firefighters. Their bright hat straps swung in tandem as they heaved the stretcher, the wheels snaping up under as it slid inside the ambulance with a rasping sound. The doors thumped closed. The quiet ambulance disappeared down the street. The crowd's volume increased exponentially, the previous reverence gone with the body bag.

Pain stung my chest and broke my trance. I had stopped breathing. Gulping, I inhaled the ashy air. I coughed, gagging. I clamped hands over my mouth, terrified of being discovered and suddenly regretting my brilliant breakout. I breathed through my nose, holding in my cough. My eyes watered.

I needed to get back. I pushed onto my heels and scrambled beneath the tree. I trembled and wiped my face with a dirty palm. Cold pain seeped into my mind. My heart seemed to briefly stop as the anxiety in my chest reached a crescendo. I exploded from underneath the tree, sprinting back toward the Zajdel's home and away from the shell of mine.

I ran as if pursued, though no one spotted me. Laces flying, arms pumping, I stumbled over a tree root but caught myself with one hand on the hard ground. For a moment I paused, and my shoulders caved inward as a scream of grief caught in my throat. No, it was impossible. Not her. I choked it down and started running again, convincing myself I hadn't seen anything. Not really. I didn't know the bag's contents.

At the corner of Carolyn's house, I slowed in the dark. My gut churned with hot nausea, but my flesh was frozen. I couldn't feel my expression. I knew one thing only. I couldn't let the horror in my heart show on my face. I buried what I had seen down deep. I just felt cold. I focused on the cold. I tried to breathe slower.

I heard voices and looked up. Through the shifting shadows near the street, two police officers headed toward the Zajdel's. Hurrying, I crept through the side yard and slipped inside the still unlocked side door of the garage. Feeling my way to the interior entry door, I cracked it open and spied down the small hallway. All clear. Inside again, I slipped into the Zajdel's bathroom and buried my face in a hand towel to cover my gasping. My hands started to throb. I ran warm water over them, but that made the burning worse. I splashed my face and used another towel to dry it. I flushed the empty toilet.

I searched my reflection framed above the sink. My bright-pink skin had faded to pale shock. Fifteen minutes earlier, I had wanted nothing but to escape. Now I wished with all my heart I hadn't. The household was still muted, unaffected, unaware of the altered girl in the bathroom. My eyes could never unsee what my heart refused to acknowledge. It was impossible to think I could calmly leave that bathroom and still pretend everything was okay, and, yet, I opened the door. Splintered between what I'd seen and how I needed to appear, I walked through the kitchen, following two policemen passing through. The faint aromas of gasoline and smoke drifted around me. I hoped it was the cops and not me.

My sister's presence on the couch surprised me, but I said nothing. Neither did she. I sank into the cushions beside her. I stared at my still damp hands. They trembled. I crossed my legs and stuck both hands between my thighs. We sat, side by side, for about ten minutes. I studied the carpet.

My heartbeat refused to slow.

I closed my eyes and lay back against the couch cushions. I pretended to sleep but could only replay the drive home from practice. One moment in particular stuck out now. Lisa had sung along with the chorus of a newer song playing on the radio. Ironically, the lyrics had talked of a housetop on fire. They had amused Lisa but horrified me.

I hadn't known anything then, not for sure, but Lisa had missed Carolyn's guarded, inquiring gaze at her mother. Mrs. Zajdel had shaken her head, the slightest movement, at Carolyn. It was the head shake that struck me then and now.

I had pinched Lisa, low and hard.

Wounded, she had made a face and hissed, "What?"

Watching Mrs. Zajdel's eyes in the rearview mirror, I had made sure she wasn't looking when I whispered, "Mom was home when I left."

Lisa had stopped singing.

Now, even a whisper was beyond me.

I found out later that Mrs. Zajdel had seen my mother's car in the garage before she'd picked us up. As a mom, she felt the same feelings I did in that moment on the couch with Lisa. She'd wanted us to have a few precious last moments of not knowing. Like her, I couldn't bear to tell Lisa what I'd seen as she'd chatted with neighborhood friends.

Panic and grief threatened to escape through the tiniest shift in the stony composure I hid behind. I gritted my teeth. A lone shudder escaped. Lisa looked at me, but I clamped down on my self-possession again. Maybe if I waited long enough, I'd never have to say it.

"Could we have a minute with the Edwards family?" The two officers I had followed in stood shoulder to shoulder in the doorway.

The room cleared. I cautiously looked at Dad. His detached demeanor throughout the entire night had been my single sliver of hope. He'd been the last one home. If anyone should be worried, it'd be him. Yet, as he sat to one side of the couch in a recliner, his expression was interested but not overly concerned.

Perhaps there were other explanations for the ominous-looking bag. It had appeared mostly empty anyways. Surely a body couldn't occupy so little space. I had jumped to conclusions too fast. For the first time in thirty minutes, my heart rate began to slow. I was taking things too far, imagining things. Everything would be all right.

The taller policeman cleared his throat.

"I am Detective Paul Brown. I am deeply sorry to tell you . . . we found the body of your wife and mother in the house." He spoke softly. "We have sent the remains for an autopsy to determine the exact cause of death."

I flinched. Despite having just seen the body bag, I began shaking from my hands to my entire body. When you understand that the awful things that happen to other people can, in fact, happen to you and just did, your life as you know it ends. My life had ended.

Lisa leapt to her feet.

"How am I supposed to graduate?" she yelled at the detective.

He looked down, not responding. She turned to me. Her white face reflected the same bewilderment I felt—which had nothing to do with high school graduation. Mom's death was impossibly wrong. This was never supposed to happen.

Lisa covered her mouth, but a wail found its way past her hand. I shrank into my seat and hid my face in my arms. Her footsteps pounded out the front door, her shriek receding.

An empty nothingness stretched on inside me. Seconds slid by until the scene from under the tree struck me. Crushed me. Gurney wheels rattling on gravel echoed in my ears.

Anger exploded in my chest. Stinging, hot grief coursed down my cheeks.

I had left her alone.

Mom was dead, and I knew who was responsible.

I was. I had known the truth since I was four.

January 1974

My parents were late picking us up, and my father's parents were weary after a long weekend of babysitting my sister and me. As Sunday afternoon turned to evening, they'd lost patience and let us watch enough TV to rot our brains and served us big bowls of ice cream swimming in crème de menthe liquor to quiet us.

Finally, hours past bedtime, Grandma Edwards looked at the clock and then at my grandfather's face. He nodded at her unspoken decision. She wiped my face, then Lisa's, with a damp dishrag. "Time for bed."

Six-year-old Lisa frowned. "But, Grandma, I want to wait for Mommy."

I agreed. "Me too!"

Our grandfather (whom we called "Papa") tossed me over his shoulder, prompting a squeal of glee from me. Lisa continued pouting as he led us into the first-floor bedroom adjoining theirs. I climbed into bed with Lisa. Grandma kissed the air above my face with a whisper of affection

"Good night, Shelly," she said.

"G'night." I was certain I wasn't tired, but in moments, the dreamy warmth of booze and sugar pulled me under. I slept deeply.

Later, I awoke upright and confused. My feet stumbled while Papa half carried me down the hallway, his hand supporting my arm.

"Wait," I said and pulled against his tugging. "What—"

"Girls, it's time to go." My father's baritone sounded from the alcove near the door. I trotted the rest of the way unaided. Mom held our coats, giving Dad mine when my sister and I appeared. He crouched, helping me button it. His cold clothes smelled damp, but his breath was warm. Coat on, I held my arms up to him. He gathered me into his embrace, and I snuggled into his neck, which smelled of Hugo.

Grandma now appeared with her hands full, stuffing things into our overnight bags. She stopped midmotion and stared at my mother. I followed her gaze, studying Mom's gray knit hat with pom-pom bouncing on top, plaid scarf, gray tweed coat . . . and sunglasses.

My eyes flitted to the front door. Its thick strip of bubbled glass reflected the foyer's pendant light against a backdrop of black—still nighttime. I examined my mother's face again. This time I noticed a raised bruise across her cheekbone beneath the wide brown frames. I winced. Whatever had made the purple bump had hurt a lot.

I looked at Lisa. She stood beside Mom, rocking on her feet, watching Grandma. Lisa looked at Dad, then Grandma again. I looked back at my grandmother's troubled face. As the youngest, I often felt I missed things, but until that moment, it hadn't seemed too significant. I wanted to understand what made everyone else so uncomfortable about my mother's face.

Mom smiled and lifted a hand toward the porch. "Oh, those icy steps out front . . . I fell leaving Friday. It's nothing, Mom."

Grandma finished zipping my bag in silence.

Mom waved her hand in front of her face as if batting away an annoying fly. "I'm fine."

With that, the moment passed. Papa took our bags from Grandma and handed them to Mom. Still holding me, Dad opened the front door and stepped into the darkness.

"Thanks again for watching the girls," he said.

I looked back as Dad carried me down the steep stairs. Mom followed, holding Lisa's hand and our bags. Grandma stood looking out the door, warm air escaping past her into the frosty night. I waved my fingers, but she didn't notice.

Our parents set us in the back seat of the still-running car, and we drove away in tense silence. I watched streetlights run across Mom's face. At home, Dad slipped into the kitchen.

"Up to bed," Mom said.

Lisa and I ran up the winding stairway, our footsteps echoing in the two-story foyer.

"Wait, did you brush your teeth at Grandma's?" Mom called as she hung our coats. We stopped at the top and looked down, shaking our heads.

"Do it now," she said.

I finished first. I slammed my faucet off and wiped my foamy mouth on my sleeve before dashing down the hall to Mom's room.

Mom smoked a Benson & Hedges Gold in her bedside chair, sunglasses removed. I approached, observing how her fat eyelid, pink above the swollen cheekbone, drooped over a crimson smear staining the white of that eye. Her face looked awful.

"I love you, Mommy," I said, putting my arms around her neck and tucking my face into her scarf. L'Air du Temps filtered through the nicotine haze.

"Love you too, Shelly-belly." She used my father's nickname for me and wrapped an arm around my waist.

I made the first intuitive connection of my life. It altered my world. Dad had a temper. Mom hadn't fallen. He had hurt her. Mom had lied. My mind exploded with questions: Are adults allowed to lie? Why would she lie about getting hurt? I understood my motivations for lying at four. I was almost always frightened I'd be in worse trouble for telling the truth.

Mom was scared. The only answer for her fear was my father. She had lied because she was scared. The mooring of my childhood, my mother's infallibility, broke free in that moment. There would never be another day in my childhood where I felt safe in her care. If Mom was scared, so was I.

She kissed my static-charged mane.

"Now, go to bed." She bent over, setting my feet on the ground.

I lay awake, holding my dolls. I fell asleep, listening for the first time. He had hurt her.

I had left her alone. Guilt eventually choked my grief silent. Dad remained in the Zajdel's recliner, his arms clasped in a prayerful grip. I searched his face. His sorrow could confirm it was a horrible accident—that I needn't blame myself or accept the guilt poised to strangle me.

Dad returned my gaze for the barest moment and stood. His expression was blank. His eyes were dry. A wave of guilt pushed me so far under I went numb. I rose. He was leaving, and I didn't want to be left alone. I followed him. He rubbed a hand across his eyes and approached the policemen. I followed. The younger one, Detective Brown, focused on me. Hat in one hand, he somehow produced a tissue with the other. I used it to scrape the salt off my cheeks.

"What was the condition of her body? What happened?" Dad asked.

The young officer gave me a sad smile and looked away. "I don't know," he said at last. Lies were sometimes the kindest part of my life.

Dad led me outside. Our neighborhood friends surrounded Lisa on the sidewalk, arms around shoulders. Dad stopped on the porch, watching Lisa and our friends shed tears he couldn't. I shivered beside him.

"Oh, poor thing." Mrs. Zajdel had noticed. She ran inside and returned with one of Carolyn's coats. "Here, put this on."

I protested, but she draped it over my shoulders.

Dad made a sound to get Lisa's attention.

Lisa broke from the huddle. Head down, she climbed the porch steps. Dad pulled us both into a hug. Neighbors huddled in small groups across the lawn and sidewalk looked at the ground in silence. Mrs. Zajdel wiped absently at her wet cheeks.

"We lost everything." Dad spoke in a hoarse voice. "The house is gone . . ."

Lisa and I patted his back. My heart sank and grew cold with certainty.

"And your mom," he paused again. "It's more than . . ."

He lay his head on mine and stopped speaking.

"It will be okay." My false words excavated any sense of wholeness that might have been left in my soul. There was nothing normal or acceptable about your mother dying in a fire. Less normal was my father's reaction.

Part of me wanted to scream accusations at Dad. The other half wished for consolation in our shared grief. Instead, Dad executed a performance that cut my soul in two. With an audience, he required me to act as usual.

My role was to comfort him as the endearing daughter.

I consoled myself that I knew nothing for sure. There was a tiny space, an hour of ignorance, where I hadn't been home. That seminal hour held my only hope of salvaging our family. If I could believe my father's story, we could survive this. His dry eyes had to be from shock and not relief. His detached manner was from panic, not cold calculation. The one benefit of self-deception was that it acted as an emotional anesthetic. I should have been throbbing with pain, but I had become an empty shell.

I wasn't the only one. Lisa looked over at me, pupils wide and black with grief. "Dad," she said, "it's all right." We exchanged a desperate glance, knowing it would never be all right again.

We lied to survive. The fire's flames had taken my mother but hadn't touched our family's primary tenet: appearances at all costs. If I stopped lying, my life would unravel.

Chapter Two

October 14, 1985

We traveled in censored silence to the house of my father's brother late that night. In the back seat, I shivered until my whole body ached. As I held a hand near the vent blowing hot air, it occurred to me that I shook with shock, not cold. All the world's warmth had dissipated at the sight of that body bag.

We parked on the street in front of my uncle Bob and aunt Diane's 1950s ranch in Southfield. I got out and stood, staring at the familiar brick and shutters. My life had been transformed—my mother had perished, my childhood home still smoldered, and I was completely undone—yet here their quiet house stood untouched. I resented it, feeling that the entire world should have changed, not just mine.

I wrapped my arms around my body and hurried behind Lisa to catch up to Dad, who was already on the doorstep.

Uncle Bob swung open the door and greeted us, "Arnie! Come in!"

Aunt Diane jumped up from the recliner and embraced us. I pulled away before taking an afghan off the couch to curl up in. The TV screen lit the cramped front room. All the local channels showed footage of our fire during the eleven o'clock news. The adults watched intently, my father swearing.

"Look at that! Hell, the entire inside must be gone." He folded his arms tightly and rocked on his feet.

White-hot flames leapt eight feet from the house, blazing through windows like a rocket launch. *They were filming as she burned?* I started shaking again as we watched Mom's death replayed. Of course, the footage panned only the exterior, but my imagination filled in the rest. I dug my fingers into the afghan's weave as her screams pierced my mind.

"The fire claimed the life of fifty-year-old Marlene Edwards, a mother of two from Farmington Hills . . . Police are calling it suspicious," Joe Glover reported.

Suspicious. The word stopped my heart. I covered a shudder by yawning.

"Can I go to bed?" I asked.

Aunt Diane led me to a small back room with a double bed. She handed me a large men's T-shirt from a drawer. Though clean, it had small flecks of various shades of dried beige paint because Uncle Bob worked for a small painting company.

I nodded. "Thanks."

My aunt gave another shirt to Lisa, who had followed us. Aunt Diane shut the door behind her, and Lisa and I were alone for the first time that night. I sat on the bed with my back to Lisa. There was so much I could have said but nothing I wanted to say. The room was silent, but we could hear the television through the thin walls.

I bent to untie the laces of my basketball shoes and smelled a whiff of smoke. I lifted my jersey to my face. It reeked of sweat, fire, and pain. I kicked off my shoes and stripped down to my underwear before pulling the clean tee over my head. I stuffed the stinky clothes in a ball under the bed with my high-top sneakers.

Dad's cursing penetrated the closed door. I pulled the blankets to my chin and lay on my side, hands over my ears. Two hours later, the floors creaked as the adults went to bed. I sighed and waited for sleep's merciful oblivion. It never came.

In desperation I prayed, "God, make this a dream. Let her wake me up in the morning."

Eventually, compassionless rays of sun brightened the small window. My nightmare appeared even more hideous in the daylight. I pushed my blankets aside and swung my feet to the floor. Remembering I was bottomless, I reluctantly retrieved my smelly shorts and snuck a peek at Lisa. Her purple eyelids were swollen, and she was unconscious. Though she had probably cried herself to sleep, I was jealous she had found oblivion. I wandered out.

A bowl of fruit in the kitchen reminded me I'd missed dinner the night before. I didn't feel hungry but supposed I should eat anyways. I peeled a banana and took a bite. Though I loved bananas, the texture and smell gagged me. Unable to swallow, I spit the mouthful into the garbage. I cut off the bitten portion and left the rest on the counter, then sat at the table and tried not to think. The house stayed quiet for some time.

Dad appeared. He dug in the refrigerator, emerging with eggs. "You want one?"

I shook my head no and wandered into the front room. Lisa came out and sat opposite me on the couch. She turned morning cartoons on, and we watched in silence until a news program started. I turned it off.

Aunt Diane entered. "You need something to wear." She looked at her watch. "Paula can drop you two off at the mall. You should get funeral outfits too."

I didn't move. Though her tone was benevolent, Diane might as well have slapped me. I could tell she thought it a huge favor to ask my cousin to drop us off at the mall—as if we wanted to hang out. Instead, she was getting rid of us, pushing us out the door to shop for funeral clothes alone.

"Shelly," Lisa stood with deep resignation in her eyes.

A cry of rebellion echoed throughout my raw soul. I'd spent my life masking my pain. Last night, the film had rolled while the façade came crumbling down in a heap of ashes. *Suspicious loss.* Those words were tattooed all over my soul.

Dad handed Lisa a credit card. I wanted to hide, not go on a shopping spree.

"Go with your sister," he ordered.

I hesitated. He watched me waver and pointed at me, then at the door. Rebellion melted into resignation. I wouldn't defy him. His wrath was worse than gawking strangers.

Outside Twelve Oaks Mall in Novi, Lisa walked ahead, hands stuffed in a borrowed sweatshirt's pockets. She swung the tall glass entry door open. My reflection startled me: unwashed hair; no makeup; baggy, borrowed sweats; and angry eyes. My mother had unfailingly given us the once-over before heading out the door. She'd never have let me leave the house in such a state. Look at me without her. Embarrassment flushed my cheeks, then grief pinned my feet to the ground. How could I care about looks or anything else? Mom died. Yesterday. Did anything else matter? I looked down at my basketball shoes.

Who goes shopping the day after their mom dies? I became angry again.

Lisa grew impatient. "C'mon."

And that was it. I pretended to be normal. I used anger to barricade my grief so I could walk inside just like any other moody teenager with their dad's credit card. I returned others' glances with glares. I didn't deserve to grieve, anyway, not when my phone call had brought Mom home just in time for the fire. No one except me knew how I'd left her to die.

We finished in twenty minutes. The day had started horribly, and it only got worse.

Chapter Three

October 15, 1985

At police headquarters, the young detective from the night before, Detective Brown, led me upstairs to a conference room. I was anxious already, but when my dad's attorney followed us into the room, my heart rate picked up. Though Lisa and Dad were also being interviewed right then, Neal Simpson had accompanied me.

I tried to not look at Simpson, afraid he'd see my fear. The lawyer perched on a desk pushed into a corner to my right. I was grateful for the noisy heater that surely covered my pounding pulse. The air smelled of stale cigarette smoke and coffee, though none were evident in the room. In front of me was a long table with manila folders and another cop, hands in his pockets. I swallowed.

Detective Brown introduced his partner. "This is Detective Keller."

Detective Keller shook my hand and motioned for me to take a seat. The detectives took seats opposite me. I squeezed my hands together under the table and tried to breathe normally. I feared these men for different reasons, but the response they all elicited was the same. I wanted to run. There was too much I didn't understand. Too much had happened the day before. I didn't know what mattered and what didn't. I had to guard my words and not be stupid.

Detective Keller began with facts I could recall.

Yes, I had been home just before the fire broke out.

Yes, both my parents had been there when I left.

No, they weren't fighting.

Yeah, Mom was smoking. She only smoked when stressed.

Yes, Dad seemed upset about Lisa's arrest yesterday morning.

He was making dinner when I got off the school bus.

Mom helped me with homework.

Reliving the moments leading to the fire inflamed my guilt, and the weight pressed on my chest. My fingertips tingled. I realized I'd been quietly hyperventilating and tried to hold each breath for a couple of seconds, forcing it deeper into my lungs. I noticed the cops looking at each other.

"You understand, Michelle, that we need to understand everything that happened yesterday, right?" Detective Keller spoke with practiced patience.

I could feel the pressure in my chest building beneath their need to wring every detail out of me to solve their case. I knew they believed the fire was suspicious—the news anchor had said so—even if they hadn't told me themselves. They thought I knew something. Somebody must have said something. They wanted me to say something without being led there by them.

In primal self-defense, I magnified any ambiguity I could find. I couldn't point the finger at my own father. I would only implicate myself in my mother's death if I had known what he was capable of and left her alone with him. I silenced the instinct that had driven me to sneak out and that had proven accurate so often. I needed my gut to be wrong because if it wasn't, not only would I never be able to live with myself, I would also lose everything.

Sitting in the small, smoky space, I decided that despite fifteen years of his threats, I didn't think my father was capable of murder. I had no answers for Detective Keller.

"Did you hear them argue in the kitchen before you left?" Keller asked again.

I rubbed my face, suddenly bone-tired, and shook my head. "No. Like I said, they didn't really talk to each other at all. Nothing."

July 1976–Six Years Old

I sprinted from my room when I heard their shouting in the kitchen. "You can gang up today, but one day you'll get what's coming!" Dad's meaty fist was in Lisa's eight-year-old face. His own flushed beet red. I stepped slightly behind her, looking at Mom.

"Know what? Someday I am going to strangle you three bitches and let everything burn to the ground." Dad swung his arms wide, gesturing to the house and ending with fingers pointed at us. "Then I'll collect the insurance money!"

My small heart broke as my father's intention impaled my soul. My father had never threatened me before, but I understood then that he meant to kill me. I had believed I was Dad's favorite, and there had been some solace in that even while he beat and terrorized Mom with religious regularity. He often ridiculed Lisa. But me? Never. Sure, I was occasionally slapped or shoved, but regardless, my status had spared me for the most part until now. He chuckled at the look on my face.

My mother stepped in front of us. "Leave them alone. You're drunk."

I imitated her, crossing my arms. He grabbed an aluminum pan from the counter and smashed it against the edge.

"Don't tell me what I am, whore. You know nothing," He swore and tossed the dented pan onto the floor before retreating to the family room.

Devastated, I watched him leave. My father didn't love me anymore, and I didn't even know why.

Taking my hand, one finger on her lips, Mom led us to the back hallway. She put her Chanel purse over her shoulder and gingerly opened the door to the garage. I opened my mouth, but Mom shook her head and shushed me.

Luckily, the noisy garage door had been left raised. Moonlight spilled into the space around Mom's new brown Mustang. She hurried to open the door and rolled the window down. She motioned for us to help her push it out. I nodded, catching the gist of her plan.

We were leaving. He'd be sorry. Maybe he'd realize he did love me—and Mom—if we left.

The moment swelled, grand as the blue summer moon low over the three of us. We pushed the hatchback onto the pad outside. The rough cement pressed cold against my bare feet. Mom looked around. I followed suit, searching for shadowed windows or late-night dog walkers. I worried what Carolyn might think if she spied us leaving like this. Still, Mom's astonishing boldness made me proud.

Mom motioned for us to hop in. She slipped behind the wheel as the Mustang gained momentum on the sloped drive. The ignition caught, then roared under her nervous foot; she'd forgotten to shift out of neutral. We all cringed. I looked behind us. Mom shifted into gear.

Dad ran onto the drive in his slippers, stalking us with a loping gait. Mom accelerated with a spray of gravel. He chased us into the street. I knelt in the back seat, facing backward, gripping the tan headrest.

I heard him through the open window. "Don't bother coming back! I'll burn the house anyways!"

All the way down Rhonswood Drive, I watched his dark form framed by the moonlight.

"Mommy, where are we going?" I wondered. I worried that I had brought nothing.

There was no reply save for a sigh.

"How long are we going for?" Lisa leaned forward between the seats.

"Hush now, girls. Just lie down and go to sleep," Mom said.

I really tried, but I kept dozing, then awakening to wonder when we'd arrive at my mother's parents' home. Going there made the most sense to me. Grandma Findlay only lived thirty miles away, but the trip took hours. We finally stopped. I sat up, relieved to get out of the small back seat. My bleary eyes found a familiar scene: our garage door, closed, in the headlights. Mom opened my car door and waited.

Confused, I dragged myself after her into our backyard. It must have been three or four in the morning, the quietest part of night, when even the frogs by the stream had hushed and the birds slept. No exterior lights shone, but the kitchen and family-room windows threw wide berths of light onto the deck. The blinds were open—just as when we'd left. We stopped in the shadows under the deck and tried the sliding door to the basement. It was locked.

Mom tapped Lisa's shoulder, pointing at the deck steps. Lisa crept up. She returned a moment later, leaving wet footprints on the stair treads.

"Dad's asleep on the couch," she whispered.

We found an unfastened kitchen window and lifted Lisa through. She opened the screened porch door and took my hand. Lisa led me to my room. She closed the door softly behind us and pushed my laundry hamper in front of it. I helped by piling stuffed animals on top. Finished, I put my ear to the door and heard the soft thunk of Mom's bedroom door locking.

That night, I realized there was no escape. I began waking at night, listening. Just listening.

Neal slurped his coffee.

"Shelly, did you hear my question?"

I blinked, realizing Keller had spoken. I hadn't been listening just then.

He raised his eyebrows. "Cigarettes. Were they lying around the house typically?"

"Um, she didn't usually smoke. She had an ashtray in the family room." I shrugged and yawned, leaning forward.

The detective switched tactics and read parts of my father's statement taken the night before. I knew he was hoping for some sort of reaction, so I gave him none.

"Your father says he left the house to buy some heating supplies for your cottage."

Dad's story had holes. The cops knew it, and so did I. We never went to our cottage on Lake Huron in the winter.

But no one ever questioned Dad except Mom when she was plastered. I tightened my jaw but didn't move. My head ached from twenty-four hours of unintentional fasting. I rubbed my temples.

"When he came back, he said he found the house in flames. He tried to enter through the garage to look for your mother but couldn't as the fire was too hot. He went in the basement entrance to call 911, then back out to get the garden hose to put out the fire." Keller consulted his notes.

Dad's stupidity annoyed me. I had seen the flames on TV last night. A hose!

"According to your dad, Mr. Zajdel, and another neighbor, uh, Stevenson, were helping when they heard an explosion and found the barbecue tank spraying propane all over the deck and flames shooting out the kitchen and family-room windows." Detective Keller paused and watched my face. I crossed my arms, only raising my eyebrows at him to continue.

Neal coughed loudly. "Do you have any relevant questions for my client?"

Keller put his hands behind his back and glared at Neal. Keller seemed sincere, but in my mind, he was missing all the salient points. He continued, trying to gauge my response to my father's story. I had already heard most of it and was able to shrug my way through it. We were almost done.

"Yes, one last question," he said. "Do you have any idea how the fire might have started?"

Neal's attention narrowed. All three men waited for me to speak.

Burning guilt flared within me, and I almost began to speak, but then I felt the surety of my dad's hands on my throat, choking me.

Heat spread from my chest up as I forced my suspicions down. I shook my head, maintaining eye contact. "No," I whispered.

It wasn't a total lie. I didn't know what had happened after I'd left, but I still blamed myself for her death even if the police didn't.

In my heart, shame compounded my grief. I should have stayed home. I should have told Lisa to go home. I should have never called my mother at work. If I had changed any one of those three mistakes, everything would have been different despite whatever Dad might have done.

As it was, my last glimpse of Dad before practice yesterday had been him soused and teary. It was his weeping that had thrown me off balance and started my panic. If only I hadn't panicked.

October 14, 1985

Every school day when the bus pulled away, I headed to the backyard. We always kept the sliding doors off the deck unlocked. My

29

parents worked opposite shifts, so the house was only empty for a few minutes in the morning after Mom, Lisa, and I left for work and school and Dad came home. Then, after Dad left for his swing shift, I'd be the first one back minutes later. I enjoyed my short time of personal freedom before practice, the house all to myself.

That day, though, I was absorbed in my thoughts. Rumors at school of my sister's friends' and her arrest that morning had made me anxious. While I'd spied her across the cafeteria at lunch and she'd looked normal, I wanted to ask her what had happened. Something must have prompted the rumors. I shook my head. I doubted she'd meant to cause trouble, but she could be impulsive.

I decided I'd have to wait until after basketball practice to ask her on the sly. She was at her own varsity practice right then, and when I got back, Mom would be there too. I didn't want to get her in trouble if it was just rumors. Our parents rarely agreed, but doing something that got you arrested meant she'd be in deep trouble with them both. I shook my head, wondering what dumb thing she'd gotten mixed up in. This wasn't like her.

Dad called Lisa stupid, but I knew she wasn't. She and I had inherited Dad's dyslexia, but instead of being compassionate, he'd ridiculed her case of the disability, which was the worst of the three. She struggled to read letters on a page, but it didn't affect her ability to decode situations. She was unusually good at that. That was why the rumors shocked me.

I reached the top of the deck stairs and turned. My heart rose in my throat. Through the kitchen window, I saw my father at the sink. Dad being home was a bad omen. Maybe there had been truth to the rumors if he was waiting for us to get home.

I took a deep breath and slid the deck door open. "Hi," I said.

Barefoot in his brown terry bathrobe, Dad grunted. He stood patting his signature meatloaf mix into a metal pan beside the sink.

His favorite cocktail, a Manhattan, sat on the counter beside it. I hurried past.

I changed into scrimmage clothes in my room. I considered staying there until my ride came, but my stomach protested. I had eaten little at lunch, watching Lisa from across the room. She hadn't seemed to notice the stares, but they had made me leave the cafeteria early.

Back in the kitchen, I rummaged through the fridge.

Dad growled, "Did you hear what happened?"

"I heard something about Lisa, but we never talked," I admitted. I closed the refrigerator door with my foot, holding a Yoplait in one hand and an apple in the other. Dad settled into the kitchen desk chair and stretched out his legs, pouring another drink. I sat at the round table and opened my yogurt. He knew more. I waited for it.

"Well, this morning, I got a call from the police," Dad started in an annoyed tone. "They'd arrested your sister for shoplifting."

He smacked the counter and snarled. "Those two-faced bitches, her so-called friends, stole some beer and let her take the rap for them."

"I knew. I knew it wasn't her the whole time. I talked the cops out of keeping her in a cell. Morons." His irritation melted into sadness. "I got her outta there." He toasted his negotiation skills, sloshing Manhattan onto the floor.

I stared at the red drops on the Spanish tile. He never even noticed. It dawned on me that he had been drinking all afternoon. I ate my remaining yogurt in two bites, swallowing hard.

Before I could escape, Dad spoke again. "Where the hell did I go wrong as a parent? What haven't I given you both? You've had every-thing I didn't."

I was stunned, unsure whether he expected a reply. His insinu-ating that his parenting was above reproach left me speechless. I was *a good liar, but not that good. Besides, never in my memory had my father asked for my opinion. He wouldn't want it now.*

I floundered for a neutral response. "It'll be okay. I mean, since she didn't do anything,"

Dad licked the side of the cup where he'd finally noticed precious droplets hung suspended, and I wondered if he had heard me. He sank deep in his glass, nursing it. His attention diverted, I stood to escape. It wasn't until passing him that I saw the tear sliding down his florid cheek and my emotional barometer plummeted. I had never seen this man cry. Not once.

I panicked. This bender was more than ten too many Manhattans. There was always an entire storm brewing beneath the surface. But after fifteen years of observing an angry drunk, I was terrified by a sad one. The whole weather pattern had changed. Tears were an unknown and therefore unpredictable and dangerous.

Dad busied himself refilling his glass. Unnoticed, I fled upstairs. As time dragged on, I alternated between hiding in Mom's bedroom and watching for my ride through the living room's corner window— creeping up and down the curving steps while listening for Dad's movements.

My teammate Sabrina's mom always picked me up for practice, and Mom dropped Sabrina off afterward. Our usual routine had just gotten complicated. If I left, Mom would come home expecting an empty house but find Dad crying instead. I wasn't sure exactly what Dad's tears meant, but I knew they scared me.

Sabrina's tardiness gave me time to think. Eventually, I locked myself inside Mom's room and sat in the bedside chair. I picked up the nightstand phone. I needed to warn Mom.

"Marlene Edwards, Mutual of New York Insurance. What may I help you with today?"

"Hi, Mom. Are you driving Sabrina and me home?"

"Oh. Hey, honey. I am planning on it. Is that all? I have someone here."

Upon hearing her voice, my urge to warn her grew.

"Dad's home still."

There was a silent moment. "Oh, really?"

I sensed her calculating the risks, weighing her curiosity against the odds of stirring up trouble. "Can I talk with him?" she asked.

I laid the phone down on the bed and opened the door, stepping out onto the landing.

"Dad, get the phone. It's Mom." I listened for the receiver's click, then hung up.

I tiptoed down the stairs and perched on the edge of the front hall bench. I was ostensibly waiting for Sabrina, but it was a good place to eavesdrop on my parents' conversation. Leaning toward Dad's unseen presence in the kitchen, I heard him describe Lisa's morning in detail.

Her friends had convinced her to stop at a party store after an early dismissal from a first-hour special district-wide class at a neighboring high school. She had watched the cashier while they stashed beer cans in their backpacks. A suspicious clerk had called the police, who had taken the girls to the local precinct and threatened to leave them in cells overnight. Dad had won Lisa's freedom after arguing that her empty bag demonstrated her innocence. For once, he'd taken Lisa's side.

"Look, she was clean. There was nothing in her bag. Even the cops knew it."

He took a breath to continue, but Mom must have gone off because he spluttered for a few seconds, trying to interrupt. Something, a fist maybe, hit the kitchen wall.

"Shut up! You don't know that. Just let me handle it. I promised that I wouldn't say anything to you before the three of us could sit down and talk. You can't say anything to her!"

He was almost shouting now. I rose from the bench and moved into the living room. I could still hear him clearly, even from farther away.

He repeated, "Don't say anything!" and slammed the phone down.

I didn't blame Mom for being angry, but my parents didn't handle upset well at all. I had done my part. Mom knew what she was getting into.

By the front living-room window, I waited for Sabrina's gray Caprice Classic—and my exit. Every passing minute gave Dad an opportunity to remember I was home. The Italian wall-clock ticked, the only sound in the tense house besides the occasional clink of a bottle neck hitting a cocktail glass.

Twenty-five minutes later, the garage-door opener thumped and then began to whine. I assumed it was Lisa returning from her practice. Sabrina was really late. After hearing Dad defend Lisa to Mom, I wasn't worried about leaving Lisa alone with him. I looked out the window and watched the wrong car turn into our driveway.

Mom. I spun, wide-eyed, staring through the empty foyer toward the kitchen. Mom must have flown out the agency's door when Dad hung up on her. She worked thirty miles away.

Lisa's absence suddenly became a major stressor. Of course, she had screwed up and didn't want to face the music at home. But someone needed to referee my parents. I couldn't leave them alone with no contingency plan.

Short on inspiration, I raced upstairs and scanned my room. Diving into my school bag, I snatched my geometry book. I leapt down the curving staircase and swung around the banister at the bottom. Running, I slid into the short hallway that passed the kitchen and led to the garage just as Mom walked in opposite me.

Mom gave me an exasperated look. She frowned at her watch. "If I'd known you were still going to be home, I'd have planned to drive you." She put her purse down and hung up her coat.

I shrugged. Sabrina's serendipitous absence gave me time. I stood between my parents with a pounding heart and my geometry book. It wasn't a great plan, or even a good one, but it had to work if I was going to leave.

I held up the math book. "I have a test tomorrow. Can you help me?"

I didn't wait for her response, stepping into the kitchen and opening the textbook on the table. After pulling a cigarette and lighter from her purse, she stood beside me and lit up. She slid the lighter into her pocket and pulled her reading glasses from her head to her nose. She read the chapter summary over my shoulder and exhaled over hers. I pointed to a problem but focused on Dad's profile in my periphery. He was silent.

"What don't you understand?" she asked twice before I realized she'd spoken.

"Oh, uh, which property should I use here?" I asked.

Dad remained at the built-in kitchen desk, mixing a fresh glass. He seemed indifferent to Mom's arrival. My heartbeat stabilized. I hadn't predicted this but took it as a positive sign. Maybe they could be okay alone, just for a few minutes until Lisa got home.

"Do you understand what I'm saying?" Mom leaned over me.

I smelled her perfume, L'Air du Temps. "Um, say it again?" I stalled.

Mom repeated herself slowly and with some irritation. I admit I was stalling, but I honestly couldn't process her explanation. I was too focused on Dad. He stood and moved behind us to the sink. Water ran into the steel basin.

A horn honked, and Mom looked at her watch again with an annoyed huff. I winced. I had moments to decide. Leaving felt wrong, but what could I tell Sabrina?

Nothing remarkable had happened. My Dad had cried about Lisa's arrest. Mom was home early. My basketball coach wouldn't accept either fact as a reason to be late. How could I make Sabrina understand without more explanation than I'd ever given anyone in my whole life? Did I bring the façade down over such small details?

I closed my book and kissed Mom goodbye.

"Love you. See you at six."

The details haunted me. I'd felt the prescient tremors and tried to warn Mom in a roundabout way, but my blunder had caused her to run straight into danger. Afraid to be clear with anyone about the danger I'd sensed, I'd left my mother behind. I had assumed Lisa would arrive home momentarily.

When Sabrina and I had walked into the gym, our coach began yelling at us for being late. It took a moment to notice Lisa sitting on the bleachers, and my heart had sunk. Mom had no backup on the way.

I had hung my head and worried. Walking past Coach to speak to Lisa would make an even bigger scene than the JV captains missing forty-five minutes of practice the day before a big game. If I'd told my sister that Dad was crying and drunk, that Mom had come home early, and, worse, that I'd left them alone, Lisa would surely flip her lid.

Still, despite being chewed out by my coach, it was the only time I'd been sorely tempted to break our family rule to never speak of family incidents even to each other. I'd had a bad feeling about leaving. Seeing Lisa sitting in the gym confirmed it.

Now, I was in agony that I hadn't brought myself to confess my terror to Lisa despite the public disgrace. I'd give anything for the chance to be openly humiliated now if it could bring my mother back.

Instead, red-faced, I had pushed my panic to the back of my mind and prayed my geometry distraction had been enough of a cooling-off period. Hope had streamed in sweaty rivulets down my face.

By the time Carolyn had nearly clotheslined me, I'd known already, somewhere deep down, that I'd lost my moment to save my mother's life. What had happened in my absence was unrepairable. You could glue, nail, or clamp a broken board. Once you burned it, though, it would never be a board again. All you had left were ashes. We had been a fractured family, but we had been a family. I had done my best to fix and mend the fissures and cracks. But the fire changed everything.

I swallowed. I could choke on so many words left unspoken:

Mom, Dad's been drinking—all afternoon by the looks of it.

Mom, I am scared; he's crying.

Mom, take me to practice.

Mom, don't fight.

Don't leave me.

Keller finished his notes, shook my hand. "I am so sorry about your mother. Thank you for coming in today. I know this must be extremely hard for you."

I nodded and stood. Neal Simpson put a hand on my back, pushing me toward the door.

"I'll get copies this week?" Neal asked Keller. The detective nodded.

I walked to the lobby, where Dad and Lisa waited. Dad searched my face with hard eyes. I shrugged and turned to Lisa, but not before seeing my dad's attorney give Dad a small nod. My father's shoulders relaxed, though he still frowned.

Chapter Four

October 16, 1985

Chilly gusts traversed the streets, depositing leaves deep in corners. Inside the O'Malley funeral home in Novi, Dad headed to the director's office. Watching the leaves swirling in an eddy just outside, Lisa remained by a window in the foyer between potted mums bright in the gloom. I wandered about alone.

I stopped in the viewing room's doorway. Inside the unlit room, Mom's gray metal coffin lay opposite. Flowers surrounded it. I rubbed my tired eyes. My dreams the night before had been brutal. In one, a paramedic had unzipped my mother's black body bag and shaken her ashes into a wooden casket. I'd awoken gasping and thrashing.

The contents of the coffin across from me in the dark haunted me. Was ash all that remained of my mother in this world? I wanted something real to say goodbye to. I wanted to kiss her face one last time and beg forgiveness for leaving. I needed her reassurance because everything since I'd left her had gone wrong. *Just let me know everything will be okay.*

Pale illumination pressed through heavy curtains behind the display table to the right of the coffin. It was covered in pictures of Mom that her sister Kathy had gathered. I entered the dimly lit room and bent over the small echoes of light captured on paper. The photographs were all that remained of Mom's face.

Guilt framed every memory and drove me to the draped casket. On my knees beside it, I leaned close. My intention was to lay my cheek against it, against her. Inches from the polished surface, I noticed fine black residue, only now visible in the dim light. Hesitating, I rubbed a finger along it. A black smear came away.

I squeezed my eyes shut and swallowed. *Why did it have to be so bad? Why couldn't she have died from a heart attack or cancer? I could have said goodbye, held her hand. Why, God?*

Opening my eyes again, I brought my finger closer to my face, mesmerized by the horror. I was suddenly certain this couldn't be her; whoever was inside the coffin wasn't my mother. She wasn't in this room. I prayed she wasn't even close to the life she'd left me behind in. Everything here was dark and ruined. I prayed she was someplace light and new.

"God, tell Mom I love her. Keep her safe." I breathed the words more than spoke them.

Stricken, I rubbed my finger on my dress. That parting smudge was crueler than any nightmare, and I felt I'd never have enough courage to describe the moment I knew she was really gone.

October 18, 1985

My mother's funeral was a production starring my father, and we were among the last to arrive. I couldn't tell if my father had planned it that way, but his appearance made a discernible stir as he approached the overflow crowd standing outside the sanctuary.

Head down, he walked ahead of us and made a striking but solemn figure in his dark suit. The crowd appreciated his grieving air and extended their hands in condolences. He paused at each token, acknowledging their mutual distress. Satisfied with Dad's execution of duties, the crowd engulfed my sister and me. But the touch of their hands on my shoulders and arms stung with reality, grounding me in a moment I had feared my whole life. I shied away, leaving my sister to calm them.

I entered the sanctuary of Our Lady of Sorrows Catholic Church to find a thousand more mourners filling the wooden pews. I caught up to Dad, who stopped several times to accept additional well-meaning condolences on the way up front to our family's reserved seating. Though I stayed by his side, I hated every step.

I hated the stares. I hated my outfit. I hated the generic flowers—stiff lilies and drooping orchids. Mom had always loved lilacs. Even if she'd never described her funeral wishes, I knew she would have wanted clusters of the purple blooms. We'd talked about so much but never what would happen after her death. Now, the memory of her voice was fading after only a few days. I would never hear it again. An angry tear escaped, but I hastily wiped it away.

Lisa had finished with the crowd outside and was again by my side. Dad shook one last hand before we reached the last untaken place up front by Uncle Bob's family. The small spot sandwiched me between Lisa and Dad.

I sat in rigid detachment. I ignored the priest and focused on my hands. Little penetrated my shield until one startling hymn began. I'd not heard it before, so I listened in unguarded curiosity as the entire throng sang. The stained-glass windows reverberated with beautiful declarations that God's love was a shield for all who loved Him. Those blessed people would be held in His hand and protected by His angels from all terrors. I clenched my jaw as a creeping, cold horror froze my heart.

It was all beautiful lies.

Angry tears fell as a new, bitter disbelief choked my throat. Despite my father's harassment, my mother had taken me to mass every Sunday. She had volunteered at the parish fundraisers, attended women's Bible study, and made me memorize my catechism. She had believed in God. I had thought I believed too. Together, we had imagined God would change things if we only mustered enough faith. Yet, despite my prayers and my mother's devotion, angels had never come. Not even when it mattered most.

Summer 1975

Fragments. Playing in my room while waiting to be told to get in bed. I stopped. The Barbie I'd gotten for my fifth birthday dropped to the floor as the angry voices escalated. I started down the hallway toward the shouting in my parents' bedroom, the wall cool against my trailing fingers. Peeking in, I could see my dad astride my mother on the bed, choking her. Lisa grabbed me from behind by my shoulders and turned me toward my bedroom. She pushed.

"Go back to your room and close the door," Lisa used her best adult voice.

I ran.

She returned to the fray behind me. "Stop! Stop!!"

When I shut my door, it dampened the vicious soundtrack of swearing and screaming accompanied by Lisa's pleading. My back against it, I sank down and braced my feet against the dresser, knees locked. My ear pressed against the wood, hot tears dripping. I cried with abandon, lacking the bitter restraint of experience.

A rosary hung on my wall. "God, change him. Make Daddy stop. I promise to always be a good girl if you stop him." I shut my eyes and crossed myself as Grandma had taught me to.

After what felt like hours but might have been twenty minutes, Dad's footsteps passed my door accompanied by a blistering tirade. He pounded down the stairs, and the house fell quiet.

I awoke the next morning, still on my side, wedged between the door and dresser. Arm tingling, I opened the door a crack and peeked out. The aroma of hash browns and sausage lured me out onto the landing. I rubbed my arm and stood, listening. Mom came smiling to the bottom of the curving staircase. Relieved, I skipped downstairs and into her arms.

"Mommy!"

She held me a moment and kissed my head, then set me down. "Listen," she said with serious eyes. "I am fine. Nothing is wrong. Daddy made a big breakfast, so remember to thank him and tell him how good it is. Don't say anything about last night. Okay?"

I bottled up my prohibited questions and fears. I took her hand and nodded. She squeezed my fingers and beamed. I shuffled ahead of her, peeking around the corner before entering the kitchen. Dad turned from the stove, motioning for me to sit at the table. Lisa appeared beside me. He filled our plates with steaming eggs. Everyone ignored the finger marks on Mom's throat and smiled as we ate.

"Arnie, pass me your cup. I'll get more coffee."

My father's violence was a secret Mom took to her grave. Left behind holding my guilt, I raged. I had not been able to save her, though I tried, and a supposed all-knowing God had chosen not to intervene. My grief at His abandonment throbbed.

The priest circled the coffin, swinging incense. Its heavy, sweet aroma, so different from my mother's, swirled into the ether under the buttressed roof. His prayer for her soul's ascent stung me. Head bowed, I refused to say amen. Why should I want her to return to a God who had refused to save her? Finally, the priest led the procession out to lay my mother to rest.

We followed. I lifted my eyes and once again saw the sea of compassionate faces. Tormented, I lowered my gaze to the priest's black rubber-soled shoes before me.

At the cemetery, people crowded us. Their many sympathies threatened to tip me off my stoic perch, so I retreated deep inside. I assumed many found me cold. My mother had raised me to be polite, but returning their kind gestures was impossible for me. Surviving that service required remaining aloof, above the darkness yawning beneath my feet. Otherwise, the abyss would consume me whole.

After the priest's final prayer, the pallbearers lowered her casket into the cold earth. Dad stood, so I did too. He swept a handful of earth from the fresh mound beside the hole and turned to offer his fist to me. I automatically opened my bare hand to receive the wet dirt. Its coldness froze my entire body. I couldn't move.

Everyone watched while Dad, then Lisa, dropped their fistfuls onto the casket. I felt the crowd's eyes on me. I managed one step forward, and then another. I could go no farther and let the dirt slip through my fingers to the grass, short of the pit. Instead of correcting me, everyone looked away.

I would have jumped into the hole with her save for the hundreds of witnesses to my grief. I'd almost hoped for that attention once. Hoped someone would see and save us. Now, it was too late. There she lay, eight feet and a breath away.

At the funeral luncheon, I wandered the Knights of Columbus hall looking for a corner to disappear into. I soundlessly entered a dark room I thought empty. I was relieved to be alone until my eyes adjusted and focused on the sole draped window. A motionless figure wrapped in the heavy curtain as though it were a shroud startled me. For a terrifying moment, I thought it a ghost before recognizing the white hair peeking out from under a black scarf. My mother's mother, Sarah Findlay, gazed far beyond the windowpanes.

1978

I was awakened by a strange series of noises after midnight. Too experienced with violence for my eight years of age, I had become a light sleeper, and even a stray cat's yowl would wake me. I couldn't identify the sounds, but they seemed to come from my parents' room.

I slipped out from under the covers, careful to not disturb my softly snoring grandmother, who had fallen asleep there while babysitting us that night. I sidled down the hall and put one eye to the crack of my parents' door. In that sliver of light, I spotted Mom faceup on the bed with Dad straddled atop her. One of his hands pinned her throat while the other smashed a suffocating pillow into her face.

I pushed the door open, running toward them. I could now see Lisa pulling on Dad's undershirt. She kicked him while Mom screamed in gasps and pulled at his arms. When I joined the fray, hitting at Dad's head, Lisa shook her head no.

"Shelly, go back. Close the door!"

Panicked, I realized that if we made too much noise, Grandma would wake up. I sprinted down the hallway to my room. Though I closed the door softly, she bolted upright and reached for her glasses. "Heaven's sake, what is going on!?"

She left my door ajar again, but I stayed under the covers. Something shattered.

"Get off of her, you devil!" Grandma's Scottish ire had been roused.

My father yelped and swore. I imagined her grabbing my father's hair or ear, twisting to make him pay attention. I knew from experience how that felt, but I didn't feel bad for him at the moment.

Dad let loose a string of profanity, but Grandma held her ground. "Get off this minute, or I am calling the police! You hear me?"

Dad roared, "Don't tell me what to do in my own home!"

"You touch my daughter, and I'll say what I want!"

I held my breath. His sulking snarl retreated downstairs. A wretched sobbing, quiet but piercing, rose from my mother. I heard the small noises of my grandmother comforting her.

Grandma eventually returned and sank onto my mattress with a sigh that sounded worn and frayed by a thousand uses. I lay awake for hours wondering if, finally, someone would reveal what I'd been forbidden to.

The next morning, Dad cooked a huge breakfast of carved fruit, sausage, hot butter syrup, and pancakes. Mom smiled and set the table, hair done and makeup on. She looked beautiful. Grandma quietly came in and sat down. She looked each of her eighty years as my smiling mother offered her a plate. My grandmother shook her head and looked away, at me.

I saw the answer then in Grandma's eyes; she too would tell no one. The tiny spark of aching hope that had kept me up all night sputtered out.

I recognized the despair in Grandma's posture. I left the room without announcing my presence. We both knew we had failed my mother. Our mutual regrets bound us in agony but not together. Neither of us would ever speak of it. I hid in a closet until the lunch ended.

Chapter Five
October 21, 1985

Drowsy, I waited for Mom to wake me. I smelled bacon and coffee. Rolling over, I glimpsed mauve walls. This wasn't my room. Mom had died. Grief crashed through my soul again. I pulled the blanket over my head.

I had played in this room as a child. Now, I woke up in it to a living nightmare. I shuddered, eyes closed. I shouldn't be in Linda's old room in the house immediately behind ours. It wasn't even hers anymore. Three years ago, her family had sold this house and moved to a larger home in the same neighborhood. The new owners had recently moved overseas, leaving it for sale. After the funeral, they had offered to let us lease the empty home until it sold. Dad had moved us in the next day.

There was a small click. Even under the bedding, eyes closed, incandescent light penetrated my gloom.

"Get up or we'll be late!" Lisa banged the door for emphasis.

"Fine." I moaned and pushed the covers off.

I rose, opening the blinds. The gray sky lightened in the east, not quite dawn. The scene flipped my usual world backward—the lawn rolled downhill, not uphill, between the properties. Yellow police tape encircled the scarred house on Rhonswood. The lawn around it was torn by tire marks and hardly seemed familiar from the window here on Lujon Street. My own window opposite was dark and empty.

Dad had wanted to be close to our house as it was repaired, even while I wanted desperately to forget. I sighed and dumped a bag of donated clothing on the floor to find something to wear. There was no escaping the physical reminders of my loss.

I had to face it. Life would never be normal again. Mom would never wake me again, no matter how many mornings I waited in bed. I found a striped tee and pulled it over my head, tears spotting the collar.

That first morning back at school, everyone's eyes slid past me. No one knew what to say. Then Sabrina found me.

"Shelly," Sabrina whispered in my ear. At the same time, her arms pulled me into a hug. After a long embrace, she put her freckled face near mine.

"I am so sorry! I can't make anything better, but can I walk you to class?"

Her kind offer, though seemingly small, brought me to the verge of a complete meltdown. I hastily wiped at my eyes. I took a deep breath and nodded. Sabrina and I had been friends and cocaptains for only a short time. Unbeknownst to either of us, she would, in fact, help make everything better.

August 1985

At basketball tryouts, I noted that the new sophomore, Sabrina Perrett, stood shorter than me by at least an inch. I smiled to myself. Despite my two-foot vertical jump, my teammates never tired of shorty jokes. Maybe they'd leave me alone now.

Sabrina and I were among the last still waiting for rides after practice. I broke the silence. "So, you guys just moved here?"

"Yes, we've only been here a few weeks. I didn't know about tryouts until last night." She laughed, pushing her bangs aside and making a face. "I am so out of shape."

"Yeah, me too," I said. I had recently returned from Europe, jetlagged and weary, and still felt off. Deflecting the topic from me, I returned the focus to her. "Where did you move from?"

"California. My dad ranches, and we own land there."

"Are you ranching here?" Michigan had its share of dairy farms, but I'd never seen ranches.

"No." She laughed. "He isn't working here, or at least not like that. It's volunteer missionary work for our church," Sabrina said.

"Huh." No one had ever accused me of being articulate, and I wasn't then, either. I leaned against the brick wall outside Farmington High School. The idea of a man moving his family cross-country to volunteer at some church, not even for money, stupefied me.

After an uncomfortable moment, I asked the obvious question. "Why?" I said, imagining her dad wearing a cowboy hat with a gold cross at his throat and pounding a pulpit.

"Well, we were supposed to go to Alaska originally," she said, missing my point. "But that changed when the guy who was supposed to come here had a family emergency, so we came instead." She beamed.

"Hmm. That's wild." Didn't missionaries go to Africa or somewhere undeveloped or heathen? Why Michigan? Why had they left their ranch and become missionaries in the first place? I nodded and pretended it all made perfect sense.

A large, silver sixteen-passenger van pulled up to the curb, and Sabrina gave me a small wave.

"See ya tomorrow!"

I could only lift my hand in parting.

Later that week, I overheard her describing her dad's new job to another teammate. On the way home from practice later that day, I asked Mom, "What is a Mormon?"

"Oh, just another kind of religion," Mom said distractedly.

"Are they Christian?"

Mom nodded. "I think so." She turned on the radio and asked who I thought should be the starting forwards for JV.

Despite her peculiar family background, Sabrina's great outside shot and enthusiastic defense got her on the team. Over the next couple of weeks, we fell into an easy rhythm. Her cheer-leader attitude and endless energy complemented my brute strength and instinct for reading the play on the court. I had secretly been hoping to be named JV captain, but Coach Diane had surprised the team and made Sabrina and me co-captains. I liked the sassy brunette from California enough that my disappointment lasted only a minute. We'd become friends.

Sabrina fell into step beside me. Our friends Vicki and Melissa joined us. As we approached huddles of classmates, conversations would cease only to resume with a frenzy once we passed. If I looked back, no one would make eye contact.

Vicious gossip followed me everywhere. Though Lisa was popular and I was well-liked, we now stood as defendants in Farmington Public High School's social court. My friends shielded me as much as possible, but I heard the savage whispers anyways.

Bathroom stalls, I discovered, were great for accidental eavesdropping. They were also the perfect place to hide and sob after the bell rang, especially after hearing Jessica Polaski tell Leslie Sallow that she'd heard I had helped Lisa strangle our mom and set the blaze because of Lisa's arrest. I was nauseated by the idea of anyone imagining me wanting my mother to die. I began avoiding restrooms.

The school hallways weren't much better. Every day reminded me how not normal I was. I had, in fact, always felt different—but I couldn't pretend anymore. A new and public level of shame tore away the façade I had always hidden my own internal hell behind.

At the center of unwanted attention and crushed by pain, I was incapable of defending myself before the most merciless judge of them all: me. I had left Mom alone with my alcoholic father, a fact I felt implicated me in the strongest terms. Staggering under my own guilt, I said nothing, which only corroborated my peers' wild theories. I hated myself and felt, in some measure, that the humiliation I experienced was just.

Only on the basketball court did I forget my transgressions. The hardwood demanded action and few words. The only sounds were the squeak of shoes sliding, my heart hammering, my teammates' labored grunting, and the percussive beating of the ball on the floor. The only shouting was for the ball. No whispers.

The discomfort in my legs and lungs muted the anguish in my heart. I threw myself into drills until I became dizzy and dehydrated. I took shot after shot and scrimmaged as if my existence was on the line. I drove teammates down the court ahead of me. It was the only space in my life where I called the plays. All I asked from the game I loved was an escape from reality.

I got more than I bargained for.

October 22, 1985

The first game I played after her death was just eight days after the fire. As I took the court in my warmups, I realized that until that night, Mom had never missed a single game in my life. As I joined my teammates jogging around the perimeter of the Canton High School auxiliary gym, I told myself to ignore the sight of parents streaming into the stands. Even if everything off the court had changed for me, once the referee blew his whistle, the lump in my throat would disappear. That's what I kept repeating to myself.

I ran the ball around my feet in a low, fast dribble, driving everything out of my mind except the plays Sabrina and I had practiced that week. When the whistle blew, I leapt into the air, surprising the Canton Chiefs' player opposite me. A full six inches taller, she wasn't prepared for the height of my spring. I tipped the ball to Sabrina and forgot about everything but the game.

Near the end of the first half, we trailed by three. I stole the ball and sprinted downcourt on a breakaway. Adrenaline flowed as Farmington Falcons fans roared in approval. Their throaty voices blended into one shout, driving me to the hoop ahead of our foes. I had just passed center court when a singular voice rang out.

"Go, Shelly!"

I almost double dribbled.

"Yeah! Shelly!" Mom called.

My feet stumbled into the paint, and I half tripped. Recovering with an awkward bounce, I scooped the ball up and stepped in for a layup. Arms rising toward the basket, I looked back over my shoulder into the stands. *There.* I saw Mom cheering with her fists raised.

I fumbled, completely missing the shot.

The ball bounced off in an empty key. The home crowd erupted, coming to their feet beside the now-groaning Farmington fans. Players thundered down the floor toward me. In the melee, I lost sight of Mom, and utter despair overtook me. I couldn't think or breathe. Cold loss filled my chest. I stepped toward the fans as players rushed past me.

Into that void flowed as vivid a warmth as the preceding chill. I gasped as it filled me head to toe.

My mother's voice spoke. "Don't worry. Everything will be okay. I will always love you."

I looked at the players surrounding me to see if they had heard it too. They bumped into me, shoving each other and grabbing for the ball. I stepped aside, dazed, trying to process the euphoria that filled me. Sabrina grabbed my arm.

"Let's go!" She pulled me into a run.

The feeling of Mom vanished. I chased after my teammates, watching them play from what seemed miles away. I couldn't comprehend the scene before my eyes or what had just happened. Coach Diane screamed something at me. I shook my head and attempted to settle my thoughts. It wasn't real. It couldn't be.

I knew I'd buried my mother. I'd stood at the edge of her dirt hole. Remembering the cold earth, my agony came hurtling back, and I found myself on the basketball court, aware I was about to lose it in front of everyone else's parents. For another two minutes, I jogged in circles, blinking tears back until the referee's whistle blew for halftime.

My coach gave me a look but said nothing. Most adults gave me a wide berth at that time. Grateful, I followed my team into the locker room and sank against a post at the end of the row of lockers while Coach tore into everyone for not having our heads in the game. I put mine down, knowing she meant me. My polyester jersey stuck to my back. Sweat rolled down my nose. My pulse raced for ten minutes straight. Coach had no idea how right she was. I'd lost my grip on reality.

I'd seen Mom. I'd felt her. I'd heard her.

Impossible. Only lunatics see or hear dead people.

Halftime was almost over, and still I could not catch my breath. Ten years later, I would recognize what a panic attack was, but at the moment, I believed I was falling apart. I stuffed my terror deep down, went back out on the hardwood, and played hard. We won, barely.

Afterward, I waited for Lisa's varsity game to end. I couldn't follow the plays on the court, the sight of Mom's face replaying in my mind over and over. Recalling her words gave me goose bumps.

Do people exist after they die? Could Mom come back? Was it my imagination? I buried my head in my hands and tried to look nonchalant, as if seeing dead people was no big deal. It had to be the stress. My grief and sleepless nights were taking a toll. I'd hardly eaten since the fire. I'd lost five pounds in a week.

After the game, I had no idea whether to congratulate my sister or not. I'd missed everything, including the final score. When she found me sitting alone on the bleachers, her expression told me that, either way, she was in no mood to talk. That happened to suit me too.

We walked out to Mom's car (which had sustained only smoke damage from the fire) without Mom's postgame chatter for the first time. Lisa started the engine, and we silently drove the twenty minutes home. Dad was gone when we got back, so we both just went to our rooms. I sat unmoving on my bed while Lisa took a quick shower and went to sleep.

I locked the bathroom door behind me and let the shower water run over my body while I went to pieces. Even when suddenly doused by cold water as the hot water gave out, I couldn't clear my head enough to make sense of it all. My brain hurt.

I shivered and turned the water off. There were three options: either I had lost my mind as well as my mother, I'd experienced a brief psychotic incident (blame stress or sleep deprivation or both), or it had been real.

I wrapped myself in a towel and stood dripping on the bathmat, contemplating my sanity. I didn't think I was crazy. I felt sane. Sane enough to feel all this pain. Sane enough to know it would never leave. Sane enough to cry alone at night where Dad wouldn't see. I eventually decided to rule out a complete mental breakdown as least likely, though I wondered if that just proved the point. Would an insane person know it?

But what about a temporary psychosis? I knew I was running ragged on every level. Could I really cross between reality and insanity as easily as crossing the center paint on the court? Baffled, I couldn't rule out the possibility.

Of course, part of me wanted it to be true. Having my mother back in any way was what I wanted more than anything else in my life. But if what I'd seen *was* possible—a vision of my mother no one else could see—it would mean taking back everything I had told myself since the funeral.

It would mean God was real and I didn't understand anything about Him. That possibility, of having seen Mom and not being crazy, was almost worse than full or partial insanity. That meant there was a God who had let my mother die—a God who had turned His face away.

Either of these last two options, temporary insanity or an unknowable divinity, sent me into gasping shivers. I got dressed at last and left the humid bathroom.

Back in my bedroom, I whispered, "Please God, if I saw her, let me know it was real. That I am not crazy."

I waited for some sign that He'd heard. If He'd managed to get my attention at the game, it was certainly even easier now. I was the only one awake in the silent house.

"God, if you hear me, if it was real . . . if you are real . . . if she really can come back, please let me see her again."

I waited. Nothing. I sniffed and cursed my stupidity. There had to be other explanations besides ghosts or madness. The dead appeared in the middle of the night to terrify and haunt the world they left behind; they didn't cheer at basketball games and wrap people in ethereal love, right?

I realized that if I had subconsciously wished for Mom to return, it would have been exactly like that, cheering me on. I missed her enough to have created the entire experience in my head. Anything else didn't make sense.

I wasn't crazy. I still did math homework and put together coherent sentences. Despite everything, I was handling all the required daily activities. I couldn't lose my marbles and still juggle everything like usual, right?

In the end, I attributed the entire thing to a weird chemical reaction in my brain, probably due to stress, an electrolyte imbalance, hyperventilating, or some other explainable combination. I told myself to forget it.

My mother's message, the comforting words I so desperately needed, turned into another awkward secret. I went to bed, but insomnia stalked me. I tossed and turned, having to shove the memory of her words away time and again. I needed sleep, but it was hard to discard the very voice I had wanted so badly to hear again.

I feared my next mental snap might not be so temporary and resolved to start eating more.

Chapter Six

November 1985

The first time Dad forced me to go back to the burned-out shell of a house, there was nothing to eat in the rental. After practice, I had come home to Dad passed out on the recliner in the rented living room. When he awoke after dark, my stomach had been growling for an hour. Our nearly empty fridge held only orange juice, ketchup, and salad dressing. I had some juice and waited. Lisa was at work, and I didn't want to rouse a sleeping bear who'd put away eight cans of Budweiser's best that afternoon (based on the surrounding floor tally). I stayed in my room, quiet.

Eventually, I heard him stir and then make a long bathroom visit. I waited a few more minutes, then came out to find him rummaging through a kitchen drawer. I summoned enough courage to ask, "Did you want me to make some dinner?"

He ignored me for a minute, opening and closing some cupboard doors and coming to the same conclusion I had arrived at. There was nothing to eat.

"Go get creamed corn from the basement."

I was puzzled. The rental's basement was crammed full of boxes of salvaged things and donations but no food. It took a moment to realize Dad referred to another basement. I looked past him, through the windows, at the shadowed outline behind us. Our home. My mom had always stockpiled canned goods. The basement was undoubtedly still full of them. My heart froze at the thought of going inside.

"Am I allowed?"

I didn't realize I had spoken aloud until Dad threw something at my head. "What the hell are you waiting for?"

I ducked, and a pair of bright keys struck the wall and fell behind a potted plant.

"I didn't know you had keys," I said.

"It's our shit still, isn't it?" he growled.

I retrieved the unfamiliar keys from the floor, then went to the closet, putting on my coat and grabbing a flashlight from the shelf above. My heart hammered in my chest as Dad rattled off a list of items to bring back and details about entering. The no-trespassing signs that roped off the property made me fairly sure I could be arrested for entering the house. I stood before the still-closed door, debating.

"Are you deaf or dumb?" Dad was super irritated. "Get the food."

My alternatives were the possibility of a juvenile record or hunger and a possible beating. I chose stealth.

I stepped into the late autumn evening. My breath clouded for a moment, visible in the porch light, before a cold gust erased it. The purple dusk whispered of snow, though none lay on the ground. Brown grass carpeted my path downhill between the trees. I left footprints in the frozen blades.

Neighboring houses glowed warmly. Before me, ours waited deep in shadow, the first-story windows boarded up. I looked down and hurried forward. Closer, I heard the dirty, frayed police tape snapping in the breeze. Cold tendrils of fear touched my soul.

Rounding the corner and coming street side, I shivered and stepped up onto the front porch. *Focus. Cans of creamed corn and soup. Don't lose it, now.* I studied the door. The original lockset hung useless. Attached above were two metal rings, one bolted to the ornate wood door and one to the frame. A chain ran through them, padlocked near the top. I considered the keys in my hand. Dad must have gotten them from the police. This couldn't be that illegal because it was our stuff. Fire investigations didn't require inventorying canned vegetables, right?

I gripped the flashlight harder. I stuck the larger key in the heavy padlock and twisted until it dropped away, pulling the chain, which zipped through the rings. The lock hit the porch with a loud clunk, and the chain coiled on top. I looked up and down the street. It was empty and quiet. I hesitated, then pushed on the oversized wooden door. It swung open with a prolonged creak. The hinges had rusted. I leapt through the dark doorway and kicked the door closed behind me.

It smelled as if I had jumped into the middle of a cold firepit. The air held an odor of heavy ash with an electrical-burn aftertaste that coated the back of my nose and throat. My eyes watered. In the darkness, my cough echoed off bare floors and through empty, frigid rooms. I stepped backward, putting my spine against the door, letting my eyes adjust. I barely made out the shadowed form of stairs climbing into darkness, black on black. Easier to see was the doorway into the living room, dimly backlit by a lone, intact window on the far wall. All else was murky.

I stretched out my senses for life in the house. Stillness reigned, scarier than creaking shutters or scratching branches. Our house was dead. No whir of heat, not even a refrigerator hum. A deep absence of life. The silence of loss.

A malevolent feeling breathed over my shoulder, enjoying my distress. Remembering Mom's ghost, I almost lost my nerve. Now was not the time to have a breakdown. I talked myself through it. There was nothing to fear. Mom's apparition was a stress symptom. There were no such things as ghosts. The house was empty. My pounding heart betrayed me, ignoring my head. The dark felt dangerously close.

My fear nudged me, reminding me of the flashlight. I brought it up and switched it on.

Sweeping the beam across the foyer, I looked for the makeshift light switch Dad had described. Spying an electrical box duct-taped to the wall next to the dining room, I started toward it. Broken odds and ends littered the floor and crunched under my boots.

I flipped the jerry-rigged contraption. A string of incandescent bulbs lit the foyer and hall with bleak frankness. I turned in a circle, taking it in. The once-adorned cream walls were now bare. They turned black as they rose, as did the curving staircase. Its dirty cream carpet became inky and crisp on the treads near the top. The carpet in the living room to my left had been entirely removed, the couches pushed against the walls. Glass and broken bits of porcelain lay under my shoes. Nothing looked familiar in this light. I crept down the front hall, pausing by the corner where I had listened from the bench to my parents' phone call. I shined the flashlight beam up and down the hallway. Flames had tattooed it from the family room all the way to the garage entry door, leaving superheated trails of white powder on the smoke-stained background.

Ash spread everywhere. I shivered with cold.

Even in my fear, questions assaulted me. I stood ten feet from the kitchen and gazed into the shadowed doorway. What had happened after I left? Where had she died? The ruined house was suddenly transformed into a lockbox of hidden secrets. I wasn't sure I was prepared to face them yet. I swallowed my curiosity. Dad waited.

I cut around through the dining room to the back hallway, avoiding the kitchen and family room. I couldn't bear to inspect them yet. The floor groaned in protest as I approached the door to the basement. I slowed, testing each board.

The basement stairwell descended into gloom. I brought my flashlight up again. Soot and rubble blanketed the steps below. I touched the blackened stair railing, and an oily film coated my fingertips. I wrinkled my nose and hastily wiped my hand on my jeans. I opted to tiptoe, arms flailing, down the stairs. My descent disturbed the tomb-like stillness. Dark particles swirled from the sagging ceiling, cutting through my flashlight beam. A light coat of ash covered me now as well.

The whole house creeped me out. These walls had witnessed the last moments of my mother's life, and even their scorched silence spoke of a nuclear family disaster. The fallout surrounded me, clung to my eyelashes, and made breathing hard.

Taking a deep breath two steps from the bottom, I jumped to the concrete floor. My feet hit at a run. Midstride, I was startled by leafy shadows moving across the glass of the sliding door in the wall opposite the storage area. The hairs on the back of my neck rose.

I slid to a stop in front of the basement pantry. The area appeared generally untouched with only small water stains on the drywall and storage boxes. I pulled open the bifold doors and faced stacks of cans, but before I could snatch and grab, a wave of grief hit me.

Mom's touch lingered like a faint aroma over the well-stocked closet. A Depression-era baby, she'd always bought in bulk and on sale. She'd haggle at Eastern Market for a baker's dozen instead of the normal twelve. Cases of soup, boxes of pasta and cereal—she had touched each one. I didn't want the dry goods she'd stockpiled as much as I wanted my mother.

I sank into a crouch and buried my face in my arms. She was prepared for everything. How could she not have escaped the fire? I lost myself for several minutes before remembering again that my father was waiting. Choking down tears, I grabbed the cans Dad had demanded, and bolted back up the stairs. Hitting the duct-taped light switch off on my way out the front door, I stopped to replace the padlock. Then I checked the street again before sprinting up the hill to the rental. I dried my eyes before going in.

The shadow of the lifeless house stretched long; it emitted a dark gravity from which I found no escape. It mocked me, pulling on my grief every time I left or came from the rental, reminding me of who had come home but never left what became a house of ashes.

I compulsively rehearsed the day she died. I berated myself for calling her, for leaving, for not insisting Lisa go home. No matter how I reprimanded myself, there was no undoing the catastrophic culmination of events. Now, a feeling that the house hid something haunted me too.

Chapter Seven

Early December 1985

Carols played in the mall, sending me into a melancholy mood. Alone and shopping for presents, I noticed a window display of fashionable elves wearing stilettos and draped in purses. I remembered Mom dragging me inside this same small store last summer for a peek.

My steps faltered, remembering her laugh at my exaggerated face of dismay. I'd known her "quick look" would bloom into a full-on hunt. Mom loved shoes and bags, especially bags large enough to fit every kind of emergency aid possible, plus snacks. Everyone on the basketball, volleyball, and softball teams knew about the large designer bags that magically produced any required emergency supplies. If anyone needed a Band-Aid, tampon, some Tylenol, safety pin, cough drops, or Kleenex, they asked my mom. If they needed chocolate and a shoulder to cry on, she had those too.

I came to a halt, thinking how much I missed having a mom. Last year, one of the girls on the team had been raped, then forced into an abortion by her parents. She and Mom had spent lots of time talking under the bleachers after games and between practices. I swallowed a huge lump in my throat.

I couldn't ever imagine a time she wouldn't be there for me like she was for others. I'd been confident that whatever the circumstances, she always loved me despite the unspoken sorrows we each carried. I hadn't minded sharing my mother. I just couldn't stand losing her. There would never be another opportunity to explain everything to her. There was so much I hadn't been able to say besides goodbye.

I looked through the window and did a double take. Mom stood beside the counter, her back to me!

I stared for a second before accelerating on every level. I leapt around a bench and burst through the entrance. The quiet store, full of racks and boxes, had no customers. I was alone. I spun slowly to make sure. Bubbling exhilaration popped in my chest, the air gone at once. I felt incredibly stupid. *I am crazy!*

I noticed a half-closed storeroom door. Unaware of my presence, the employees behind it conversed in low tones. I looked back out to the packed mall and hoped no passing shopper had witnessed my insanity.

How had I been so easily duped again? Disappointment filled the space hope had vacated. Head down, I walked to the door. At the threshold, I heard almost the same message:

"I will always love you. Don't worry. Everything will be okay."

Joy filled my heart. I looked back into the empty store, half expecting to see her there again. The shop remained empty.

Outside the store, I collapsed onto the bench I had catapulted over earlier and covered my face with my hands. I had seen my mother twice. Could you really make up stuff that weird? And the feeling that came with her words . . . I couldn't deny the euphoria and peace coursing through my being. For a moment, I wasn't alone, and I felt all would be right. Was that part of psychotic breaks? Was it the stress, or could it be real?

I let myself consider believing for a few moments, though I knew nothing had changed. I would still have to go back to the rental and Dad's drunken stupor, but I sat for a long while as angels sang over loudspeakers and in my heart. Then I quietly picked up my small bags and dismissed the memory.

Christmas Eve 1985

Snowflakes swirled, blanketing the lawn. I watched the neighborhood lights turn on one by one. Inside, all was quiet. I'd been homebound with Dad for two weeks, having herniated two spinal disks the week after the mall visit, just as volleyball season began. He'd been surprisingly patient and helpful.

It reminded me how incredibly gentle he'd been in moments a lifetime ago, when our family was happier—when cotton candy strands had melted in my mouth and Dad held a sticky hand to pull me along.

March 1978

"Hurry! We don't want to miss Cinderella!" Dad smiled down at me. Disney World was everything a seven-year-old dreamed of, including the food vendors.

We found Mom and Lisa on Main Street. They'd been saving spots for the Electric Parade while we bought cotton candy. I stuck out my blue tongue for Mom to admire, and Dad handed Lisa hers. The crowds roared as fireworks burst overhead and we danced to the music of the giant box speakers. When the magic came to an end, Mom folded up the blanket, and everyone headed toward the gate.

I sang happily to myself on the way back to the van, even though my legs ached and my flat feet were sore. Mom took my hand. Around us, people talked and laughed.

"What was your favorite?" she asked, squeezing gently.

I considered. "Space Mountain, or maybe . . . no, Space Mountain."

Mom swung our hands in rhythm. "I liked the shows."

We piled into our customized van for the seventy-five-mile ride to Tampa, our next stop. On the way, my legs began cramping. I instinctively flexed my feet to stretch my calves but grew agitated as the contractions refused to relax. I began to scream. Mom tried to help. Lisa put her hands over her ears, and I fell apart. Dad drove as fast as he could, making it to Tampa in just under an hour.

Dad knelt beside me in the hotel bathroom, rubbing my legs as I sat in a hot bath until well past two o'clock. The water became tepid long before my muscles relaxed. Finally, Dad lifted me from the tub. Eyes closed, I let him wrap me in a towel, get my pj's on, and place me in bed next to Lisa. He pulled the covers over me and kissed my cheek. I had never been so grateful for him.

I tuned the radio to a Christmas station. Dad helped me finish my English assignment, and I stretched, tired of sitting all day. Something in the kitchen smelled good. He had been drinking less because of all the help I needed, and a small hope lodged in my heart that my accident had been a blessing in disguise. Life had taken on a kind of normal routine for the first time in months. I found I craved it. Besides, Dad's cooking was a definite improvement over my attempts to feed myself.

Dad appeared outside my doorway, wearing his slippers and robe. He smiled. "Let's try sitting at the table for Christmas Eve," he said.

He wrapped an arm under my shoulders to help me stand. I sniffed. Dad smelled like he'd been baking. I loved Christmas. No matter what else happened, it was a season of hope. Mom had loved Christmas more than anyone I knew, and her messages had delivered exactly the promise I needed to make it through this holiday without her.

Christmas 1984 -Fourteen Years Old

"Shelly! Lisa! Let's go!" Mom yelled up the stairs. I put on earrings and looked one last time in the mirror before racing downstairs in my new dress. I smiled at Dad, who was looking handsome in his suit. The Children's Mass on Christmas Eve was my favorite mass. The organist played Christmas carols instead of hymns, and children hung hand-made decorations on the tree in the chapel.

"Oh, my ornament!" I ran back up to my room to retrieve it. I had carved a wooden star, then carefully painted and edged it with glitter. It sparkled in the bright foyer lights as I descended the curving staircase once again.

At the bottom, Mom had donned her long mink. Dad held out my rabbit-fur coat—identical to Lisa's—and I shrugged it on. In the cold car, my parents chatted, and I held the star up to show Lisa. She stuck her lower lip out and showed me her paper snowflake.

"It's pretty," I said. She shrugged.

"Oh, look at that house!" Mom pointed to a rooftop Santa, his rein-deer galloping along the ridge of a Tudor near downtown Farmington.

Dad made a wisecrack about Santa being high, and we all laughed.

After the service, we hurried home to change as Dad retrieved paper luminaries from the basement. Mom had crafted them weeks ahead of time. We carried the lanterns out to join our neighbors digging small holes in the snow. Along the frosty street, families exchanged season's greetings.

Mom placed a lantern in the hole I had just finished. Dad grunted as his long match lit the luminary's paper edge along with the tea light. I giggled as a huge flame promptly consumed the entire bag, then died just as quickly.

He stomped the charred ashes into snow, and Mom handed him another bag. I dug another icy hole. Lisa brought out cups of hot chocolate. Carolyn joined us with her own steaming mug.

"Here he comes!" she said, pointing to a red F-150 with flashing lights, rolling slowly down the street.

Kids raced toward it. A Santa wearing a stuffed, rented suit tossed candy over the side from an overstuffed La-Z Boy in the truck bed. I stepped over a glowing luminary and into the street with Lisa and Carolyn. A preschooler who lived across the street joined us. She looked up with wide eyes as Santa's horse-powered sleigh rolled to a stop in front of our group. I realized she couldn't reach the offered candy.

I handed my cup to Lisa. "Here." I hoisted the small girl onto my hip. She giggled and stretched her hands out. Santa gave her a striped candy cane and a tap on the nose that made her laugh again. I set her down and took my hot chocolate back.

"Merry Christmas." Santa tossed a candy cane my way. I recognized Mr. Zajdel's glasses above the white beard and winked at him.

"Merry Christmas, Santa!" I said with a laugh.

With a flourish, Dad set a casserole and cornmeal muffins made from basement-raid items on the table. I frowned. I missed Mom's traditional holiday cooking and remembered her prime rib and potatoes au gratin. While I'd hoped for ham, I refused to sulk on Christmas Eve and ate without complaint. While Hamburger Helper and Jiffy mix weren't perfect, at least Dad was giving it a try. Like Mom said, everything would be okay—even if it was different.

Dad made an announcement as we finished. "I think we should skip the Christmas Eve Children's Mass tonight."

My face betrayed me.

He gave my hand a pat. "It's too long for you to sit in hard pews."

Disappointed, I went back to my bedroom and picked up the small sheep ornament I had made from clay. The little black face looked lost.

"C'mon, let's hang you," I limped slowly to the tree in the living room and found a spot.

Outside, I heard the neighbors talking and laughing in the street. I smiled wistfully. Christmas was Christmas, after all. My back injury was just a hiccup. Everything would be okay, and next year would be even better.

Christmas morning, light filtered through dense clouds, too weak to leave a warm impression on the gray carpet beneath my window. I had slept in longer than I'd planned. It was almost nine, but it seemed I was the first awake still. There was no music or smells of breakfast cooking already. The house merely sighed as a strong wind whistled by. The furnace clicked and began to hum. I wished for a crackling fire and the smell of bacon or Mom's apple pies baking for Christmas brunch. Christmas morning didn't sound or smell any different from any other morning since Mom's death.

Still holding on to hope, I turned on my clock radio to carols, volume low, and waited for Lisa and Dad to wake and help me out of bed. Two hours later, I sat in a chair by the tree. A paltry pile of presents lay underneath, covered in cheap paper with jagged edges and no bows. I coughed to hide my dismay. Mom had always made Christmas beautiful. Dad's shabby gift wrap bordered on sacrilege.

Dad handed me my first present. "Here."

I hoped until the moment I tore the last paper scrap away that there could be something amazing inside. Instead, a red ice scraper lay in my lap.

I looked up at Dad blankly.

"You know, for your new car," he said with a wounded look.

"Oh, sure. Thanks, Dad." I forced a smile. I didn't have a car or license yet.

Next, I unwrapped a black knit hat, its drugstore label still attached—men's size small, perfect for robbing a bank. I put it on my head and thanked him for random gifts I assumed he had thrown into a basket while getting my prescriptions or more alcohol the day before.

I'd spent hours picking out my gift for him at the mall, debating which Dremel tool set would make him light up. Now, he barely glanced at the set's contents. As for me, I already had three winter hats, all donated by people who'd given more thought to clothing me than my own father had. A heavy gloom settled in my chest. Disappointed didn't cover half of what I felt.

After visiting Dad's mom at the nursing home that afternoon, we went to Uncle Bob's. I tried to ignore the cheesy movies on TV and drowsed on one end of the living room couch.

Dad and Bob came in. Bob sat in the recliner opposite, and Dad sank into the other end of the same couch I lay on.

"You still going?" Bob asked in a low voice. Lisa and my aunt and cousins were chatting in the adjoining kitchen, and I guessed that my father and uncle had come in here to avoid the girls overhearing them. I kept my eyes closed and pretended to be asleep.

Dad shifted. I felt his attention focus on me. I tried to breathe deeply and relax my face. Dad quietly cleared his throat.

"It won't work," he said.

Bob grunted. "What's the insurance amount?"

"Not enough," Dad said.

Bob began to ask another question that I wanted to hear, but another person entered, and Bob swallowed whatever it was. I heard Aunt Diane. "I made coffee—with Baileys."

The men changed the subject, Bob complaining about having only Christmas Day off.

"I lost $500 last week on the horses," he said. "Gotta work overtime to pay for all the presents Diane put on credit."

Dad laughed. "When you going to stop throwing good money after bad?" he asked.

Bob whined, "Well, I don't have a white-collar paycheck, and I've got two more kids than you. What else am I supposed to do to make ends meet?"

With a final slurp, Dad finished his mug and tapped my foot.

"Time to go."

I made a noise and stretched, stiff from holding still. I wondered what Dad needed money for as Lisa silently brought me my coat. We waited by the door while Dad borrowed paper to wrap his gift for Grandma Findlay, whom I hadn't seen since the funeral.

At Grandma's Redford Parish home in west Detroit, Aunt Kathy unfastened the door and greeted my father with a pinched face. "Arnie."

I hadn't seen Aunt Kathy since the funeral either, though I knew she'd come to help my dad and Aunt Diane write thank-you cards for all the flowers and sympathy donations while we were staying with Aunt Diane immediately after the fire.

I was doing homework in the spare bedroom of the small ranch when Kathy's voice alerted me to her presence. I'd begun to come out, but her next words stopped me cold.

"Excuse me?" she had said with an icy edge.

Aunt Diane had mumbled. "Nothing. Never mind."

I'd shrunk back into my room, not hearing a response from my dad if there was one. He'd probably ignored the women, not wanting to be bothered by whatever drama they'd conjured up. My mother's sister had left a few moments later, and I'd been too afraid to say anything. My father had kept his distance from my mother's family ever since.

My aunt Kathy explained years later that she'd heard my aunt Diane muttering to herself. The painter's wife had said something to the effect of, "With those spoiled bitches (meaning my sister and me) out of the way, (Diane's kids) will be able to have what they need."

My grieving aunt Kathy had been stunned at first but grown angry and distraught, while my father had said nothing, and she'd had to leave before another murder was committed—as Kathy put it to me.

But that Christmas, all I knew was that there had been a family rift. I'd worried that my father's attitude had created a gulf between them and me also, but Kathy hugged me with genuine affection. I felt warm for the first time that day.

That was before I saw the thin, papery smile stretched across my grandmother Findlay's face as she waited for her turn to embrace me. Despite her "Merry Christmas," her eyes lacked joy. She had aged years since October. She ignored my father's offered hand, turning back to the kitchen.

"Give me ten minutes, girls. It's almost ready."

I trailed Lisa upstairs to see Aunt Kathy's young boys but hid at the top when I heard my aunt address my father.

"How are the girls?"

Dad answered, "Well, you know. It's been hard on all of us . . . I just don't know how I can go back to work with their mother gone."

The atmosphere chilled despite the warm smell of prime rib and potatoes. I wondered if that was what Dad had been hinting at with his brother. If so, it seemed silly. Lisa and I took care of ourselves; we were almost adults. We did most of the cooking and cleaning. Lisa was even doing the shopping. We didn't need a babysitter. The house had been paid for and insured. So were our cars. I was confused by his apparent fear of running out of money.

A long moment passed, and I almost walked away, but then Dad continued.

"They really need a mother figure to be there for them . . ." His words almost sounded like a question.

Indignation swelled. Was this about money or Mom? If it was about Mom, I recalled all the times he had mocked and belittled Mom. For years, he'd shouted about how irrelevant she was. Now he said we needed her? The irony made me want to march down those steps and tell him how miserable this Christmas had been without Mom, how unloved I felt by his thoughtless presents, how magical she'd made Christmases, and how desperately I missed her every day. Of course, I still needed my mother at fifteen! Was he asking my aunt to take us on because he didn't want to? Or he couldn't?

I couldn't ask because I had eavesdropped. Any confrontation would halt at that particular point with my father, and there would be consequences for that betrayal.

Then a thought struck me. Maybe I had it completely wrong. Maybe Dad had finally realized how much Mom mattered. Maybe he really was concerned. Maybe as a single parent now, he at last recognized her contribution.

I let that possibility quash the rage. Did he miss my mother beneath the drinking and rage—or was he just trying to guilt my aunt into caring for us? Unsure which was true, I kept silent. I sensed there were gaps in my understanding of the factors at play in my life, so I kept listening when I shouldn't have but not asking the questions I should have. Though I rationalized that it was the threat of violence that silenced me, my self-contempt accused me of fearing the answers more.

We stayed barely long enough to eat dinner and exchange gifts. Grandma cried when I unwrapped hers—a picture of Mom taken at her cousin's bridal shower a week before she died. They weren't happy tears. I hugged Grandma, ashamed that my family always caused her grief.

I went to bed disillusioned. I'd believed Christmas lived and breathed joy; instead, Christmas had died with Mom. I mourned them both.

Chapter Eight
January 1986

Dad sent me to the old house weekly. If it happened to be light out, I'd snoop around, trying to put the puzzle pieces together. I wanted to know where Mom had been found, how she could have been trapped. I wanted the truth. He wanted cans of green beans, boxes of pasta, and tools.

First, I explored the main floor. The worst of the damage was concentrated in the family room. The blackened ceiling sagged like old skin, fragile-looking and dry. Cobweb-like dust had settled in corners. If touched, it collapsed into flakes. All that remained of our couches were dark springs lying in three or four inches of debris, patches of carpet fibers buried beneath. The thick glass top of the coffee table had shattered as its wooden legs made a bonfire beneath it and collapsed. Heavy shards of glass lay scattered among the ashes.

A smaller pile of charcoal dust lay between the couches and coffee table. I imagined the room as I had known it. I recalled nothing that could explain the smaller pile's existence. I contemplated the spot often from the doorway, trying to imagine what might have been there. I avoided examining it too closely for several weeks.

One sunny January afternoon, a rarity in Michigan's deep winter, I summoned enough courage to sift through the smaller ash mound. In a moment, my searching fingers uncovered Mom's wire-rimmed reading glasses, twisted and black. I remembered her putting them on as she read my geometry book and puffed on her cigarette. She had slid them atop her head as I kissed her cheek goodbye. I sobbed, holding the corroded frames to my chest, kneeling.

"Holy Mary, Mother of God, pray for us sinners, now and at the hour of our death. Amen."

I repeated that phrase thirty or forty times. I lost count. I didn't know what else to do. She'd drawn her last breath here as the fire swirled around her and I'd run laps at basketball practice. These glasses stayed with her to the end. In my hands, I held a physical connection to her death. Until I held those frames, she had just disappeared. Finding them felt like goodbye at last.

I rose, tucking the bent rims into my pocket. On my way to the basement, I paused in the kitchen doorway. The inferno had melted the refrigerator doors, now an ashy white glob on the floor. Stepping inside, I checked the oven and found a large pan of petrified meatloaf. Opening the cupboards by the pantry, I saw mom's stash of chips and graham crackers. The cans of peas and pears over the built-in desk remained identifiable. Everything had been flash-seared in a time I could never return to. The two missing things were the only ones that mattered. My mother and our family's future had disappeared, leaving only a throbbing ache. I lifted my foot to kick at the puddle of refrigerator but stopped midmotion. Another memory interrupted the silence.

I turned to leave.

June 1979

Lisa had been babysitting while my parents attended a wedding.
She was eleven, and I was nine, too young for a cocktail reception. I

was drowsy and almost asleep when I heard the garage door open. I sat up, eager to hear about the party, when I heard muffled shouting in the garage.

When the door to the house opened and Dad's "You lying whore!" pierced the night air, both Lisa and I left our rooms and tiptoed to the top of the stairs. Despite knowing we were supposed to be in bed, we eavesdropped with tense concentration. At Mom's scream, we barreled down the steps and into the kitchen.

Dad had Mom up against the refrigerator.

"Never again!" he yelled.

He attacked in his suit jacket, a flower from the wedding still pinned to his pocket. She had dropped her purse to the floor, clawing at his forearm, which had pinned her neck against the fridge door. His other hand forced Mom's jaw open as he tore at her mouth. She had set her jaw tight, but her lip was bleeding. He took a sideswipe at her face with his free fist to knock her mouth open.

I intuitively understood his intent to rip out her tongue.

Lisa and I used everything—hands, heads, shoulders, fingernails, feet—to wedge between them. Mom gagged.

"Get off! Leave her alone!" we shouted.

Lisa pummeled Dad's stomach with her head and hands. I pushed on his legs. He swore and backed away, panting as he cradled his fingers. Mom must have bitten him hard. He kicked at Lisa while the three of us fled to their bedroom.

Lisa locked the door. Mom sank into the olive-green bedside chair. She held her throat, hands crossed. Lisa and I came to stand near as she rocked in agitation. I stroked her hair.

"Should we stay . . . or leave?" Mom rasped.

I pulled my hand back as if stung and looked at Lisa. My mother had never wavered in her devotion to her marriage. I'd internalized her belief that the only thing worse than an unhappy family was losing one altogether. I was desperate to keep mine no matter the cost.

My neighborhood friend Jenny had had to move two years earlier because of her parents' divorce. I had seen her mother crying. Jenny had been so sad that I'd cried for her. Now, my own mother was on the verge of tears, contemplating leaving my father, and it terrified me.

"No! We can't leave!" Lisa cried. Her wide eyes mirrored mine.

I joined her. "No, Mommy!"

She grasped us each by the elbow and looked into our eyes. "One of these days, you girls won't be here, and he's going to kill me," she whispered, her eyes haunted.

My hand clenched hers. "No, don't leave him. We won't let him hurt you."

I had done my best for years, but I'd made several miscalculations that doomed my family.

I walked out of the kitchen. My family had been held together only by lies. Lisa and I thought we could corral the rage, control the alcoholism, do damage control. Control was a lie. We thought we could hold together what, in truth, was already gone. I had mistaken proximity for love. Lies bound my parents together, not love.

I had left my mother in the kitchen that afternoon—telling myself everything would be okay—believing the fragile lies I'd spun. With just a few breaths of bad luck, my self-deceit had proven fatal to my mother. Now, consuming guilt shadowed every step I took. I had promised her my protection, then left her alone. I had lied to and betrayed us both. My penance was being left behind with him.

I remembered he was waiting, so I gathered several cans from the basement and left. Back at the rental, I wiped my feet on the doormat and opened the front door. Canned laughter from a sitcom greeted me. I spied Dad asleep in the living room recliner. I tiptoed past into the kitchen and opened a can I'd brought and dumped it into a pan. I whisked the congealed soup with water until it was hot and bubbly, then ate alone in the fading light, lost in what might have been—had I kept my promise.

Late in January, Dad sent me over to the house one afternoon, a Saturday, I think. Closing the front door behind me, I noticed light pouring into the dark foyer from the second floor. The upper windows hadn't all been boarded up, and light streamed through my bedroom door, which stood ajar.

I hadn't dared climb the charred staircase previously, but the house had become less intimidating over time. I took a deep breath and ascended, testing each riser before putting my full weight on it. The hallway carpet remained, though grimy and melted on the foyer side. With a gentle push on my smoke-stained door, three months rewound before my eyes.

Everything was exactly as I'd left it—my school bag lay open on top of my unmade bed—fixed in time and covered in soot. I walked to my dresser and touched a finger to the jewelry spread across the top. Except for a string of pearls Grandma Findlay had given me at communion, everything had melted fast to the laminate top. I wiped the pearls on my shirt, then stuck them in my pocket.

Water marks and thick dust swirled together, making strange patterns on the wrinkled surfaces of the art projects I'd tacked to the wall. Dad had been so proud of the now-ruined sketches that he'd bought the drafting table still in the corner as a Christmas present the year prior.

A gust swept little drops of snow from the ceiling. I raised my face to a hole chiseled by axes above my bed. The winter sun, now low in the sky, threw soft puffs of pink across the new skylight. It would be dark before five o'clock. Looking around the room again, I decided to rescue the drafting table.

Hefting it, I started downstairs, but while trying to balance one side on the railing, I tripped and fell. I barely caught myself from a full-flight tumble with the maple desk by grabbing onto a sagging banister, which, impossibly, held. With a sigh of relief, I carefully dragged the table down to the front door.

I climbed the sooty steps once more and opened the door to my mother's room. I remained in the doorway, terrified any intrusion might break the spell—and the scene might vanish. There were no ashes here. Aside from a slight odor of lingering smoke and the melted television, nothing looked different. Her clothes hung in the open closet. A pair of heels still sat by the full-length mirror. Her bottles of perfume, including my favorite, L'Air du Temps, lay scattered across the dresser. The bed pillows, still arranged and plumped, seemed expectant. The olive chair remained by the phone I had used. A time capsule perfectly preserved.

After a few minutes, I gently closed the door and ran down the stairs, stopping to lift the desk before stumbling out the door. A nagging desire to return grew more insistent.

The first opportunity came on a cold evening three days later. Dad complained that we had no milk for gravy, and I remembered the evaporated milk in the charred kitchen pantry.

"I think there's still canned milk back there," I offered. I inclined my head toward the house behind us. He nodded at the key drawer. I grabbed a flashlight before heading out into the early-winter nightfall.

I used the makeshift emergency lights to make my way upstairs, headed for her room first. Digging under the bed's decorative shams, I retrieved her pillow and smelled the underside. Her scent lingered. I collapsed to the floor, dropping the flashlight, which rolled under the bed while I sobbed in the dark room. I slowly climbed under the covers, dirty shoes and all, to be as close as possible to my mother. I lay there weeping in the shadow of her life.

Next, I went through purses in her closet, looking for something of her, but only found grocery lists, receipts, lipsticks, and gum. I frowned. In her bathroom, I rubbed her skin cream on my wrist to smell at home later. I put everything back exactly how she'd left it before I softly closed the door behind me and returned to Dad with the cans of milk.

Days later, I came home from school and noticed the county coroner's return address among the opened mail on the rental's kitchen desk. Intrigued, I peeked into the living room to confirm Dad was blacked out as usual in the recliner. I knew Lisa was working late as usual, so I returned to the desk and pulled the envelope from the pile. My hands trembled for a moment before opening it. I imagined the cause of death spelled out in murderous letters but then decided if that were the case, they wouldn't have simply mailed it. I held my breath as I pulled the contents out.

The death certificate inside recorded Marlene Findlay Edwards's death to be by natural causes. I studied it and the raised seal. It looked official. I let a deep sigh out and surrendered my suspicions to the certificate's authority.

My fears were silly nonsense. How could Dad do something as insane as commit murder? Sure, he had a temper, but there was a difference between heated words and the actual crime. What more evidence did I need to let go of the haunting echoes of the past?

My guilt took a turn, and now I wished I had stayed to help her get out of the fire. Believing that it had all been some cosmic accident and not cold-blooded murder relieved some of the pressure but changed none of the consequences. The house still lay in ruins, and my mother was gone—but my visits stopped.

In fact, sifting through the ashes had to cease. With the official cause of death declared, Dad received generous life-insurance disbursements. Almost immediately, hired hands gutted the house and emptied my previous life into dumpsters.

Dad soon received another large envelope in the mail. He tore it open and dumped the contents into his hand one evening when we were all home. He stared into his hand for a moment, then turned to me.

"Here, take them."

I held out my hands, and he quickly dropped my mother's diamond solitaire and band into my possession.

"What is it?" Lisa asked.

"They should go to you both," was all he said.

He turned away and threw the packaging in the garbage before washing his hands at the sink. I showed Lisa. She appeared pained at the sight of the jewelry and didn't ask to keep them, so I put them with the twisted frames I'd hidden in my jewelry box.

He never mentioned them again.

Those small tokens and my nightmares were my only relics of Mom.

Chapter Nine

One awful dream replayed with torturous regularity. It always began with me outside a glass door, watching my parents fight in the kitchen. I yanked at the locked door, but it refused to give. Next came the horrible recognition that this scene was after I'd left them alone. Shouting, I banged both fists against the glass. Though I heard their every word, they always ignored my pleading. Growing angry, I either kicked the door or rammed it with my shoulder. That varied. Regardless, I was powerless to intervene every time. I usually watched Dad take a swing at Mom. She ducked or pushed him aside and then disappeared into the house.

If the dream continued and I didn't wake drenched in sweat or calling Mom's name, I'd watch Dad drive off in a rage. At this point, there was always a small sense of relief, knowing she was safe with him gone. I would go back to searching for Mom, circling the house and peering through locked windows. I called her name, unable to find her.

"Mom, he's gone! Come out!"

I'd call until I noticed a flame licking the baseboard in the hallway. Then I would go berserk, pounding on windows and screaming.

"Mom! Mom! Get out!"

Fire ran along the walls, climbing to the ceiling . . . Then the worst part came as her screams started—and wouldn't stop. I tried to break the glass but found nothing able to shatter the freakishly thick panes. Despairing,

I put my face against the window, seeing into the family room as flames engulfed her on the couch.

"Somebody, help me!"

With the effect of ironic horror only fantasies can produce, the greater effort I used in shouting, the less noise my throat produced, leaving me to pound the glass with silent sobs. I never made it past this point without waking in the middle of a mute scream.

I would tell myself they were just dreams, not real, but the tears on my cheeks always were. Her "natural" death haunted me. How could dying in a fire be considered, much less termed, natural? I couldn't imagine a worse fate than being burned alive. I didn't understand why she hadn't escaped. There were glass doors ten feet from where I'd found the frames. She'd lain so close to living, ten feet from an alternate reality.

In all my searching of the house, I had assumed if I could discover what had happened, it would make things better. Knowing the fire had killed her solved nothing.

One night in January, I lay awake. Unable to bear the thought of witnessing Mom's death in my sleep once again, I grew angry with God. I was tired of the pain. I was haunted by not knowing why or how my life had suddenly gone from a tolerable kind of dysfunction to horribly excruciating. What had I done to deserve any of this?

How could I trust God with my life when He had allowed my mother to experience such unspeakable agony? She had been a better believer than I was, and still the evidence suggested my mother's faith in God's goodness had been grossly misplaced. He hadn't saved her, and all He'd left me were ashes.

Absolute hopelessness pressed into every part of me. Everything good I had believed in was gone, and I had been left alone with the alcoholic.

Like everything else in my life, God was a lie. I wished to end my pain by the only method I knew—ceasing to exist. I began contemplating a void swallowing me whole.

The room emptied of feeling. I wanted to feel nothing. I closed my eyes and turned on my side, away from the door. A shade of blackness darker than I'd ever imagined pressed around me, a yawning shadow that could extinguish thought and breath. It invited me to embrace it, to give myself to it. Without fear, I considered the promised relief.

Warm light filled the room.

With it, the dark specter fled, but I'd barely registered its retreat when I rolled over and gasped. My eyes widened and then squinted in response to the brightening glow. Though I dared not remove my gaze from its center, I knew that if I'd turned my head, my room would have been as visible to me as if it were high noon and the house made of glass. All this dazzling energy radiated from a single person at its core.

I put a hand over my eyes. A familiar smile came into focus. I jolted upright with recognition and joy. The woman I saw had longer hair and was perhaps younger looking, but there was no mistaking Mom's shining face. She radiated so much peace even her clothes and skin shone with it. I couldn't have described any color; she was just bright.

I opened my mouth to speak, but before I could utter a syllable, love struck my chest with physical force. Her tender feelings poured into the emptiness that had driven me toward the void.

"Shelly. Don't worry. Everything will be okay. I will always love you."

I stretched my hand toward her, wanting to feel her once more, but already the light was fading. In a moment, she was gone. I exhaled a soft breath. Gentle warmth lingered in the again-dim room. The shadows were no longer cold and hungry, only silent. I hugged myself, preserving the warmth, and wished I could have asked her why everything had happened. Why had she come back to me?

84

I'd told myself for months that hallucinations due to physical and emotional stress explained her earlier visits. I hadn't wanted to accept her appearances as anything else. This time was different. I believed she knew I had been succumbing to the allure of self-annihilation and had come to save me. I wrapped myself in her words and slept deeply for the first time in months.

Even if it meant I was crazy, God help me, I believed in heavenly messengers.

The ongoing press coverage and watercooler gossip among his colleagues drove my father to take a leave of absence effective the first of January. Without any reason to remain sober, he never was, and he left the house only to stock up on booze or go to bars.

I sought ways to escape being home alone with him. Lisa picked up extra shifts and did the grocery shopping on her way home from work. I rarely saw her. Our only "family" time was Friday nights when I shadowed her to parties. I was grateful to hang out on the fringes with a paper cup of beer and watch anyone besides Dad get drunk.

Because of my back injury, sports had been put on hold, and I had few options for avoiding the house besides wandering the cold streets. The week after my mother's visit, Sabrina stopped me in the hallway and asked if I had plans for Saturday. She offered to take me to the volleyball game and invited me to stay overnight afterward at her house. I jumped at the opportunity.

The experience was eye-opening. Sabrina's home overflowed with a boisterous happiness opposite the tense silences and roaring obscenities that filled mine. It amazed me how two parents, three kids, and random church people (there were lots) could come and go all evening with comfortable ease. It was harmonious chaos, and I loved it.

The only awkward time was waiting for them to finish praying that evening. My family had only ever prayed together briefly over holiday meals. I thought praying every day a bit much, but Sabrina's family was different in general. Even if they were extra religious, it didn't change the fact that I enjoyed being away from home. At least, at the Perrett's home, no one yelled at me.

That night, I waited in Sabrina's room while they finished downstairs. I sat on Sabrina's spare twin bed and pondered my mom's visit the week before. Growing up, I had supposed after dying you went to heaven or hell. Simple enough, as long as you didn't have to spend much time in purgatory.

Mom had lacked a purgatory vibe; her glowing countenance spoke only of joy and love, with no hint of pain or suffering. That was a relief, but Mom's visits left me wanting to know more. Ironically, I had always asked Mom any religious questions before, but that seemed impossible despite her appearances. I sighed. It was frustrating that her messages were exactly the same and left me with more questions than answers.

Sabrina's feet pounded up the stairs, and my thoughts shifted to her. Sabrina's family was overtly religious, so I assumed she had an opinion on the next life. Maybe I could ask her.

Sabrina entered and closed the door behind her. Diving headfirst into whether Sabrina believed in angelic visits might sound crazy. I needed a more natural way to come at it.

"Thanks for waiting," she said.

"Yep, no problem." My mind churned.

She pulled open a drawer and took out her pajamas. The perfect segue occurred to me while she changed. I cleared my throat.

"So, uh, what is the difference between your beliefs and mine? I know you are Christian, but what makes you Mormon?"

"Hmm." Sabrina sat on her bed and thought. "I suppose the biggest difference is that I believe God still speaks to people," she said.

I wasn't sure what she meant by God speaking to people, but her answer wasn't the summary of dogmatic differences I'd expected. I bit my lip.

"Who . . ." I stopped, curious who she thought God spoke to but afraid my question might sound overeager.

Sabrina smiled. "I believe that God can talk to us, like He did to Moses," she said.

"Okay . . . like the pope?" I asked, relieved to have made a sensible connection by myself.

"Yes, I guess." She blew out a breath. "But people like me too."

I blinked, trying to absorb that thought. "Like, He talks to you?"

Sabrina nodded. "Not like you think of talking, maybe. I get thoughts or impressions that I know aren't mine. It's like someone whispers them to my mind."

I tried to process what she had said. Could God—would God—really talk to regular people?

She gave me a weak smile. "I know it sounds a little funny, but the thoughts bring me hope and peace." She shrugged at my astonished look.

Sabrina looked a bit sheepish. "I sound like I'm schizophrenic. I don't know how to explain it better. It's like I suddenly understand something I'm sure I didn't get a moment before, or when something I was confused about is suddenly clear."

I wasn't sure whether to laugh or cry. I had talked *at* God all my life. With all my pleas for help, for protection, for penance, I had never heard a reply or expected one. I had always assumed God's response was limited to either granting my petitions or not. That was it. God speaking was an Old Testament thing or to apostles in the New Testament, not for twentieth-century believers. He had given us His Word then, and now we followed it. What would He tell me that I didn't already know? That I was faithless? That I had failed my mother? That I was broken and lost?

I looked down at my hands, trying to work through what all this meant. Sabrina thought God talked to people. My dead mother was talking to me. Was she crazy? Was I?

Sabrina rolled over to grab a paperback from her nightstand and opened it. "This man started our church." She pointed to a painting of a young guy kneeling in a forest and two men above him in the air, bright light emanating from them—glowing robes and hair. They lacked halos or wings. Men of light.

I took the book and stared. My heart raced as I looked at the small picture, and I almost fell off the bed. I had thought I would have to come at the angel thing in a roundabout way, but she had handed it to me practically unprompted! I realized my jaw had dropped, and I closed my mouth.

The picture was crazy. Six months ago, I might have smiled politely and laughed into my pillow when the lights turned off. Now, a surge of interest filled me. I handed the book back in silence. She turned the lights off and instead of a smirk, my brow furrowed at the stunning parallels to my own experience—the darkness in the background, the illumination, his hand raised to shield his eyes.

The concept of angels was familiar to me. An angel came to Mary and the shepherds, one stopped Paul on the road to Damascus. Angels ministered to Jesus. But angels were great beings of light with halos, wings, and music who appeared at significant times to great people. I had neither importance nor distinction. I had little faith in anything to do with God, in fact. My angel had been the one person most familiar to me in the world—my mother. All I knew was that I believed she had come and that the picture in Sabrina's book looked astoundingly similar to what had happened to me.

Though Sabrina believed this man's story, I wasn't about to share mine, even though I had seen something amazing too. Sabrina showing me the picture seemed more than coincidence. I took it as a reassuring sign that

God wanted me to understand that He did send messengers to his children on occasion—a small mercy to calm my fears of being insane.

Still, even if God sent her, why? I didn't envision starting any new religion. I had never been a passionate parish member. I'd gone to church with Mom. That she believed had been enough for me.

I let the conversation lapse and lay awake while Sabrina slept, wondering why God had spoken or, rather, had let Mom. Miraculous visitation or not, nothing made sense.

Chapter Ten

January 31, 1986

Coming in behind Lisa after school, I slammed the door shut. It echoed in the empty house. The television was off, and so were the lights. Dad's recliner was vacant.

I dropped my school bag. "Dad?"

"Shelly!" Lisa called from the kitchen.

She pointed to a plate dumped in the sink, spaghetti noodles sliding into the drain. She looked at me, eyes wide. Dad hadn't left the house for four weeks. Now, he had vanished. We searched for a note but found nothing. We checked the garage. Inexplicably, Dad's car remained parked there.

I was left grasping at straws to explain his disappearance. "It can't be an emergency if he just went for a walk, right?"

Lisa shook her head. "No, someone must have come and taken him out."

I nodded. It was a Friday night. Maybe he'd gone with a friend to a sports bar to watch the Pistons game. Unsure of what else to do, we did homework and made sandwiches for dinner. At six o'clock, we left for the varsity boys' basketball game. When we returned around midnight, we heard the phone ringing in the dark kitchen as we opened the house door.

Lisa ran and picked up the handset. "Oh! Hi, Aunt Diane."

The answering machine blinked with eight messages. I pressed play.

"This is Dad. Pick up the phone."

"Shelly, Lisa, pick up! I need you to come get me."

"Lisa! Get the phone! You guys need to bail me out!"

I turned to Lisa, terrified. "Dad's in jail."

She hushed me with an abrupt slash of her hand. "Shh! I know. Diane's telling me."

I waited, listening. Dad had been arrested and charged with first-degree murder and arson. They had handcuffed him and taken him to Pontiac shortly before school ended. The knot in my stomach that had relaxed since holding the death certificate in my hands was back and bigger than ever.

Stupid. I'd been so stupid to believe the shiny seal. I sank into the kitchen desk chair and stared at the floor. He'd done it after all.

"But we can't get his money out!" Lisa pulled at her long hair. "Wait, we both have $40,000 in our college funds. How much does he need?" She paused as Diane answered.

"Okay, see you then."

Lisa hung up and swore. She looked at me. "They're coming to get us at eight tomorrow morning."

"What about the money?" I asked.

"Diane said we'll figure it out tomorrow."

We went to our rooms in shock. Part of me waited for another call, hoping Grandma Findlay or Aunt Kathy would come get us. I assumed they knew of my father's arrest—didn't cops tell the victim's family about that stuff?

No one called them that night, not even me. I was too embarrassed. I knew my mother's family also suspected my father and would probably be both relieved and furious to have their misgivings validated. I couldn't confide to them how upset my father's arrest made me if it was justice at last. Still, I was devastated.

He was my father, and as awful as the charges were, he was all I had left.

No one called or came that night. Trying not to panic, I went through the motions of getting ready for bed. I brushed my teeth and caught my reflection in the mirror. A mistake. A murderer's daughter stared back at me.

I suddenly doubted Mom's assertion that everything was going to be okay. My hands shook as I rinsed my toothbrush and shut off the water.

That my intuition had been correct provided no comfort. My insides twisted in fear. The lie that I had a normal family had just been exposed. Any kind of normalcy I once possessed had been consumed by the fire. I just hadn't been able to face it.

I realized that seeing Mom after her death might have meant I was sort of crazy, but refusing to see Dad for what he was should have been my one-way ticket to the looney bin.

I turned my lights off and looked out my window at the dark form of our house behind the rental. I'd dedicated hours to my obsession of finding something there but had missed something right here. Now, crazy or not, I shuddered.

From now on, I was on my own.

That night, an ice storm coated the roads and trees, and when Uncle Bob arrived the next morning, he drove us to Pontiac at a snail's pace in his 1977 Cadillac. He parked in a mostly empty lot adjacent to a three-story granite building near Woodward Avenue.

Lisa and I followed our aunt and uncle into a vaulted entry with marble floors. The courthouse lobby stretched several hundred yards to my right. Neal Simpson stood to the right at a tall counter and waved us over while continuing his conversation with a female bailiff. She looked up and made eye contact with me. I looked away, my attention drawn to the glass doors at the end of the atrium. They swung open, and two policemen emerged. They flanked a third man whose hands were cobbled by steel cuffs. Dad looked rumpled and angry.

I had never spent much time contemplating whether Dad was a good person or not. He was just . . . Dad. He scared me, he took care of me, and he was part of me. Now, the man standing before me seemed a stranger.

I studied his face as if for the first time. The booze had dissipated and left him defensive. A thin web of red veins stood out just beneath the surface of his cheeks and nose, and a large one at his temple throbbed defiantly. His brown eyes were clear but distant, as if calculating the odds of coming out on top. There was no regret, no contrition, no explanation. For the first time in my life, I saw my father as he was—a selfish, murderous drunk.

As Dad rubbed at his wrists after they removed the restraints, I wondered if the strangers milling around us in the lobby also saw his true character. Anyone arrested for murder must, by default, be bad. One who had killed his own wife? Worse.

I felt tainted by association. I wanted to believe I was a good person. I had never intentionally harmed anyone. Mom was a good person. Lisa too. We had never wanted anything but a normal, good life. And yet this man had ruined everything for no possible good reason. Divorce was normal. Murder was not.

I had made a mistake and aligned myself with the wrong side after the fire. With Mom's death, I wasn't sure what to believe. Surviving with any sense of normalcy had required I hope Dad's lies were true and hang on to what was left of our family. I saw now that he had manipulated my desire for a happy family. I hung my head, wanting to leave as soon as possible. I had been a fool, and that shamed me.

I had done it to myself again. Both times, before the fire and afterward,

I had let my burning desire to have a normal homelife persuade me that the worst-case scenario couldn't or didn't happen. I hadn't wanted to believe our family had been that bad and still was.

Dad swore at the bail amount as he gripped the pen tightly above the page Neal put in front of him. He was free to go after the papers were signed. Our family reunion was about what you'd expect. He ignored Lisa and me as we walked out to the car and used every cuss word in his extensive foul vocabulary to describe his attorney, the cops, and the prison guards.

"I have to pay Neal a hundred grand! I swear the judicial system is rigged! It's all about making money!" He slammed his passenger door closed.

Aunt Diane winced slightly beside me in the back seat. She made a noise in her throat but nodded her agreement. She, like all of us, had tensed under his blistering tirade. He was wound tighter than I'd ever seen him. You could feel his need, his wanting, to throttle something or someone.

Dad struck the dash with a fist. "They bleed me before a trial can even prove my innocence."

At that last word, a wave of humming anger swept the fear and shame from my mind. *His innocence?* I wanted to scream at my dad—to fill Uncle Bob's 1977 Cadillac with the whole truth—from the first bruise to the last threat. He had been trying to kill my mother for at least as long as I'd been alive, probably longer.

I opened my mouth, but my survival instincts choked me into silence at the same time Lisa gripped my arm. Her face held the same warning. We lived with him. My mother's killer slept two doors down the hallway. My fists clenched quietly in my lap. *Liar.*

The three of us split up as soon as we got home, disappearing into our own rooms. It felt exactly like the morning after a big fight when nobody talked and everyone pretended everything was fine, though nothing was.

Just before lunchtime, Dad banged on my bedroom door. I jumped, startled.

He growled. "Get up. We gotta go transfer some funds."

I had no idea what he needed me for, but I wasn't about to contradict him in his surly mood, which hadn't improved from that morning despite the cocktail in his hand. He herded Lisa and me into his car and drove us to the bank.

On the way inside the bank, I spied the Saturday paper in the coin-operated newsstand outside and gasped.

Our family had made the front page once again. I realized every grocery-store checkout stand and newspaper box in town screamed the same headline: "Farmington Hills Man Arrested for Arson and Murder." Suddenly, I imagined every person in that bank and every citizen in the city having eaten their breakfast while devouring the agonizing details of my horrible life. The whole world suspected that Dad had murdered Mom.

Even worse, I agreed. That made me an accomplice because I had left her alone with him. I wanted to disappear. Shame and agony ate at me.

Why had Mom said that things would be okay? Things had gone from bad to worse.

I looked at Dad for his response, but he ignored the newspapers and went inside. Lisa saw the headline and paled, but she jerked her head at me to follow. Neal was waiting. He and my father began a terse conversation with a bank manager while I tried to pretend everything was normal.

I numbly signed the papers Neal pushed under my nose. I didn't care if Dad was a co-signer on my accounts or not. My life was ruined, and I couldn't envision a deeper pit of shame and torment. Apparently, my imagination lacked depth.

Chapter Eleven

February 1986

The week after his arrest, Dad sat Lisa and me down. We had lived in oppressive silence for days, and I wondered what new explosive announcement he was about to unload on us. My shoulders tensed, and I kept my feet under me, poised to escape.

Dad rubbed his hands together. The waves of expectation rolling off him confused me.

"I have a surprise for you girls." He smiled, waiting for a response.

I stole a glance at Lisa, whose eyebrows were raised. She was nervous too.

"Okay," I said and sat back, arms crossed. Lately, surprises were bad things.

"I booked a vacation a few months ago. I thought it would be nice to get away from it all and make new memories, as a family."

Silence. I drew my eyebrows together, trying to imagine a vacation that included Dad checking in with his bond officer.

"A few months ago?" Lisa asked first.

Dad's smile wilted a bit. "I booked that hotel in Mexico a few weeks after the fire." He paused. "I wanted to surprise you."

He was repeating himself. I didn't believe a word of it. Nothing was ever about us.

"But you can't go anywhere now." I failed to see what his revelation had in it for me besides a shocking display of his narcissistic mind. He'd booked travel a few weeks after murdering my mother? To my parents' annual resort? My stomach dropped in revulsion.

I had been to the resort once and hated it.

"Yes. Unfortunately, recent events preclude me leaving the country," Dad continued.

Good, I thought. I huffed under my breath.

"I don't want to go anyways," I said.

What was a family vacation without Mom? Besides, it seemed like a blown escape to me. I had a strong premonition we would never have come back. Dad's words to my aunt Kathy began to ring in my ears. A tingle went down my spine.

I was grateful he was being closely watched now. His weekly check-ins (due to his retirement status) were the one safety net I now possessed. If he disappeared, if we disappeared, there would be an instantaneous manhunt.

I was blindsided by his reaction.

"I paid for the resort already," he said, his voice hardening. "You are both going."

And that was it. I was on my way to Mexico whether I wanted a vacation or not. My pleas to stay home only infuriated my father, who called me ungrateful and then other more colorful adjectives. I relented.

Last time had been horrible, but I consoled myself that this time would be different. I was no longer a child.

February 1982 - Eleven Years Old

I wandered the Acapulco hotel grounds alone as an eleven-year-old.
Lisa and I were the only underage guests at the exclusive hotel—a
favor for my parents' long patronage—and the owner's granddaughter

Etelivita had spent every moment she could taking advantage of our presence. I sympathized with her usual lone existence as I made another boring round of the grounds.

The exotic flowers and trees had been interesting at first, but after a week, I had grown tired of the flora and pool and only wished for a playmate during the hours Etelivita was at school or in bed. That night, I had no idea where Lisa had gone, and my parents were off doing something with friends as usual, trusting me to the quiet resort's amenities. I sighed.

"Aren't you Arnie's daughter?" A man's voice interrupted my thoughts.

I recognized a graying Italian man in his fifties at a nearby table. He held playing cards and smiled, straight teeth shining from his olive face. A younger blonde woman, his wife, lowered her tall glass containing something pink and fizzy. Her short sundress matched the cocktail.

After a glance, taking me in from head to foot, the blonde returned to her cards, shuffling them.

"What's your name, sweetie?" the woman asked.

"Shelly." I clasped my hands behind my back, shifting my weight and flushing with the unsought attention. I knew better than to talk with strangers, but my parents had chatted with these two the previous night. They were all part of a large group who had vacationed there for a decade.

"Do you know how to play gin rummy?" the man asked, leaning back. He glanced at his wife, who nodded at him.

I shook my head no but quickly added, "I like to play card games, though."

"Well, would you like to learn?" the woman asked. She motioned to a nearby chair, and I dragged it over. I listened, brows furrowed, as

they explained the rules. We played a round with open hands so they could coach me. I picked it up quickly.

The woman called the man Tony, though I never did remember hearing her name. Tony talked to me and grunted at her. I won the third round.

"Wow. Good strategy!" The wife smiled at me. I beamed.

I ordered a Coke with lime to celebrate.

"Whatever!" Tony put on an offended face but winked at me. "Beginner's luck! I bet you can't beat me again!"

I laughed. That night and the next four raced by with no recollection of my parents' or sister's whereabouts. Tony admired my skills. I was happily occupied with new friends.

That week ended with a birthday party for Etelivita at her grandparents' villa, a Spanish colonial perched above the coast. A tennis court, flower gardens with fountains, and an outdoor pool filled three terraces descending to the beach. White-coated servers holding silver trays floated by with drinks and canapés. A mariachi band played music poolside.

I lounged in my navy bathing suit and white terry cover-up on a vinyl-strapped deck chair, not far from my parents. A smiling waiter placed a hairy coconut trimmed with a paper umbrella in my hands and nodded, watching. I took a tentative sip through a blue straw. The creamy sweet juice was delicious.

"Piña colada," the waiter said. I grinned at him and looked in vain for Lisa. I stood to see better.

The pool patio opened onto wide stone steps bordered by palm trees and ferns. The natural staircase led down to a rocky beach. I spied Lisa and Etelivita picking their way through the tide pools. I ran down the sandy stairs and joined them in gathering sand dollars and starfish. I used my cover-up as an apron to carry my treasure back to my lounge chair, depositing the crusty pile on the pool deck next to my distracted parents. On my fourth trip, Mom glanced down at my growing collection and sandy arms.

"I think that's enough dead sea creatures for ten little girls!" She tweaked my nose. "No more, okay? Why don't you just swim for a bit?"

I nodded, though my lip stuck out in a small pout. A couple of my parents' friends, including Tony, cajoled me, asking if I'd tried body-surfing. They invited me to come swim. Mom sent me off with an encouraging smile and a message for Lisa.

"Lisa, Mom says no more shells. Do you want to swim?"

I looked down the beach to where the tide pools turned to rolling waves and sand. Lisa shaded her eyes and looked up at our parents, then to where our adult acquaintances ventured into the water.

"Okay, come on, Etelivita." Lisa led the way. We splashed and screamed as the waves knocked us over. I chewed my lip, watching Lisa and Etelivita as they rode in on a wave, imitating the adults. I was a decent swimmer, thanks to summers on Lake Huron, but I had never been in the ocean.

Tony floated nearby. "Do you want me to show you how to body-surf?"

"Sure." I shrugged my shoulders and swam toward him. He crouched down into the surging waves and reached out for me. One hand wrapped around my chest and the other touched my bottom. His fingers shifted underneath the elastic of my suit.

Shocked, I froze. Tony's caresses confused me. He moved gently, but I knew it was wrong. He looked into my eyes. I silently looked away, paddling my arms.

He laughed and called to someone else as he adjusted his grip while he floated me along in the water. I looked toward the pool. Even over the surging crash of waves, the trumpets could be heard. I saw my parents. They were absorbed in their conversation.

Look at me, look at me! My heart raced with an urgent need for them to see what was happening.

Tony whispered in my ear, but I couldn't understand his words over the roar of the water and my confusion. I turned my head aside, away, and he shoved me ahead of a wave. It pushed me to shore and away from his touch. Crawling out of the water, I looked up again at the pool deck. My parents laughed and gestured for more drinks. I was invisible to them. From where I'd come, I watched Tony swim toward his friends. Lisa played in the surf with Etelivita farther up the beach. I padded down the sand until I stood near them. I didn't join in their play but followed them everywhere they went.

My secret settled into my belly. I said nothing to anyone. It had happened too fast, and no one had seen. If I explained what had happened to my parents, and I had a sense it was bad, I worried I would get in trouble. Dad was drinking a lot, and that meant getting in trouble would be painful. Instead, I maintained a constant vigil on Tony's location—in relation to me—and kept my distance.

The next day at breakfast, Mom ordered coffee at the bar.

"Black, please."

Tony appeared at her shoulder, sunglasses on. "What a party, eh?"

His slicked hair and freshly showered smell made me feel unexpectedly dirty. I stepped back, behind Mom.

"What? Oh yeah." Mom smiled. "It was an amazing house."

Dad leaned over. "The booze wasn't bad either." He laughed.

As I held my orange juice and watched the adults chuckling, it occurred to me that maybe it had been my imagination. Maybe I had overreacted. Tony's touch might have been accidental, and not meant anything. I relaxed. I dismissed my fears.

I sat alone in the lobby that afternoon, drawing. Tony walked in. I tucked my feet under my chair and concentrated on my picture.

He stood behind me and looked over my shoulder for a moment. I continued coloring, not speaking.

"Nice artwork! Are we on for gin rummy tonight as usual?" he asked.

I hesitated but agreed. I wanted things to be normal. I needed everything to go back to the way it was. I won again that night and went to bed happy. Everything would be okay.

I sat alone by the pool the next day. Tony and his wife passed, waving, on their way to their room. He returned without her a few minutes later.

"Still here? Are you bored?"

I nodded. He went to the pool bar then returned to hand me a Coke with lime.

"For you," Tony said. The lime must have been especially sour because it had a funny taste. I squinched my nose but swallowed to be polite.

"Thank you."

After a moment, Tony sat down beside me. "Do you want to see the basement? It's unlike anything else you've seen."

I sipped my drink and tilted my head, considering. I had roamed all the floors of the hotel and the gardens but didn't know about a basement. My favorite place was the roof, six floors up. From the lounge chairs there, I could see the cliff divers and a beautiful view of the ocean. If the basement was as beautiful as the rest, I wanted to see it.

"Okay," I said.

It turned out that the same staircase that went up to the roof also led down to the basement, just through a door I'd not tried previously. Strictly utilitarian, the basement had three cinderblock walls and a dirt floor. The fourth wall was simply a high chain-link fence. Pipes and wires ran along the ceiling. Tattered beach chairs and various boxes lined the walls. I wondered what Tony thought was so great about this creepy place.

"Come over here and see." He walked to the fenced wall, which was the sole source of light for the basement. I followed, hoping to understand Tony's enthusiasm. I pressed my forehead to the cool metal and gazed out.

The terrain dropped steeply down the hillside. Below us, the bright Mexican sun reflected off corrugated roofs and blue tarps covering shacks where locals lived. I watched a toddler wander between the huts, clothed in only a stained T-shirt that hung to his knees. He had thin legs, and the damp shirt clung to his small buttocks.

A wave of sadness swept over me. How did families live in those conditions? I tried to imagine how different my life could be. I had my own bedroom and bathroom. I had a backyard with a swing and a creek to play in. Drawers full of clothes and enough toys that my mom threatened to throw them away if I couldn't keep them tidy. I watched the boy retrieve a dirty tennis ball and throw it at a dog.

Lost in thought, I had forgotten about Tony until his voice interrupted. "Amazing, huh? Come sit over here."

Thinking about the dirty child, I walked out of the light, blinking in the gloom.

Tony squatted on a bench a few feet from the opposite wall, in the shadows. "You know, it's good to be fair. I touched you nice the other day. Now it's your turn."

Not understanding what he meant, I searched Tony's face. He looked down. Following his gaze, I saw that he had unzipped his pants. Embarrassment reddened my cheeks.

"Don't be afraid. People do this all the time. It's supposed to be secret, but it's fun!" He took my hand in his and placed it where he wanted.

My embarrassment turned to disgust and then to abject terror as I came to understand that I'd been trapped. For the next three days, he threatened to tell my parents unless I complied with his every wish.

His threats were less powerful than my shame. I could never admit to my parents that my hope that what Tony had done was an accident had led to something so much worse.

I was forced to hide what a bad girl I was.

Despite my best attempts to forget that I was going back to that same hotel, I awoke the morning we were supposed to fly to Mexico with certain dread. This was going to be miserable. Uncle Bob's daughter and her husband met us at the airport and escorted Lisa and me to the gate. I could tell they were excited, especially since Dad had paid their way. Before we boarded, they took us aside.

"We know what it's like to be young," Paula said and winked.

Her condescending tone made me want to gag. My cousin was only in her early thirties. What time had she had to forget? Her husband John chuckled and gave us a knowing look.

"She's just saying we know how to look the other way. As long as you don't make trouble, we'll stay out of your business. Got it?"

I understood. They wanted to be on vacation, too, not nursemaids to a couple of teenage girls. Lisa clapped her hands in excitement.

"You guys are the best!" she squealed.

I gave my cousins a weak smile and got in line to board. *This is definitely going to be the worst vacation ever.* On the plane, Lisa went on and on about our last visit to the resort and the open bar, which she planned to make good use of this time. She elbowed me when she noticed my attention wandering. I managed to nod and gave her a thumbs up. She turned to gush about the resort's amenities to Paula, a more willing audience. I closed my eyes.

I wasn't assuming some moral high ground. Drinking just depressed me. I had followed Lisa to parties ever since my mother's death, looking for a way to escape the house and my life. At first, I had laughed at others' ridiculous performances during drinking games and only sipped at my own beer. But since Dad's arrest, binge drinking had become my new normal. I had passed out drunk every weekend for almost a month. Alcohol tasted of grief, not rebellion or freedom.

I turned toward the window and tried to sleep, feeling a deep tiredness in my bones. I'd had my fill of booze, and it changed nothing. I wanted a family. Traveling alone, without parents, on an exotic vacation was a charade. We weren't living the good life, or any life, for that matter. I was barely surviving. I resented Dad for forcing us to pretend everything was okay. It exhausted me.

The plane wheels hitting the ground jolted me conscious.

"This is going to be the best trip ever!" Lisa giggled as the plane coasted to a stop.

"Just don't kill yourself." John clapped me on the shoulder as we exited on the tarmac.

"Not planning on it," I said, rolling my eyes.

Mexico wasn't quite as I remembered. Everything that had made Mexico exotic as a child now looked old and unsafe. The brightly colored buildings had dirty paint peeling along the edges. The taxi had no seat belts, so I gripped the seat in front of me, my duffel bag in my lap as we wove through traffic. The bumpy highway, narrow turns, and passing busses made me close my eyes in terror.

When we arrived at Hotel Vita in Acapulco, John paid the driver of the pink taxi while Paula went to check us in. I shouldered my light bag. I had tossed a few random things into it the night before and now momentarily wondered if I had packed my swimsuit.

"Take this, will you?" Lisa shoved a purple, oversized suitcase at me. She retrieved two more, one in each hand, from the trunk. I sighed. Lisa would have duplicates of anything I might have forgotten.

Under the bright sunshine, Lisa grinned at me and cocked her head. "We're here!" She arched an eyebrow at my sour face. "You can be happy now!"

Suddenly my resentful disposition wilted, and I felt ashamed. Why did I have to be such a wet blanket? Mom wasn't here, but neither was Dad. I decided to try harder for Lisa's sake. All I had to endure was a week of boring tanning. Then I could go home. It wouldn't be so bad.

I smiled at my sister and took one of her bags. We walked inside and a bellboy took our luggage. Paula handed us our room key, and we strolled together toward the stairs.

A couple entered the lobby from the gardens. The blonde woman laughed and put her hand on her companion's shoulder. His profile seized my attention. I turned away, heart racing, and swore under my breath.

Tony.

Perspiration broke out on my upper lip as a nasty taste came back to my mouth.

I looked for a place to hide.

Chapter Twelve

They hadn't noticed us yet. Four years later, the sight of him reduced me to a voiceless child, lost and desperate to hide. But if I ran, it would draw attention, and the last thing I wanted was his attention. I stood very still while my brain went into hyperdrive.

Shame from my childhood converged with the disgrace of my father's arrest. Dad and I both had secrets. They were catching up with us, but he had quit working and become a drunken recluse who avoided anything public. I suddenly understood his desire to hide.

An ominous conviction filled me. I knew my vacation would not be boring; it would be horrendous. I needed to disappear right then. I rehearsed possible options as the hotel clerk checked us in.

I couldn't run without drawing unwanted comments. If I screamed or hid, Lisa would think I'd gone crazy. I couldn't accuse Tony four years after the fact; everyone would wonder why I hadn't said anything before. I'd look like a liar. No viable options existed.

Fear rooted me to the spot, bound and gagged me. If my sordid past was exposed, I knew everyone would look at me the way Mrs. Zajdel or my aunt Kathy looked at Dad—with suspicion and judgment. My secrets multiplied in a horrific way. I'd thought I could bury what had happened. My naivete had created a nightmare of my own making.

The blonde woman turned and saw us. Her face paused in recall, then her hand lifted. Lisa noticed and returned the greeting. Happy to see a familiar face, my sister walked over. I followed a few steps behind, stiffening as I went.

Tony's wife hugged Lisa, then turned to me. "We were so sorry to hear about your mom. It must be so devastating."

Tony nodded and stuck his hands in his pockets. He smiled at me.

A tired rage built. I had had enough of pain, of loss, of surprises. I lifted my chin and stared him down, arms crossed. I summoned all my defiance to build a stone wall between us. Tony shook Lisa's hand, and then he and his wife left.

He kept his distance for three days.

Lisa sat beside me at the pool. I noticed Tony's approach. I pretended to read a magazine as he wandered closer, first stopping at the pool bar and then strolling behind us. My heart skipped a beat when his footsteps stopped behind me.

"Hi there! What do you say to a friendly round of cards tonight?"

My stomach dropped. His voice, the same one that had threatened and cajoled me, now sounded so casual. I wanted to throw up.

"I'm not in the mood. I'm still jet-lagged."

I looked out over the pool, not meeting his eyes, and yawned to emphasize my point.

"Another time, perhaps." His footsteps faded away.

I put a towel over my face and pretended to sleep.

I kept running into him—at the restaurant, in the lobby. He wouldn't let me escape without repeating the same casual but petrifying invitations.

"Hey, how about some gin?"

"C'mon, you were so good at cards. You must be even better now!"

I knew his persistence should move me to action, but defensive strategies required energy, and I suffered from battle fatigue. Six months of enduring a constant need to appear normal had taken enormous effort. Tony's presence threatened to tear my thin façade to pieces, and the best I could muster was not falling completely apart. Fighting back was beyond me.

I reassured myself I was no longer a child and had control. I was too smart to be lured with a Coke. Still, Tony's relentlessness worried me. I could sense him circling.

My small sense of self-preservation shouted for me to run, but there was nowhere to hide. I was stuck at the resort. If I stayed in my room, Lisa would harass me until I spilled my guts. If I admitted how scared I was, I would have to explain why. I had never imagined facing this monster again and was unprepared for the renewed peril.

I shadowed Lisa and was never alone except when she went drinking at night. Then, I stayed in my room and watched cable television with the door bolted.

The night before we flew home, I sat by Lisa at dinner. Paula and John had left on an excursion, taking advantage of every last moment. Lisa told me about running into Etelivita the evening before. I half listened, head down, relieved the nightmare was almost over.

"Hi."

I jumped. I'd let my guard down for only a moment, and he'd appeared before I realized he'd left his table across the restaurant.

"Have you been avoiding me?" Tony grinned, noting the look on my face.

I shrugged. "No, just busy." I straightened my back to lie with authority. "We are leaving tomorrow, so we've been trying to fit everything in."

A small sense of victory spilled into my words. I looked across the room at his wife. She waved, watching.

I gave her a small smile. I pitied her, married to such a lowlife. A sense of superiority washed over me. I had done it. I was almost to the finish line and could taste victory.

Tony sighed. "In that case, tonight is our last chance to try and beat you."

I turned to him. "Yeah, I guess so."

My words surprised me. I had spoken without pause, caught up in my rush of elation at having nearly run the gauntlet. I ignored the small flutter of panic in my stomach and lifted my chin. "But don't expect to win."

He smiled and stepped back. "There, it's settled. Come to our room—suite twenty-eight. I'll tell her. She'll be so pleased!"

He left with a wave.

Lisa leaned over. "He's so rude, not giving you a minute's peace about stupid cards. You beat him good. He deserves it."

I looked at his retreating back and nodded. I cut my chicken into small pieces and chewed slowly. I assured myself it would be okay. Nothing would happen with his wife there.

I found the bungalow number Tony had given me and knocked on the brown wooden door. The sun had set, and the hotel had turned sleepy, with few people by the pool. The air smelled of tiki torches being lit. My vacation was almost over. I was a card game away from victory.

Tony answered dressed in white linen pants and a loud Hawaiian shirt.

"Come in!" He swung the door half open, partially blocking my view. Forced to turn sideways to slip by, I heard him close and bolt the door behind me. I spun to face him as the echo of the lock sliding into place bounced off the tile floors in an empty room. No blonde wife.

I understood then that this had been an unbelievably bad idea. Cold adrenaline rushed through my body.

Chapter Thirteen

I threw my hands up as he leapt on me.

He grabbed the back of my shirt, pulling it over my head, and kicked me several feet onto the bed with a foot to my stomach.

"Noooo!" My voice tore my throat. "Noooooo!"

He hit my hands away, pinned my arms, and sat on top of me just as my father had often restrained my mother. I continued to scream as he tore the button off my shorts, pulling them down. I kicked at him, losing my flip-flops. I bit his forearm, and he slapped me hard across the face, my head snapping back. The download of chemicals in my system blocked the sting.

"Help, somebody!" I screamed.

At least this time I could scream.

July 1985

On my last night in England, three months before the house fire, I walked with Lisa down a narrow dirt road in West Sussex. Not far from the coast, seagulls circled above us as the sun set. My second cousins had accompanied us, laughing and telling stories of conquests and drinking. Their home was maybe five kilometers or so from the outskirts, and they led the way to a local tavern on Bognor Regis's High Street.

Mom and Dad had looked at each other when my cousins offered to take us along to their pub night. Lisa had begged to go. Mom's cousin, Colleen, and her husband, Granger, reassured my parents.

"Robbie and Steven will keep an eye on the girls," Colleen said.

Granger nodded. "Eh, boys? Right?"

Robbie and Steven had nodded enthusiastically. "Of course! Just some music and dancing."

Mom considered me. "Do you promise to be safe?"

It was a loaded question—and not about my father's drinking.

It'd been two years since I'd been grounded for a month following my first real taste of alcohol. The issue hadn't been sneaking one sip, I'd had weekly sips of wine since first communion, it was that I'd had about eighty—and an entire airplane bottle of vodka.

As Mom's question hung in the air, I remembered her disappointed face when she'd found out I'd lied to her. Carolyn Zajdel's mom had called to let her know it wasn't a mysterious stomach flu that had caused Carolyn's case of vomiting early that morning while sleeping over—we'd dared each other to sample every single bottle in my house.

Though we'd only taken small swallows as we'd traded bottles, there'd been nearly eighty bottles, and we'd quickly become drunk. So drunk that we'd forgotten our stealthy strategy, and each downed a small vodka. Apparently, I had inherited my father's iron stomach, but the colorless 50 ml bottle had been the last straw for Carolyn. Her stomach had rebelled at the copious combination of liquors, not only causing her to puke all over the family room couches and carpet, but sick enough to tearfully confess at home later that day.

I had felt ashamed for making Carolyn sick and hadn't repeated my transgression since.

Now, I nodded in response to my mother's unspoken question. I'd learned my lesson and wouldn't drink to excess like before.

Mom turned to Lisa. "Don't do anything stupid."

Lisa looked at me. Mom was putting her in charge of me. "We won't."

We left with their blessing. On the walk, I became keyed up with anticipation. I was in a country where it was legal to drink at fourteen, and our parents had given us implicit permission.

I wasn't sure whether I was excited, a little scared, or both.

It wasn't that I'd even liked the taste of anything other than peach schnapps during my and Carolyn's experiment. It was the idea of being drunk and carefree that intoxicated me. I remembered the buzzed euphoria that I'd felt just before Carolyn and I had tipped our heads back to down the vodka that would eventually give us away. I'd been invincible and on top of the world—nothing could touch me.

As a fifteen-year-old who'd experienced frequent violent nightmares while asleep and awake, feeling bulletproof was a seductive emotion to pursue.

The sky was almost dark when we arrived at a squat brick building with few windows and large metal doors. We followed Robbie inside. Everyone, from preteens to adults in their early thirties, convulsed to the rhythm of the music and the clunk of mugs on wood tables. Roach smoke and crass laughter floated above the crowd. I entered the secret world of adults with some trepidation.

We squeezed our way through the crowded tavern. I traded a five-pound note for my first Lager beer. My head hummed after downing it. Lisa and Steven joined the dancing. I turned back to tell Robbie how much I hated dancing, but he'd disappeared.

Alone in the crowded room, I suddenly wanted to go home.

A surge in the crowd pushed me into the person behind me at the bar, causing me to spill my drink on myself and the floor. I turned. A

114

twenty-something Middle Eastern guy sporting a decent Don Johnson beard was looking down at his shoes, which my Lager had splashed across. I blushed and felt caught like a naughty child holding an emptied mug, covered in beer. I ducked my head.

"Sorry," I apologized.

"No worries," he said before looking me up and down and leaning closer. "I think fate meant for us to meet."

It was an odd thing to say. I looked at him blankly, wondering if I had heard him correctly. He smiled and pointed to my clothes, which I now realized matched his. White jeans and pastel-pink tops.

"Oh yeah. Funny," I stammered. My hand was dripping. I flushed and automatically licked it, which made me feel even more juvenile.

"Here," he said and handed me a few napkins from the bar.

Grateful, I sopped up the puddle at my feet. I wanted to disappear. Drinking at a pub had sounded so exciting, a perfect end to our quaint romp through Britain. Reality had been a letdown. I left the empty glass on the counter and gave a weak smile to the barman, who took the pile of soggy napkins.

"I'll order you a better one," my new friend said.

"Um, no. Don't worry about it." After half a beer, I didn't want any more. My mother would have been proud.

He ignored me and signaled to the bartender. I sighed, not wanting to be rude. I turned my attention to the cuff of my white jean jacket. With another napkin, I tried to blot the stain on it. Coming home soaked in alcohol would be defined as excessive behavior by my mother.

The handsome, dark youth tapped my shoulder. "Try this. It's an English whiskey."

He held matching shot glasses and demonstrated as he downed one in a single gulp. He held out the other to me. I accepted the small glass and tilted my head back to swallow. My eyes widened as a trail of fire consumed my entire esophagus. I coughed, embarrassed.

There was a deep laugh by my side. "Some kick, huh?"

I nodded, a bitter burn coated my mouth and throat. I finished the whiskey with another gulp and hid my teary eyes by turning to look out over the parquet floor. There Lisa was—dancing in the middle of the crowd. Seeing her made me feel better.

I continued to watch. The music grew louder and the colors brighter. At the time, I thought I had finally relaxed—but later I would hear of being "roofied" and realize that the young man had slipped something into my glass.

I enjoyed chatting with my new friend until he took my hand and pulled me to the dance floor. I protested, but he insisted. He held me close and danced fast. He twirled me, and I fell over. We laughed out loud as my vision swam. I pressed my hands to my forehead and wiped away beads of sweat. My head felt strange. I looked for a break in the crowd, suddenly breathless.

"Do you need some air?" my partner asked.

I nodded. He took my hand and led me to the exit. I followed, forgetting everything but him. I'd never had a boyfriend, never held a boy's hand, even, until now. I didn't even know his name, but already my heart fluttered at the thought of sending postcards crossing the ocean. I was so drugged that all I could think of was how cute he looked under the pulsing neon lights.

The wood door swung closed behind us, and the volume dropped immediately. I removed my jacket, wrapping it around my waist. The fresh country air cleared my head a little. It was easier to stand on my own. I wondered if he would kiss me, and I leaned against him with a sigh. He smiled, but his eyes scanned the street instead of gazing adoringly into mine. I guessed he was nervous about people watching. How sweet.

"Come." He pulled me away from the tavern and across the road into a fallow field of waist-high grass. I stumbled behind, caught up in the midsummer beauty around me. The breeze raced through the stalks with a hush. A bird called out. The moon peeked out from behind dark clouds sliding by. I thought I'd never seen a more beautiful sight than the abandoned field.

A hundred feet into the tall fronds, the young man stopped and faced me. We were alone at last. As he put his arm around my waist, I lifted my chin and closed my eyes. A sweet anticipation raced through my veins as he leaned in.

His hand covered my mouth. He shoved me to the ground, falling onto me. I inhaled to scream but his forearm shoved my jaw back and up, pinning my head against the ground while his large hand covered my mouth and nose. I couldn't get enough air. I fought, but my attempts felt blunted and weak. He easily overpowered my petite frame.

His beard scraped my cheek and forehead. His elbow dug into my shoulder. Beneath me, an iron irrigation pipe crossed just below my shoulder blades. It dug savagely into my back. The sharp grass stung my arms as I thrashed. My white jacket ground into the earth beneath me.

My rapist had seduced me with the promise of my first kiss, but violence doesn't touch, it takes. He forced my soul open and inserted his will while I breathlessly begged for mercy.

Thumping music spilled out over the field from the club, then quieted. Someone had exited; a moment later, car lights passed us on the road. I tried to scream, but he tightened his grip, and my panicked gasps went unheard. Despite being within a stone's throw of the entrance, I remained invisible.

He knelt on my hips while he zipped his pants. With one last push on my head, he discarded me and walked out of the field without a backward glance. Torn, bruised, bleeding, and clothes askew, I pulled my pants up, then yanked my bra back up over my chest. I heard his car drive off.

Pain set in. It clarified my thinking.

I bolted upright, grabbing my jacket. I hadn't told anyone I was leaving, and if Lisa was looking for me, I'd likely be in big trouble. The combination of that thought and the reality of the trouble I had just gotten myself into hit me like a ton of bricks. A sob burst from my chest, followed by many more.

I hadn't been cautious enough, and I'd been very stupid.

Eventually, I decided I had to return before someone found me there like that. I made for the pub's bathroom, first cleaning myself with paper towels in the stall. Next, I checked my face in the mirror. Though my chin felt bruised, it didn't show yet. I wiped the dirt off my cheeks and scrubbed the black smudges of mascara from around my eyes with warm water. I soaked paper towels in cold water and held them over my eyes and face, trying to reduce the puffiness. I turned my new white jean coat inside out to hide the dirt and grass stains.

I finished with what I could fix and returned to the pub's common room. There, I found a corner table and sat down, absolutely undone. My makeup was gone, my eyes were red, and my clothes were dirty. I hid in the shadows, silently berating myself for leaving. My head pounded, my body hurt, and I wanted to go home, but I willed myself into numbness. Finally, after midnight, Lisa found me.

"Hey, ho. What's up?" She leaned heavily against me, and I could smell marijuana on her breath. At least she'd been having a good time.

I waved a hand in front of my face and shrugged, unable to speak for fear of crying. She pulled me to my feet, and Steven came over.

"Anyone seen Robbie?"

Lisa laughed. "Last I saw, he was putting the moves on a blonde in a purple top. Try looking somewhere dark."

I repressed all but a small tremor no one noticed.

After finding Robbie, we walked back to my cousin's house. I took the hottest shower possible without scalding myself. As I sat down in the tub, the sound of the water hitting the porcelain covered my crying.

Three weeks later, the morning of the second day of basketball tryouts, I cried in another bathroom with relief. My period had come a day late, and I had spent the last twenty-four hours desperately debating how to secretly buy a pregnancy test. Afterward, I forbade myself to think about it. No one ever need know how stupid I'd been.

When Tony finished, I lay weeping on the bed. I grabbed the corner of the sheet and rolled over, wrapping it around me. I faced the wall.

"You know, I prefer younger girls. You were prettier last time."

I squeezed my eyes shut. His words cut through my soul. He had hunted and used me, and now he'd tossed me aside. I had no strength to disagree. I had walked into this room. I was as stupid as he meant me to feel.

"Listen. You tell no one, *no one*, about this. You talk, and I will find you and make you wish I had killed you instead." His footsteps walked away. He slammed the door. I shattered.

Pain descended. Shock set my teeth chattering. I cried while I bled. Eventually I quieted, exhausted. I must have spent an hour alone in the room before a small fear that Tony might return made me sit up. I pushed myself up and began to dress. I couldn't find one shoe, so I left barefoot.

Even though the grounds were deserted, I wandered the shadows unseen. I needed to avoid my sister and cousins, and so I avoided our rooms. I couldn't pretend anymore. I hadn't beaten Tony at cards; I had lost everything. I couldn't pull myself together.

Kinetic energy seemed to be the only way to keep from imploding right there on the sidewalk. I headed up and up the hotel stairs. Three flights up. Four flights up. The pain followed me, building with each step. Tony's words echoed in the stairway, taunting me. I stopped at the fifth floor, shaking.

God had abandoned me again. How could I believe my life was worth anything since God had left me so utterly alone? Just after Mom had said things would get better and I had started to hope, Dad had been arrested, and now this.

I looked up. One more set of stairs. I started moving up again. I would contemplate my options from the roof.

It had become so late it was early morning. The hotel was quiet, asleep. No one was around to intervene as I approached the roof ledge. A brick wall three feet high separated me from eternity. I sat on top of it, bare feet dangling. From my vantage point, I watched the white crests of waves a half mile away, the only thing visible in the dark ocean. The black horizon was lost to me. I couldn't see anything beyond the breakers.

I folded forward and inspected the ground six floors below. My mind, predisposed to mathematics, became coldly detached. I calculated the drop.

A long way. Maybe a ten-second fall?

I weighed my alternatives. My mom was murdered, my childhood home lay in ashes, my dad appeared to be on his way to prison, and I had just been raped *again*. No one cared. Not even God. My life was that worthless.

God had watched and walked away. If Mom had come before, why not tonight? There was no heavenly visitation, no sudden light to fill the empty rooftop, not even a whisper. Nothing but pain. I looked out on the world and saw darkness. I stared at the ground below, and a new thought came to me.

I had created all of it. It was my fault. I should have known better. I shouldn't have called Mom when Dad was crying in the kitchen or left her alone with him. I should have told Lisa to go home. I shouldn't have gotten drunk in England or left the pub. I shouldn't have followed Tony into the basement. I knew better than to let him talk me into cards again. My life was a wreck, but it was all self-inflicted.

What could God do with a stupid idiot like me? How had I been so incredibly dumb over and over? I hated myself. I shifted and imagined releasing my body to gravity. What would the scene below look like in twenty minutes? It would be over. I would be lying there beside the palm tree below, my pain at an end, God willing or not.

In my mind I saw the commotion, as if I really heard the maid frantically calling for help. Lisa waking to the screams and coming out onto our balcony. Doors opening, people pointing. Lisa screaming. Lisa holding my body. Blood pooling in her lap.

Lisa wouldn't handle it well.

I put my head in my hands. I realized that if I jumped, I would not only end my life but hers. I had no desire to ruin my sister's life with my death. I loved her. But how could I go on? I had ruined everything.

I thought for a while. The only other thing that stopped me was the mess. I disliked the thought of somebody having to clean up my bloody remains. Making someone else clean it would be cruel.

I got off the ledge, paced, cried again, and berated myself. Making Lisa go through losing someone again would be beyond cruel. I grew increasingly miserable and felt trapped. How had I allowed this to happen? I wanted to strangle myself for agreeing to meet Tony. Why had I imagined anything had changed? I'd avoided him all week and then betrayed myself at the last moment.

I straddled the wall again, one foot dangling above the pool deck below. I leaned forward. The dizzying height pulled at me. There, hanging on for life, I finally realized one thing I had never seen from below.

My entire life, I had never admitted what really happened around me, to me, and that was why I'd acted stupidly. I'd remained silent when I should have screamed. My fear of people finding out about one thing, then another, had left me voiceless.

I hated myself for my weakness. Normally, I would have laughed at my stupid psychotic breakdowns, at Mom's assurances—except that everything hurt too much. I'd used them as a crutch to ignore reality. Reality had gotten way too real.

Now I hung from a hotel roof, driven by my fear of people knowing how stupid I was. My fear had compelled me to act in stupid ways, made me pretend and ignore reality. That was the actual stupid part—the fear of what others thought.

I had known to not leave Mom. I'd wanted to leave the bar before being drugged. I had known Tony was a predator.

I sat up in amazement. I wasn't stupid. It was just that I'd been taught to fear what others thought more than listen to my instincts. My mother had been terrified of letting anyone know of Dad's abuse. She had been more afraid of others' judgment than the monster in the room. I let out a small cry of anger.

How had we not been more afraid of the real danger, the men who broke us? How had I not called Tony out? Why had I ignored my instincts?

My self-disgust served one preserving purpose. There, that night, I vowed to never again let myself be silenced by my fear of what others thought. I vowed to fight the real Goliaths in my life.

I put both feet on the rooftop and looked over my shoulder at the drop one last time. I would prove to myself I could stop being afraid. I would do something right for once in my life. Then I could do whatever I wanted. Taking my life now would prove I was what I feared. A stupid coward.

I was not stupid.

I was not a coward.

I walked away from that precipice and back downstairs to my room. When Lisa's alarm blared two hours later, she groaned and rubbed her temples. Her hangover made her irritable and nonverbal, but I appreciated not having to talk. I crammed everything in my duffel while I shoved the rape, the hurt, God's abandonment, and my fear into the deepest recesses of my memory.

I recognized that I should have screamed when I first saw Tony but decided there was nothing to be done after the fact. I would never see him again and had zero desire to relive the night by reporting it. (Though I should have, I lacked the emotional strength.) From this point on, staying alive was my victory.

Two weeks later, I got a tampon from the quarter-fed dispenser in the girls' bathroom and locked the stall door. I washed my hands afterward as the white-faced girl in the mirror stared at me accusingly. My hands shook as I dried them on the rough paper towels. I had pushed Mexico so far down that I hadn't even considered the possibility of pregnancy. I had been so afraid of my fear that I'd not let it get a single word in.

What would I have done with Tony's baby? Just the thought of it, even after the prospect was safely dismissed, made me shudder. I discarded the panic and thanked God for this one break. I grabbed the hall pass from where I'd left it on the sink and exited the bathroom. I'd never be that stupid again.

Walking back to class, I remembered that Lisa had mentioned a senior party hosted by the basketball captains the next night. I vaguely wondered what could have happened had I been unknowingly pregnant and gone. Didn't alcohol screw babies up? I dismissed the thought with a jerk of my head. Worrying now was a waste, a moot point. I had enough on my plate.

I don't want to be home alone with Dad on a Friday night.

I went with Lisa to the party, revealing nothing. Even though our relationship kept me from jumping in Mexico, I had complicated feelings about Lisa. In our natural state, we might have gravitated to opposite ends of the spectrum, but the hostile environment we endured made it clear that if we didn't have each other's backs, no one would. It was a compromise of survival. Sure, we fought in small ways every day—over things like who'd left the milk out or why I ran the shower too long—but Lisa protected me at her own risk. When mom died, it was Lisa who stepped into the ring with Dad to take the heat.

Lisa's sacrifices made me more willing to put up with her bossiness and snide comments about me being nerdy and annoying. I *was* nerdy and annoying, especially when I proudly presented Dad with my report card. I admit I had hidden a smile a couple of times as he'd ridiculed hers. And yet, Lisa let me trail her to the endless parties to which I was never actually invited. She was my nemesis and my salvation.

I needed her. I never had to explain to Lisa why I flinched at the sound of sirens, or why I counted bottles in the trash before coming in the house to predict Dad's mood.

We were bound by more than blood; we were bound by loss. She alone understood my silence, even if she chose a different way to grieve. Anger, drugs, rebellion, and fighting were her way of keeping her pain at arm's length, but she let me quietly cry in a corner without calling me out. Just as I knew that losing me would undo her, I couldn't fathom losing Lisa.

Chapter Fourteen
April 6, 1986

Dad and I walked through the Metro Detroit terminal shortly before nine that morning. That familiar feeling of impending disaster had settled in my chest. Anxious to leave for Florida, I checked the airline ticket again. Lisa had left two days earlier to drive her friends to Fort Lauderdale for spring break, and I had refused to go. Mexico was too recent for me to want to travel anywhere. An early-morning phone call had changed my mind.

I set my backpack down on an empty chair. "This is the gate. We have an hour."

Dad took the chair beside me, leafing through a discarded newspaper. After five minutes, he stood. "I'll be right back," he said, jerking his thumb down the hallway. I shrugged, and he left. I crossed my arms and closed my eyes, exhausted.

All I could think about was Lisa. I hadn't slept since the telephone rang.

Yesterday, Lisa's lead foot had gotten the van full of friends to their Florida resort too early to check in. Meanwhile, rumors spread that a hopping party was already in progress at the Howard Johnson across the street. They'd left their stuff in the van and walked across the boulevard. That's when Lisa had spied a vacant parking spot in the Howard Johnson's parking lot that would make it easier to keep an eye on their things. She had gone back to move the vehicle.

While backing the van out of its spot, Lisa had accidentally hooked its bumper on a parked car. She'd shifted into drive, but the wheels merely spun. She had floored the gas until the bumper broke free with a squeal of tires that propelled the van toward the side of the hotel.

Lisa had panicked. Instead of the brakes, she hit the right accelerator, which launched the van over the curb and straight into the side of the brick building. She'd failed to put her seat belt on and shattered the windshield with her head. The cab was wrapped around her, and the emergency brake impaled her knee.

Emergency responders called us after landing with her at a level-one trauma center. She'd sustained multiple injuries, all of which needed immediate attention. Her head had massive intracranial swelling and numerous lacerations with embedded glass shards. The impact had broken ribs, torn her spleen and liver, and caused internal hemorrhaging. The emergency brake had shattered her patella and ripped through the ligaments in her knee. She was a mess.

Dad needed official permission to leave the state and spent all night leaving messages on answering machines. Meanwhile, I had lain shaking under my covers, certain the unthinkable was happening again.

Alone at the gate, I tried not to break down. Enough horrible things had happened in the last six months that I believed one more was not only possible but probable. I sank lower into my seat. God had cursed me; there was no other explanation. A dark misery ate at the edges of my hope. Lisa was still alive but for how long?

The morning news came on the TV at the gate. I straightened when the anchor mentioned the date. It was my sixteenth birthday. I had forgotten all about it. Would God take Lisa on my birthday? Would He take her to punish me further?

Tears filled my eyes. He wouldn't do that. He couldn't. Even God had to have limits on callousness. Even if I deserved some pain, Lisa didn't.

I prayed silently. "God, if you even care, listen to me. Don't take her, not today."

The aching echo of my mother's words, "*Don't worry. Everything will be okay,*" cut into my heart. The hope that had filled me then seemed almost laughable now. I wanted to believe in the peace I had felt, but how? Everything had only gotten worse.

The flight attendants began boarding passengers. I checked my watch again. I waited until the passenger line grew short before boarding the plane. I threw my bag in the overhead bin and took the window seat. When almost everyone was buckled in, Dad finally dropped into the seat beside me. I ignored him and opened the in-flight magazine. It was my birthday, Lisa could be dying, and he smelled like whiskey.

Lisa lay unconscious, hooked to tubes and machines in an intensive-care room. Her face was swollen and lacerated. When I saw her, my anger at Dad melted into a puddle of distress. I turned to him with a small gasp. Dad let me cling to him while he peppered the tall, bespeckled doctor with questions. He assured us that she had endured the surgery better than they'd hoped. After he left, I released my grip on Dad's arm and ran my fingers through my messy hair. I sat down with a sigh.

Lisa's cautiously optimistic prognosis was a wonderful birthday gift after twenty hours of anguish. The miserable prospect of losing my sister lifted, and I could breathe again. Dad kissed Lisa's forehead in relief. Touched, I watched from the chair beside her bed. The bedside clock read 9:40 p.m. My stomach growled, reminding me that all I'd eaten that day was the peanuts on the flight.

"How about we get something to eat?" Dad pointed to my stomach.

I nodded and smiled. We usually ate out on birthdays. Maybe Dad had remembered today's significance.

I turned the rental car's radio on. Dad rolled down his window. I grinned and rolled mine down too. I stuck my arm out and let the warm Florida breeze fly through my fingers.

"Does Italian sound good?" Dad gestured at a sign.

"Sure!" I smiled. Italian was my favorite. It was my birthday. I was still alive, and Lisa hadn't died. Maybe Mom was right. Things would work out. In the end, we would be okay.

The restaurant smelled amazing. I could practically taste the steaming garlic bread stacked inside baskets waiting in a nearby serving window. Tea lights flickered on white-papered tables, and a cute college-aged waiter pulled out a chair for me. I sank into it, ready to eat the entire yeasty loaf he set in front of us.

He handed us menus. "What can I get you to drink?"

"Coke, please," I answered with a smile.

"A Manhattan and Coke to start, then another with our salads," Dad said.

I looked down. I could tell from my father's tone that it would be one of those nights, so I buried my face behind the menu to gain control of my disappointment. My appetite disappeared. This dinner was not about me. I swallowed my tears before the waiter came back with the drinks.

Dad ordered round after round. Our dinners came. I tried to keep a conversation going at our table, even as Dad got trashed. His alfredo was barely touched, though he was on his sixth Manhattan.

"Hey, this is really good. Did you try yours?"

"Do you want to finish that pasta?"

He ordered another glass.

"More breadsticks?"

I saw the glances from the table behind Dad. I pretended to understand Dad's rambling conversation instead of asking him to repeat himself. I watched the waiter's eyes flash in concern as Dad ordered another highball.

"Uh, can we get the bill too?" I pasted on my widest smile.

The waiter brought both. I eyed the slip. Over a hundred dollars, mostly booze. My lasagna and salad had been twelve.

"Here, give me your wallet," I said. Dad handed it over while he sipped.

I led him to the car. He fumbled in his pocket for the keys. I held out my hand for them. He ignored me at first, trying to stick them into the keyhole. Finally, he relented. I unlocked the door and pulled it open. Dad fell behind the wheel.

I held the keys for another moment, debating whether I should call a cab. Holding my breath, I watched the restaurant door. The waiter was fully aware of my father's inebriated state. Was he watching to see who drove? Would he call the cops?

Dad snatched the keys, and I wasn't about to get into a fistfight, so I relented. He drove us to the hotel, where he drank tequila from the minibar until he passed out.

I cried myself to sleep. *Happy birthday*, I told myself.

May 1986

One Friday night or, rather, early Saturday morning, I stood swaying on our front porch. One might think, with the living embodiment of alcoholic self-centeredness that was my father, I would have caught on sooner. I didn't.

My eyes crossed in a vain attempt to focus on the small front-door knob. I jabbed at the keyhole, trying unsuccessfully to fit the key into it. I tried over and over until I finally dropped the key chain in frustration. It hit the porch floor with a small *clunk*. The image of Dad in the parking lot on my birthday, keys shaking, came back to me.

I sat on the concrete steps and bawled like a baby. Dad had ruined everything with his drinking. I knew it, yet here I was, taking the same path.

"This started it all! You dummy!" I said out loud—at least I think I did.

I was disgusted with myself. I was not only drunk but high. I had added weed to my Friday-night partying. I was running from the fire, from England, from Mexico. I was trying to forget what I had done or, rather, not done. I hated who I lived with and what he did to us. I hid in corners in strange basements to cry in Dixie cups of beer and smoke joints. Partying had become a necessity, but it wasn't fun.

The drugs and alcohol had an effect, but they were losing their ability to dampen the misery growing inside me. They just left me disembodied and staring at my life from a distance. But it wasn't until I saw Dad in myself on that porch that I decided to stop.

Seeing his disease in me was another moment of truth. I had spent my life pretending for other people; now I realized I had deceived myself. Mexico had forced me to see that hiding what abusers did to me in order to appear normal was a dysfunctional strategy that let others harm me at my own expense.

That night, I had my first real glimpse at my self-inflicted abuse, and it was ugly. I'd tortured and hated myself. I'd made myself an idiot and was on my way to being an addict. They didn't hear my detestable self-talk. That part of me was all walled-off by a singular brand of solitude that came with self-hate.

I lay back on the cold cement porch and curled into a ball, weeping with despair.

Finally, shivering in the chilly spring night, I picked up the keys to try again. I leaned against the door, squatting, trying to steady myself. The door opened suddenly, and I fell inside.

I looked up. My dad stood above me, looking down with his hand still on the inside doorknob. After a moment, he walked away without a word, entered his room, and shut his door. I finished rolling over the threshold and closed the house door behind me, keys still in hand. I was embarrassed and angry.

I had assumed the higher ground all that time, ridiculing him in my mind, making comments to Sabrina. I was horrified to realize I was just as out of control. I stopped partying. I went cold turkey with the drugs and alcohol. The only exception was the one-year anniversary of my mother's death. I remember almost nothing from that night, so I won't mention it again.

Chapter Fifteen

Early June 1986

One Saturday afternoon, Lisa was helping me pack up the rental. We emptied the dining-room cabinets of what china and crystal had been salvaged before the Rhonswood house had been gutted that spring. I had smashed most of it in a rage during one of my secret trips eight months earlier. It was the only time I'd left any clue that I'd been there, and I'd later regretted the destruction.

Lisa had fully recovered from her accident, which was a miracle. But almost immediately after she'd come home, the rental sold and we had been given a month to pack up and leave.

I wrapped the last china plate in paper and looked around. Boxes dotted the room. There wasn't much left to do. "About done," I said to Lisa. She smiled and checked her watch.

"That's good. I got to go soon anyways."

I tried to not let my disappointment show.

The doorbell rang a few minutes later. Lisa left with friends I had watched for months at parties. They'd all be hammered later that evening.

I waved goodbye even though, in my opinion, closed-head injuries and booze were not a healthy combination. But I felt like a hypocrite saying so and assumed Dad felt the same. With my new sobriety, I spent a lot of weekends alone in my room or at Sabrina's.

I sighed, looking forward to another quiet evening. I decided to pack my closet and headed to my room.

Sometime later, I brought a taped box out of my bedroom and stopped at the top of the stairs when I heard Dad talking on the phone downstairs. I hadn't heard him come home some minutes before, and I was hesitant to intrude on him, not knowing his state of mind. But as I listened, he mentioned Mom. He must have assumed both Lisa and I had left for the evening. Curious, I hunched against the wall above the foyer, listening. The tiled foyer floor and empty dining room amplified his conversation.

"Exactly. They got nothing. Her body was so burned, the legs and arms detached."

Dad paused for effect, then continued. "Only a spot on the back of her head, they say the size of a dime, left unburned . . . Yeah, Neal told me."

I slowly put the box down and covered my mouth with my hand. I closed my eyes, trying not to breathe loudly.

". . . She was on the floor. Must have rolled off the couch. Head toward the door . . . I don't know what they can do with that."

I felt nauseated. I left the cardboard packing box and eased my way back down the hallway toward my room. Inside, I closed my door and opened my jewelry box. I held everything I had left of her in my hands and lay on my bed with a pillow over my head so he wouldn't hear me weep.

With this accidental revelation of how bad Mom had been burned, a wave of grief pulled me under again and renewed my compulsion to investigate.

I tried to hold my life together despite these new details, which threatened to send me into a tailspin. I had to hide each new discovery, whether that discovery was made through eavesdropping, reading a newspaper leaking grisly details, or steaming open the mail before my dad read it. If I'd shown any grief, I would have been discovered and punished for snooping.

I'd had no idea how badly Mom's body had been burned, and the upcoming trial press-coverage leaks contained facts that colored my night-mares. Neighbors had reportedly made statements that refuted my father's story of when he'd left and returned. Accelerant was found splashed in the house. The second autopsy had different conclusions from the first. Though unspecified, it all pointed to violence.

It was all so overwhelming. Tired of grief, I threw myself into packing the entire house. Dad barely had to lift a finger.

The Rhonswood home was slowly being renovated, but only for selling. We would never live in it again—we all agreed on that. Dad was building a new condo, but it wasn't finished, so he decided to move into our cottage the summer between my sophomore and junior year. Instead of going with him, Lisa and I accepted Grandma Findlay's offer to stay with her. I had just gotten my driver's license and saw it as an opportunity to test my wings as an uncertain future bore down on me.

Besides, memories haunted the cottage.

July 1978

I shifted in my kitchen chair at the cottage, peeling my legs off the tacky brown vinyl, and reshuffled my cards. The horizon beyond the screens grew purple, the hour far past bedtime. Mom set the orange oscillating fan on high and stood to open the sliding glass doors on the opposite wall. With the rush of damp, cool air, I gave her a gap-toothed smile. She grinned back, patting my head as she sat down next to me.

"Your turn," Lisa reminded her.

Mom won that hand. Dad swore. "You cheated somehow."

He glowered while Lisa and I giggled at Mom's swagger to the fridge. Mom poured herself a glass of wine. "One of us is smarter, that's all." She winked at me.

"Oh, right. That's why you had to trick me into marrying you,"
Dad replied.

I stopped laughing. Their banter had transformed to arguing in
one sentence.

Mom slammed the fridge door shut. "How can you lie like that in
front of the girls?"

Panic began to rise in my chest. I stared at Mom. Shut up, shut up.

Dad swore again, sticking his chin out, "I'm lying? Really? The
truth is, you are a conspiring whore who trapped me. Remember?"

This was an old argument. Though I was only eight, I knew my
mom had had a miscarriage shortly after their marriage that my dad
resented somehow. He stood and took a step toward her.

My eyes flitted to the open patio door to see if any neighbors were
outside within earshot. The lawn was empty, and the light had all but
faded. Good. No one would see or hear whatever happened next. I
waited, tense.

"Remember?" His voice reverberated over the fan's damp air. He
took another step, and Mom moved backward, bumping into the
counter. He wanted her to relent, to admit her fault. She did neither,
so he took one last step.

Mom pushed him back with her arm, and it began. He seized her
throat. I leapt from my chair and hooked my small arms around Dad's
elbow. I yanked while Lisa wedged herself between our parents and
screamed, "Let her go!"

For several moments, our efforts had no effect, and Mom strug-
gled for air. I switched tactics and hung from Dad's elbow, lifting my
feet off the ground, willing gravity to aid me. Lisa pushed her head
into Dad's stomach and anchored a foot against the cupboards behind
Mom. Dad's grip began to slip. Clawing at her, his nails left a red trail
on her pale chest before he grasped her nightgown's neckline.

We were grunting, locked in a brutal contest of wills. He tightened his hold on the gold fabric as Mom inched away with our help. The polyester failed to give, even under that force. Mom suddenly shifted her weight down and back, wiggling out of the gown until it popped over her head.

Dad fell back with a snort. I landed on my feet and watched my nearly naked mother flee through the sliding glass door into the dusk. Dad sneered at the form in white panties racing toward the wooded lot behind the cottage. Then he began laughing and dropped the gown to the floor.

"Mom!" Lisa snuck a glance at Dad snickering, then slipped out to follow Mom.

Dad opened the fridge for another beer. I crept to the bedroom and hid under the covers, breathing hard. I was alone with Dad, but he seemed to have forgotten about me as the minutes passed. There was silence save for the occasional creaking of the old sofa springs from the living room. Dad must have taken up watch there, where he could see both the front and kitchen doors.

I prayed Lisa had found Mom. Eventually, I thought to peek outside to see if any of the neighbors' lights were on. I swallowed in relief at the darkness surrounding us. Mom might be able to sneak home.

Maybe an hour later, Lisa crept into our room. I hadn't thought to make sure the back door was unlocked, but luckily it had been. She nodded at my anxious face and climbed into the double bed with me. All was quiet, but I lay awake. After midnight, Mom tapped on our window. She pointed toward the side door. We tiptoed down the back hallway to let her in. She followed us into our room.

"Go back to sleep," she whispered.

I nodded, though I hadn't managed to sleep at all. Rather than lie on one of the two other single beds in the room, she wedged herself between our double bed and the wall.

136

"Where were you?" I whispered to the wall above her.

Her answer floated back in the darkness. "Shhh . . . I hid behind the priest's cottage."

The small stone dwelling, unused on the adjacent St. Edward's Church property, was hidden by overgrown bushes. Even then, I thought it an ironic but perfect choice.

"Now, shush," my mother quietly admonished.

For most people, a family cottage sounds idyllic, a cozy escape from life. Not for us. Some of the worst abuse we experienced happened at our cottage. On vacation there, my parents had no limits on drinking, and any bruises had a week to heal.

June 15, 1986

Driving past Mom's cemetery row to park my car in the neighboring lot, I noticed a bare plot in her section. My heart squeezed in sympathy for whoever had recently lost someone. Turning the engine off, I picked my bouquet of lilac stems off the front passenger seat and headed toward my mother's grave site. I walked to the edge of the fresh site and froze, disorientated.

Unless the trees immediately beside her site had been moved, the new site had replaced hers. The freshly turned earth was still wet with dew, and I could smell the warm grass seed and straw spread on top. How was I so turned around? On my last visit, I had lain on her resting place atop seven months of grassy grief grown over it.

I stood, brow furrowed, contemplating the spot. Was I in the wrong section? I looked around and back down again. No, this had to be the right place, though it looked like the wrong grave. I finally thought to brush off the large headstone above the muddy rectangle. The granite marker had been covered in dirt and grass clippings from a recent mow. I removed the debris and read it.

Marlene Findlay Edwards.

The sympathy I had felt for another family soured. This was my loss still, just freshly turned.

I set the bouquet of lilacs I'd brought on the black headstone Dad had had engraved with both their birthdays and the date of the fire for my mother's death—only he'd gotten Mom's birthday wrong. I covered the date and shook my head. Seeing the error made me upset, but the state of the grave site troubled me more than Dad's drunken incompetence.

Why was her site bare again? There seemed to be an unending list of things I still didn't know. A tear slid down my cheek. Every time I turned around, I found myself sidelined, not understanding my life. I was sure now that Dad kept everything from me. Mom had died, but I only grasped tiny pieces of how or why. I knew her body had burned until it had fallen to pieces. I swallowed. Why had someone disturbed what was left of her? What more could her ashes reveal?

Two days later, in Grandma's kitchen, I found a newspaper article that had been cut out and folded in a stack of papers on her counter. Its headline read "Police Exhume Body in Search for Clues." Marlene Edwards's body had been unearthed for another autopsy. The article didn't say why, just that the investigation continued. I reread the clipped article and saw what I had missed the first time through. The prosecutor had been changed and was a woman now. I slowly refolded the paper and placed it in the same spot on the counter. Even the new prosecutor knew more about my mother's case than I did.

Everyone was hiding things.

Chapter Sixteen

September 1986

Once school started again and I had moved back in with Dad at his condo, I spent most weekends at Sabrina's. I arrived on Friday nights and stayed as long as her parents could tolerate me, usually until Sunday evenings. I slept in while they went to church on Sunday mornings, and I avoided their family prayer time. They didn't seem bothered by my preference to keep their religious observance at arm's length.

The only time Sabrina refused to back down was when she occasionally insisted that God answered prayers. Her unwavering faith that the divine force behind the universe had time to speak with someone like me earned her a rueful grin. She had no idea the extent of the mess my life had become. I found her determination to believe in God's love refreshing in its simple way, but not applicable to me. Her life was uncomplicated, and, therefore, so was her belief.

Following one basketball game in late September, I told her about the newspaper clipping and my confusion about what had happened the night of the fire. She repeated her mantra.

"I know if you pray and ask God, He can help you find answers."

This time, she surprised me by holding out a small book. I looked down and recognized the cover. It was the book she'd shown me with the painting inside almost ten months earlier. I didn't think the answers to my mother's death were inside, even if this guy had seen angels too.

"Take it. I marked the promise near the end that God answers prayers." She flipped open the pages to a verse she'd underlined in red pencil.

Simple resignation made me take the sacred text her church was known for. Sabrina had become my best friend. I had confided some parts of my misery at home. Refusing Sabrina meant rejecting the one person who knew anything about my real life. Not my whole life, but the big parts. She knew I had misgivings concerning the fire. She knew I hated Dad's drinking. She knew more than anyone besides Lisa.

I looked into her hopeful eyes. Accepting the book was a small price to pay for her friendship. She meant no harm.

"Okay." I put it in my bag.

I doubted I would read it. I was dyslexic. I never read anything besides school-assigned books. More importantly, my family had been Catholic forever. What would a reading-challenged parish girl like me do with a Book of Mormon? I didn't even read the Bible and had no idea where my mother's copy had disappeared to. Besides, I had already asked God to change my life. Multiple times.

He just never answered.

December 1986

Christmas music played as I unpacked in my new loft bedroom. We had moved into the condo months before, but mountains of boxes still filled the garage. Humming, I knelt beside a box Dad had brought up a few minutes before and began emptying its contents. Halfway through, I pulled out Sabrina's religious book.

I stopped and turned it over in my hands. How had it gotten in there? Strangely, I didn't remember packing it. My curiosity was piqued as I recalled the picture of the young man and angels, and instead of discarding it, I looked around my room for a place to hide it for looking at later.

That night I cleaned the kitchen, said good night to Dad, and went upstairs. I brushed my teeth and climbed into bed. I reached over to set my alarm and remembered the book stashed inside the nightstand drawer.

I decided I'd wait until the next morning to read anything. My dyslexia required enormous effort to force my brain to remain focused on the page, until I recognized the words, one after another. I hated the exercise and only did it when necessary.

I lay back, eyes closed. A sudden urgency to read the book surprised me. I tossed and turned for a few minutes until I gave up and threw the covers back. I grabbed the book and my duvet and crossed the room to a couch in my loft. Comfortably seated, I turned on the lamp and opened the book, braced for battle. I flipped through the second half, looking for Sabrina's highlighted passage.

I found it near the end and pulled the book closer as I ran my finger along the print. The old-fashioned phrasing reminded me of Shakespeare's *King Lear*, which I had barely made my way through that semester. Still, I understood the gist. The verses promised readers that God would answer their earnest questions. I set the volume in my lap and thought. I had not been on speaking terms with God since the trip to Mexico when He'd been silent as I'd fallen apart on a hotel roof.

With Lisa's accident, my thoughts were more about disbelief that God would allow more suffering than pleas for anything. I was fairly convinced that no kind of heavenly intervention would magically fix anything in my life. Despite my mother's inexplicable visits, life simply moved on and dragged me with it.

So, the question remained—why I would ever pray again?

I hadn't experienced God as anything but disconnected, but constant exposure to Sabrina's faith had eroded my anger at Him. Her unyielding belief that a loving someone listened had chiseled away at my barriers. To be honest, it wasn't that I *wanted* God to be aloof and unconcerned. I simply believed He was.

Growing up, I'd enjoyed the mystical sacraments of the Holy Church, which instilled in me a sense of God's power. The Eucharist, which looked and tasted like plain bread and weak wine, was transformed into Christ's body and blood with a priest's prayer. Likewise, I had believed that someday God could alter my life if I prayed enough rosaries. I didn't understand how or when but, for a child, that hope had been enough.

But during every mounting catastrophe over the past two years, God's continued absence had drained my faith. If God didn't respond to such pain and loss, He wasn't who the priests pretended He was. The heavens had lost any sense of compassion.

God was unmoved by my pain.

Though I'd tried to hold on to my mother's comforting message, the memories had been transformed into a painful mockery of how bad my life had gotten. Nothing was okay, and I definitely didn't feel loved.

The contrast between Sabrina and me was excruciating. Sabrina's family had everything I wished for—love, stability, patience, laughter, and hope. I was both devastatingly jealous of them and eager to bask in their warmth. And this amazing family believed in God's love.

I reread the marked passage and felt the book's weight in my hands. I decided to gamble on God one last time. I would pray, for Sabrina's sake, and see if heaven answered. I wagered on silence, but curiosity prodded me on.

At least I could tell Sabrina I'd tried.

I slid from beneath the duvet and knelt beside the couch like I'd seen Sabrina do. I crossed myself out of habit, then stopped, wondering why I did that. Sabrina didn't. I thought about it, suddenly unsure.

Did Jesus cross Himself?

Had I been praying incorrectly all these years?

July 15, 1973

"You know what you can do when you are scared and alone? You just pray, and God will send his angels to watch over you and protect you," Grandma Edwards said to me, a child barely past the toddler stage. She stroked my wet cheeks. I remember her presence as a large softness.

My eyes widened. *"But, Grandma, I don't know how to pray."*

I had dropped Dad's bowl of homemade BBQ sauce at his birthday cookout. It was an accident; I was trying to help him cook. A beer in one hand, Dad had laid me out flat on the lawn. My mother had defended me, stepping between us. Her defiance had crumbled when he'd taken a swing at her, and she'd fled inside the house with him roaring at her heels. The other adults had followed, but only after looking over at the neighbors' yards first.

Forgotten in the grass, I'd sobbed until Grandma Edwards appeared and swept me into her arms. She had ambled a few steps with me to the swings to sit, and now we rocked back and forth.

She smiled softly at my confession and pressed my open palms together. *"Put your hands like this."*

I held them together tightly.

"Kneel by your bed and bow your head like this," she said, lowering her chin. She closed her eyes.

I copied her, squishing my eyes tight. A tear slid down my cheek.

"Then say, 'Dear God, please protect me from harm.'" Her lips brushed my ear. *"Or you can ask for anything else you need. Then end by saying, 'In the name of the Father, Son, and Holy Ghost. Amen.'"*

I opened my eyes. Grandma looked at me. *"Can you remember that?"*

I nodded.

She began to swing more vigorously. Her chest filled with air against my shoulder. She crooned softly, sweet and cracked with age, "This little light of mine, I'm gonna let it shine."

I decided that making the sign of the cross was not going to make or break the bet.

Now, to pray. No words came despite having uttered thousands of petitions in my childhood. Fear crept into my heart. My unanswered prayers indicated a problem with either me or God. I had blamed God until that moment, but what if I was wrong?

Maybe it wasn't how I prayed but who I'd become.

My heart filled with shame. As a child, I had believed in my innate goodness. I'd known I'd tried my best to do what was right. But after the basement in Mexico, that had changed.

I had lost my sense of wholeness. I knew I had sinned against God, against my mother, and done what I knew was wrong and vile. I had lied and hidden so many parts of myself that I'd lost who I was and tried to duct-tape my soul together with accomplishments. Honor-roll student, captain of the basketball team, three-sport athlete . . . it was all an attempt to redefine a girl falling apart.

I bowed my head and mustered enough courage to speak five words.

"God, can you hear me?"

I had lost so much that a simple query was all I had the strength to venture. Having finished my brief prayer of sorts, I sat back on the couch and pulled the duvet back over my legs. I opened the book to the beginning.

Depressing but familiar thoughts surfaced. I was cracked in the head. All this stuff about seeing my mother and angels. Praying on my knees. If

I admitted any of it out loud, my father would have me committed. I felt sane, but if the definition of crazy was losing your grasp on reality, then, no matter how hard I tried, I wouldn't know whether I was losing it or not. Right?

Nothing made sense. I wasn't even sure if there was a God anymore. Maybe I really was delusional.

Still, I read my way through one page, then another. I didn't notice the subtle arrival of warmth until the feeling began to swell. I recognized it from my mother's appearances and praying at Sabrina's house. Peace. Love. Energy lighting me up from the inside out. I looked around my room and saw nothing.

"Is this you?" I asked aloud at last.

The only answer was that burning in my heart. I kept reading. I barely comprehended the text, but I began to grasp the warmth as coming from God. It certainly didn't originate with me. It couldn't. My soul had known nothing like this comfort. But why did it come only now? If God cared, why hadn't He told me before?

A simple answer occurred to me. I'd only ever asked God one question: whether my mom's first visit was real. Didn't I already have that answer? Two subsequent visits had seemed to affirm it was. Other than that, I had only yelled and screamed and pleaded at Him to change people's choices.

Understanding flooded my heart. He had listened to every word, but despite His infinite power, He couldn't change the people around me. In this one area, He seemed powerless.

My mind struggled to grasp the paradox. God loved me. I felt His love flowing through every particle of my body. Simultaneously, I tried to comprehend His unwillingness—no, His inability—to alter things that had wounded me.

Still confused, I focused on the peace that filled me. He knew me. He saw me. I realized He was answering my real question: Did it matter to

God that I, tormented by suffering and loss, had experienced such crushing pain?

The answer was a soft but resounding yes.

Tears ran down my face and dripped onto the thin pages. A couple of hours passed swimming in these waves of conviction that God heard me. I started to feel anxious and put the book back in the drawer.

While I comprehended little of the text, I understood I had received an answer to an unspoken question that had plagued my soul. God had confirmed He'd heard, but more than that, He saw me and loved me. The unexpected answer fanned to life the embers of hope I had long thought dead and cold.

At the same time, I wasn't sure what my gamble had won me. If God answered prayers, why had such awful things happened? What about my entire Catholic childhood? Had I ever really known God? What did that mean for Mom? Had He meant for her to die? If not, had I been the one person He couldn't reach out and change in time?

My guilt returned, and everything confused me.

Chapter Seventeen

Late December 1986

I sat up in terror, sending my covers flying. My heart thumped beneath the hand I'd pressed to my chest. The house was silent, dark. I lay back on the mattress and forced myself to breathe slowly. Tears of relief sprang to my eyes.

Sabrina hadn't moved away and left me. The whole horrible scenario was just a nightmare. I turned over and pulled the covers tight around my shoulders. With a shaky breath, I released an impulse to sob.

The dream had seemed so real. But lying in bed, I rehearsed why it couldn't be. I'd seen Sabrina two nights ago at her house. We'd rented *Pretty in Pink* from Blockbuster Video. She'd only been here for a year and a half and said they'd be here for at least three. She wasn't going anywhere. I closed my eyes and sank back into dreams, forgetting the strange episode. After all, it was one bad dream among many.

Christmas's bleak dawn didn't surprise me that year, which made it better, even though Dad skipped the presents. I had expected nothing, so when he handed Lisa and me each a check, it was better than the year before.

After visiting his mother in her nursing home, we drove to brunch at Uncle Bob and Aunt Diane's home. Dad started drinking there, and the conversation quickly turned hostile toward my mother's family.

Though we'd followed the same Christmas routine my entire life— first brunch with my father's family, then dinner with my mother's family—now Dad fell into a rage about us going to my grandmother's for dinner.

"Those bitches are sending weekly letters to the prosecutor's office," he screamed at my uncle Bob, who tried to placate him. Lisa and I stood by the door, keys in hand, ready to go but too afraid to leave.

My father had taken great offense at my aunt's and grandmother's perceived betrayal, and he'd stewed all morning about whether he should let us go to dinner without him. He wasn't uninvited but everyone knew he wasn't wanted, including him.

My grown cousins flanked their father, hands on their hips.

"Arnie," Bob pleaded. "It's just a few hours. Stay here and play some cards, they can't do anything to you. It's a holiday dinner, not a trial."

Dad's brother calmed him down enough to allow Aunt Diane to sneak us out the back before Dad knew we were gone. Leaving him behind was the highlight of Christmas Day.

Dinner with Grandma and Aunt Kathy's family was a somber affair, but it lacked the frost of the prior year. We received our first presents of the day and enjoyed being fussed over. Afterward, we returned to Uncle Bob's to pick up our wasted father and went home.

Life assumed a rhythm, a kind of horrid normalcy. Dad behaved badly, and I escaped to Sabrina's whenever possible. Lisa also found places to hide out. The three of us maintained different orbits while tethered together by the fire at the center of our lives. We did our best not to collide.

Just after Christmas, Sabrina and I dropped her older brother Steele off at basketball practice. The wet streets wound through cold neighborhoods of bare maples and oaks. Gray clouds lowered, letting the sun peek out now and again. I drove, humming along to a popular Wham! song. I turned the volume up to liven the dreary day.

Sabrina shifted in the passenger seat and faced me.

"I need to tell you something," she said.

I gripped the wheel and stopped humming as the forgotten nightmare sprang to mind. I swallowed and blinked quickly, trying not to cry.

"Okay, what's up?" For once, my voice didn't give me away.

I refused to look over, afraid I'd lose my composure if I did.

Sabrina sighed and turned off the radio. She slumped in the seat.

"Well, my parents just told us we are moving back to California a little early. Next month, actually . . ."

I tried blinking the tears away, but they only rolled down my cheeks. Just when I had started to believe God loved me and maybe things would get better, I was being left behind again.

How would I hold on to hope?

January 1987

It was the Saturday before Sabrina's move, and I was lying on her bed as she sorted and cleaned her room. "What if you came to church with us tomorrow?" Sabrina asked.

I didn't respond, already feeling morose about everything.

"We are having an open house afterward to say goodbye to everyone. There will be lots of food." She grinned.

She knew I was jealous of her mother's cooking. I had to cook for myself. I looked away, thinking of my mom.

I had not told Sabrina about my praying. Trying to reconcile those feelings with my Catholic background overwhelmed me. Did one answer mean my entire life before had been wrong? It was too confusing.

I had begun to participate in prayers and Bible study with the Perrett family since then, but I still slept in while they went to church. That was as far I felt comfortable taking things. I just couldn't imagine myself in any place of worship other than Mom's.

I wrinkled my nose and started to shake my head.

"Please! Please!" Sabrina cut in. She fell onto the bed with hands clasped as if it were a desperate plea.

I laughed in wonder, and her grim expression twitched in amusement. Only Sabrina would be excited about church. She was so different from anyone I'd ever known.

Mom would have appreciated the good friend Sabrina had been to me. The thought struck me, along with a surprising assurance that Mom would have given her blessing for me to go, insisted, even, if she were here. We were Catholic through and through, but she would have expected me to support a friend who'd done so much for me. Going wouldn't betray Mom; it would show Sabrina my gratitude.

I gave Sabrina a small smile. "Okay, I'll go."

Sabrina jumped up and did a little dance. I pretended to groan at her excitement. I couldn't fathom why a church service meant so much to her, but if it made her happy, I was glad to go.

Sunday morning, I drove to the corner of Merriman Road and Six Mile Road. Small evergreen bushes and bare trees were dusted with the previous night's snow. I parked near a redbrick building and hurried in out of the blustery wind.

No holy water or marble floors greeted me in the vestibule. Instead, the small foyer, carpeted in tight commercial fibers, held a few chairs, a couch, and paintings of Christ. Open wood doors led to a larger sanctuary. Inside, families filled long padded pews without kneelers.

It was simpler than what I was accustomed to. The absence of stained-glass windows, candlesticks, crosses, and ornamentation made the cream-colored room trimmed in oak seem plain. Still, it wasn't bleak. Several floral arrangements brightened the wooden lectern in front. Sabrina smiled from the second row.

I was relieved to see her waiting and made my way toward her. Every few steps, though, kind-faced strangers stepped into my path and introduced themselves.

They each offered some version of "We're so glad you're here," and shook my hand.

The attention was unexpected, and I wasn't prepared for it. I felt the Catholic greeting, "Peace be with you" wasn't the right choice for the situation, so I improvised with "Nice to meet you" and "I'm just visiting." Finally, Sabrina rescued me from a group of older women who had surrounded me, explaining I was a friend from school. She pulled me through the circle and cleared a path so I could sit beside her family up front.

Piano music began, hushing the assembly. I raised my eyebrows at Sabrina. She leaned toward me, and I whispered in her ear. "How does everyone know I'm new?"

Sabrina chuckled under her breath. "Because everyone here knows everyone else."

I stole a glance around me. While Our Lady of Sorrows' sanctuary could fit over a thousand parishioners, this small chapel only accommodated a couple hundred. I couldn't decide if the idea of being so intimately connected to a congregation terrified me or appealed to me.

After the meeting, Sabrina's friend who attended a neighboring high school found me and handed me a piece of paper with an address. "If you want to come again, be at my house by eight and we can go together."

I gave her a feeble smile. "Thanks."

I had nothing specific against Molly Snow. I'd met her several times before at Sabrina's house. I'd liked her then, and I appreciated her gesture, but I shoved the paper into my purse without a second thought.

There really wasn't any reason to come back. Sabrina was leaving.

A Week Later

I had a bad habit of kicking my covers off in the middle of the night, and I awoke that gray Sunday morning feeling tense and cold. I pulled the covers up and wondered what time it was. A glance at the clock revealed I hadn't slept long; it was just after seven. After Sabrina's departure the day before, I'd cried all evening in my room. I guessed I had fallen asleep sometime after 1:00 a.m.

Cynical, thanks to my new loss, I noted that my life had endless varieties of the same rotten flavor to look forward to. I could stay home by myself. I could go to the mall by myself. I could watch movies by myself. I could study by myself. I sighed and closed my eyes, finally starting to get warm again. Maybe staying in bed—alone—was the best option.

For the first time in months, I had slept at home all weekend instead of at Sabrina's. I already felt the hole Sabrina's absence was leaving in my life. I had lost my refuge and had no prospects of finding another.

I could feel the self-pity gaining hold in my soul and decided nothing else could be worse than drowning in it all day. I got up to get dressed. I would think of some way to get out of the house after that. Maybe the library.

In the shower, I remembered Molly's invitation. If I went with her, I would have something to do and people to be with. I rubbed shampoo into my hair as hot steam filled the bathroom. Why would I even consider this? A Catholic girl wouldn't worship with the Mormons.

I tipped my head back under the stream of water. One tiny, amazing answer came: I believed Sabrina's claim. God had answered my prayer. My eyes opened wide at the realization. I believed that He had answered my prayer, and part of me was curious if there was more.

Oh no.

I scrubbed my anxiety out with a loofah, then rinsed off. I could simply visit a different church on Sunday, right? It would be no big deal if I explored what others thought. I wasn't leaving my mother's church.

Careful to not wake Lisa or Dad, I got dressed and ate a bowl of cereal. I spilled some milk on my lap and had to change again. Then I left the quiet house with my shoes in hand, closing the door softly behind me.

If my dad suspected my intent, he would belittle and torment me for choosing to go to any church—much less an unknown Christian sect. Depending on his blood-alcohol level, he might even forbid it. Not that he cared about Mormons in particular; he just hated believers.

I doubted Lisa really cared about God, but if she knew, she would rat on me to our grandmother. If Grandma Findlay suspected defection, she would be undone. You didn't have to be Catholic to attend Mass or Jewish to attend Shabbat service; churches opened their doors to any seekers. But if I went through any door other than the Holy Roman Church's, my grandmother would see me as defecting from our family. In her eyes, it was no different than if I'd jumped off that roof in Mexico.

I had attended mass at Our Lady of Sorrows every week until Mom died. Her funeral was the last time I had darkened our parish doors. Now, at last, when I finally went back to God, it was in a little chapel that I had to sneak away to. Yet my hope was throbbing again because, for once, my choices were driving events. It was the first thing that felt right after Mom's death.

My first few tenuous steps out on my own were quickly challenged.

Chapter Eighteen

February 1987

I curled up on my bed, hyperventilating.

Nobody was forcing me, but I had forty-eight hours to secure my dad's approval to become an official member of Sabrina's church, and I was terrified he would beat me for asking.

I had told myself that going to church with Molly didn't imply any kind of commitment, but the longer I went, the more I wanted to commit to this new path. I'd thought the transition might take several years, if not a decade, to where I fully considered myself ready to do something so drastic. But just weeks later, I was desperate to get my father's permission.

I attributed my expedited shift in desire to a growing sense of my mother's approval. At first, I'd worried that joining a new faith was a betrayal. As I continued to pray, however, I felt God understood my fears. He didn't take long to send a gentle response that included a further sense of meaning in my mother's "I will always love you." She meant for me to know that this new path would never diminish her love for me. She agreed with my choices.

When I told Sabrina over the phone of my amazing experiences having prayers answered, she whooped with excitement.

Molly was also thrilled, but I wasn't quite prepared when she asked, "Does this mean you want to officially join our church?"

Taken aback, I considered how my life had assumed a new level of peace and hope. If being baptized brought more of what I was experiencing, I was in.

"Yes," I'd said, unaware of the implications.

Then Molly's parents dropped the bomb on me. As a minor, I would need my parent's permission. "He doesn't have to sign anything since membership carries no legal obligations; we just have to know he is okay with your baptism."

I'd floundered to explain the wave of incredulity that swept me off my feet. I wanted to continue in the path I'd chosen. I'd come closer to God than I'd ever known was possible. But now, my father, who hated religion, could stand in the way of even that. The man ruined everything.

Tears of frustration filled my eyes. "You don't understand. He doesn't care about me."

This was about my faith and relationship with God. Why did my father need to sign off on that? He had ridiculed and beat my mother while cursing her faith. He could do the same to me.

The Snows had been sympathetic but unbending. No permission, no baptism.

I debated for several days. I could continue attending church without becoming an official member. But avoiding the confrontation would mean Dad had won by default. He still controlled my life. The only way to pursue my path was to own it. I finally chose a date and promised Molly I would ask before then.

I had just hours left.

I had prayed for courage for days. That night, I prayed again for safety and tried to calm my breathing. This was all too familiar. I had prayed for protection without success my entire life.

My tiny seeds of faith were just emerging, and the possibility of life taking a drastic turn for the worse felt extremely probable. I envisioned in detail a scene that would end everything. I knew the taste of blood in my mouth, the smell of alcoholic rage and primal fear, the smack of my head against a wall. I just didn't know what it felt like to die.

Then again, I was desperate to hold on to the feeling of love and to be part of something happy.

Finally, I got up from my bed and wandered into the living room with the dread of an empty-handed girl facing Goliath. David had trusted God enough to refuse King Saul's armor. I would have taken anything anyone offered in that moment, but my hands were empty. The only thing I had was a determination to live my life with the love I had found in God, even if it lasted only moments more. *I need a miracle. Now.*

It was late, past dinner, and Dad lay sprawled on the couch watching basketball. Beer bottles littered the coffee table beside a cold, half-eaten Little Caesars pizza sitting in its greasy box.

"What?! You call that a foul? C'mon, man . . . Dumars had both feet planted." Dad pounded the arm of the couch.

We watched the replay of the Chicago Bulls player charging to the basket while Dumars defended. Dad was right.

"Bad call," I said.

He snorted and nodded at the screen. "Should have put money on this one." He stretched as the Bulls took a time-out after missing both free throws. "Pistons are up by eight. Bulls can't hit their outside shots for nothing."

Dad seemed relaxed and not totally wasted.

Knowing this might be my best chance, I decided to go for it, even though my heart thumped as if I had just come out of the game myself. Words spilled out.

"Dad, is it okay if I get baptized into Sabrina's church?"

He didn't look away from the TV, letting a long moment pass.

"I figured you'd ask me that sooner or later," he finally said. "I don't care. Whatever." He pointed to the pizza box. "Put that away, will you?"

"Sure, thanks." I could barely breathe.

I threw the box away and left before another Stroh's could change his mind.

I didn't know if the miracle was that he didn't hear me right or didn't really care. Not hearing me seemed more likely, considering his opinion on the topic, but I wasn't about to clarify. He'd said he didn't care what I did. That was permission.

It wasn't my fault if he hadn't understood my question.

March 23, 1987

I had spent half of the school year coming home to an empty house. My dad would leave for days at a time and go north to party with friends he'd made the previous summer. I didn't mind the quiet evenings.

One Monday, I caught a glimpse of Dad sleeping on the couch as I came in after school. I gently set my bags down and slipped my shoes off. There was no telling if it's been a good weekend or not, and even though I was hungry, I went straight up to the loft to do homework. I didn't want to rouse him.

Later, I heard Dad moving around in the kitchen. The phone rang, and Dad answered it. He started listing options for bars to meet at that night, so I figured it was a drinking buddy. My stomach growled. It was almost six-thirty, and I hadn't eaten anything since lunch.

I had started down the stairs when I heard a nasty laugh from the kitchen.

"Ha. Yeah, right." Dad snorted.

Something about his tone cautioned me. I halted just out of sight, halfway down.

"No, I don't have to be home this weekend," Dad said. "We could go up Friday and see Donny."

He laughed. "I'm serious. Hell, Lisa is never home, always out partying. And get this. The other one joined a cult—"

The blood drained from my face.

"Yeah, it's one of those weird ones. Some voodoo shit." He laughed mockingly. "I never know where she is, but as long as it's not here, it's fine with me."

He paused. "Okay, I'll call Don and make sure. See ya."

He hung up. I went back to my room with a sick stomach. I knew he hated believers; I just hadn't realized how little he cared about me. I sat on my bed and let it sink in that he had willingly let me join something he believed twisted and dangerous. For all he understood, they might kill me off for some sadistic or insane self-satisfaction. He thought I had ignorantly imperiled myself, and it made him laugh.

It didn't matter that none of what he believed was true. It only mattered that he believed it but hadn't cared enough to object. He had heard me correctly. After everything he'd done, I was surprised by how much my heart still stung.

I went back upstairs and didn't come down for food until he'd left. When your own parent cares so little for your well-being, you begin to believe they might be right.

I wasn't worth the effort to save.

April 6, 1987

I had smarted for a couple of weeks following the phone conversation, so when Dad handed me shiny keys and led me to the garage, I couldn't process what he was saying.

159

"Do you like it?" he asked with a grin.

I stood back and admired a midnight blue '87 Mustang GT convertible parked there. It was beautiful.

"Is it really for me?" I slowly said, half expecting it to be some kind of joke.

Dad nodded, and I squealed. I leapt toward my father and hugged him. Tears sprang to my eyes—a real present for my birthday. Whatever he had said or done lately, his generous gesture filled my soul like nothing else.

He laughed as I released him to jump up and down.

"Are you going to drive it?" he asked, satisfied by my reaction.

I opened the door and hopped in. I stuck the keys in the ignition before I noticed the stick shift and frowned.

Dad had rounded the car and was sliding into the passenger seat beside me. "It's easier than you think."

A bit deflated, I looked at him. He patted my hand.

"Trust me. Let's take her out." He grinned. "I loved driving her home. This baby can fly."

Dad was in his element. "Now, put the key in and put your right foot on the brake and your left on the clutch."

I managed to back the car out without hitting anything. My hands were sweaty.

"Good job!" He began explaining how the flywheel integrated with the engine and what I needed to do to make the little sports car go.

We circled the neighborhood, eventually putting the top down just for fun. It was chilly, but I drank in his patient attention. Dad waved to the neighbors as I shifted while going uphill. The engine stuttered, then roared up and over the top. I grinned in triumph but forgot to shift into neutral when I hit the brakes coming down the other side. The car jerked to a halt, engine dead, just short of the stop sign at the bottom.

Panicked, I looked at Dad. He threw his head back and laughed.

I couldn't help but laugh too.

Three days later, I killed the engine on purpose and left the top down. Climbing out of the muscle car, I unzipped my coat in the gorgeous spring evening. From one day to the next, Michigan weather flipped from snow to steamy heat all through April. It was an incredibly remarkable day with sunshine that promised to break us free from winter's grasp at last. Audible laughter came from the backyard.

Molly slammed her passenger door on the other side of the Mustang and ran ahead of me. A dozen teens jumped on a trampoline in the backyard. There wasn't a beer can in sight, and trays of cookies and pitchers of lemonade filled a patio table.

It was my first real party since I'd quit drinking the summer before. Sure, I'd gone to movie nights at church kids' houses over the winter, but this was an all-night birthday affair for one of the girls—a good, clean celebration that kicked the boys out at ten that night. Eventually close to twenty kids milled about, either showing off on the trampoline or teasing those bouncing.

Joining the melee atop the trampoline, I sprang into the air with both feet kicking sideways, Karate-Kid style. With hoots of approval, I continued my flying acrobatics, to everyone's amusement.

With a powerful kick, I soared higher into the air. I had bounced on trampolines a million times before, but never with so many others, and the landing that followed ended uniquely. My left leg caught a "double bounce," which caused my knee to collapse sideways.

I fell. My left knee audibly snapped as my lower leg hit ninety degrees, then bent farther, my leg doubling over sideways on itself. Screaming as my left foot lay twisted under my left hip, I rolled onto my back and pulled my knee into my chest with my hands and physically pushed my foot down into place with my left arm as my friends continued bouncing.

They interpreted my screams as shouts of delight—until they noticed my face. The jumping ceased. I sobbed. One girl ran for her mom.

In minutes, my knee had swollen and filled my loose pantleg. Someone handed me a cordless phone, and I left frantic messages for Dad. He'd been home when I'd left less than an hour earlier, and I begged him to pick up. He didn't.

In his absence, the moms decided to take me to urgent care without him.

Several of the boys volunteered to heft my dead weight to the host mom's car. When they lifted me down from the tramp, one pair of hands that gripped immediately above my left knee sent a spasm of pain so absorbing I lost my vision. I surely screamed but have no memory of it.

I came fully conscious while my guy friends pushed and pulled me into the sedan's back seat. I panted and groaned as they securely positioned me. They felt awful hurting me, but it couldn't be helped. Any movement was excruciating.

The mom drove as slowly as possible over the unpaved washboard road, but I screamed with each bump. I could barely breathe the first half mile. Once we got on to the pavement, it wasn't far to a small urgent-care center. Molly ran in and returned with a nurse pushing a wheelchair.

Reversing the process to get me out of the car was just as bad. When I was finally loaded into the wheelchair, we went inside and had a few moments of desperate debate over whether the center could treat me because my legal guardian wasn't present. A nurse began to wheel me back outside. I went into hysterics at the thought of another car ride, then remembered an important detail as the doors opened.

"Wait! Wait! I was here last year for my back injury. My dad brought me here!"

The nurse pushing me out looked over her shoulder at the admissions clerk, who tilted her head to the side, then nodded. "Okay, I think I can make it work. Bring her back."

As the wheelchair swiveled around, Dad came through the doors, which made me start crying again. He was dressed and didn't smell too bad, which were small miracles. He signed papers while two nurses took me back to a room. They closed the door behind them.

"Let's get those pants off." One nurse smiled and began undoing the buttons. Just that small jostle provoked currents of pain.

"No, no, that hurts. Just cut my pants off!" I said breathlessly, trying not to scream. But she continued tugging my high-waisted pants down around my hips. I screamed as another nurse joined her, wrapping her arms around my shoulders and chest. She lifted and held me above the gurney while the other yanked the material past my rear.

"Just cut them off! Cut them off!!" I screamed, giving in to panic. They persisted, pulling harder. I had those pants in every color from Limited. These peach ones were my least favorite. I yelled at the nurses, but they just ignored me.

"Listen to me! Cut them off!!"

The pants went over my knee, and without the tight fabric cuff, the joint gave way. Each tug tore at my suspended knee, pulled between the quad that spasmed with pain and my still-trapped calf.

A litany of cuss words streamed from my mouth, and I blindly punched backward at the nurse. I would have knocked her flat if possible, for ignoring me.

"Ugh!" I gave a final shriek as my freed leg thumped onto the bed.

They wheeled me off for X-rays. The tech carefully captured every possible painful angle. My teeth chattered. I will admit using four-letter words quite a few times again and having less than charitable feelings

163

toward that man also. I shook uncontrollably. Someone draped a blanket over me before finally leaving me alone.

Dad entered a few minutes later. I began to tell him how they'd tortured me, but the doctor knocked a moment later. I shut up while he bustled about, clipping X-rays to the light box. I studied them, unable to identify anything besides bones. The rest looked like one dark mass.

"Well, Miss Edwards, to put it bluntly, that was some fall. As we can see here, there is nothing broken, which is good news. Unfortunately, the bad news is there is nothing holding your lower leg and upper leg together except small tendons and skin. Your ligaments were all torn, which destroyed the joint. I am going to refer you to an orthopedic surgeon."

He continued, but that was all I needed to hear.

I wanted Mom.

Chapter Nineteen

The condo stairs were out of the question, so Dad helped me into in Lisa's room on the main floor that night. Her waterbed moved with every breath, making my knee spasm. Halfway through the night, I yelled to Dad, who had the television on in the next room.

"Dad! Dad! I need to pee!" I tried to get up on one elbow to yell louder but fell back onto the wobbly mattress. I had to rock back and forth a couple of times to get enough momentum to finally prop my elbow under myself. Extra-strength Tylenol was no match for any movement.

I swore to myself.

"Da-ad!"

No answer.

I lay back and reached over my head, then desperately banged the wall with my fist. Maybe if Dad had passed out drunk in the living room, Lisa might hear my pounding from the loft.

"Lisa! Help!"

If I wet myself, I would lay in it all night before going to the hospital in the morning. There was no way I'd survive a shower or getting redressed. I kept shouting every few seconds.

"Dad!"

"Lisa!"

Canned television laughter mocked my repetitive pleas. My voice grew hoarse. Helpless, I prayed.

God, why is everything so awful all the time? I wanted to give up. *What more can I do?*

With a flash of inspiration, I recalled a childhood trick. I stretched over the bed, barely grasping the tangled phone cord falling over the night-stand's edge. I yanked the handset free with the cord and reeled it in to dial. I punched the buttons and waited. All the house phones rang in unison. It took at least twenty times before Dad answered.

"Y-yah?" he slurred.

"Dad! I have to pee, and I can't get up!" My voice squeaked on the last word.

"Shelly? What? Where are you?"

"Lisa's room!" My bladder started to cramp.

"What? Oh, hell."

Exactly. "Hurry!" I hissed.

"You better have broken ten bones, or I'll break them for you," Dad said.

It was the morning after the urgent care doctor had definitively shown us the damage on film. I wasn't sure how much Dad remembered, though, so I kept quiet. He was more bothered by having to drive with a pounding head to Royal Oak than the state of my knee. I didn't want his resentment to take a worse turn.

Luckily, Dr. Mayo, a top orthopedic surgeon at Beaumont Hospital, took one look at my X-rays and immediately sent me to the adjacent facility. I sighed in relief.

Dad stayed until I was assigned a room. "I need to get back. See you later."

A nurse walked in as he left.

"Can I get something for the pain now?" I asked. It had been eighteen hours with only Tylenol and Advil. All I really cared about was relief.

166

The nurse brought a shot of morphine. I dozed all day.

Dad called that night. I muted the television.

"Hey, how are you doing?" he asked. I heard a basketball game in the background, lots of voices.

"I'm fine. The pain meds helped." I was touched he had bothered to check on me. He'd not acted the least bit concerned that morning, so it was a nice surprise.

"That's good," he said.

Awkward silence stretched between us. The crowd around him burst into cheers, so he spoke louder.

"Did they schedule a time for surgery?"

It hit me then. He needed to know how hard he could party. It was the only reason he'd called.

I frowned in disappointment. "Tomorrow morning at nine."

"All right. Well, I'll see you later."

"Okay, bye—"

He hung up.

—*Love you.*

The next day, Dr. Mayo spent five hours reconstructing my knee, removing tendons from my thigh to fashion new knee ligaments. Afterward, I awoke in the recovery room with a leg cast from groin to toes and suspended in a sling above my bed. A triangle handle dangled above my waist to allow me to reposition myself.

Whether it was the sight of the monstrous cast or my morphine wearing off, it suddenly became clear that despite beating the odds to have returned to play varsity basketball and volleyball that year after intense physical therapy, not just my softball season had prematurely ended.

I would never play anything again.

I covered my face. "God, when is enough, enough?"

It had been such a small moment, one second on the trampoline that could have gone a million other ways. Like everything else in my life that I couldn't go back and change, I hadn't seen it coming.

A wave of despair came crashing through my heart. Sports had been the only arena in my life where I was powerful, where I controlled the outcome by working harder and playing smarter. I'd just lost it all.

"Oh, God," I prayed. "Please, please, help me survive this."

Two days later, my leg hurt so much I begged my nurses to knock me out. Unable to administer more pain medication without risking stopping my heart, Dr. Mayo decided they could slice the side of the cast near my knee to allow some expansion and hopefully relief.

It helped for a couple of days, but once the post-op inflammation subsided, they needed to replace the cast. I was awake as they lifted my leg out of the cracked cast and set it with new plaster bandages. They worked quickly as I gripped my bedrails with both hands, trying not to scream. It was ten minutes of pure agony.

Back in my room alone, I could feel perspiration still covering my upper lip and forehead, though the nurses had changed my soiled gown dripping with plaster and sweat.

I had no one to talk to besides God, so I poured out my confusion. Sabrina's church had taught me that God loved His children and desired our happiness, that there was purpose for my life. I wanted to believe even though I struggled to understand the need for so much pain. So far, my disappointments far outweighed my happiness.

"Is this part of your plan for my life?" I spoke aloud.

Honestly, with recent answers I'd never imagined possible, the love and hope that came and lifted me had caused me to believe in His existence. But I still failed to reconcile that with the constant barrage of distressing circumstances.

Had I understood God's intent, I'm certain I would have bolted my recovery-room door. Instead, I remained upset by my circumstances and unwilling to risk doing the very thing that might provide the love I so desperately needed. The solution to both would enter through that door in a wool coat holding Kentucky Fried Chicken.

But first, my secret had to be revealed.

April 14, 1987

The knock and a familiar face brought an instant smile to mine.

"Hey there!" Molly's mom, Leslie Snow, hugged me and set some flowers on a side table in my hospital room.

I rang the nurses' bell for them to take the remains of my lunch and began to chat with Leslie. There came another knock at the door, but instead of the expected nurse, my aunt Kathy walked in.

"Shelly!" She kissed my cheek.

"Aunt Kathy!" A sense of alarm set in.

Kathy looked over at Leslie on the polyester love seat. Leslie nodded to Aunt Kathy. They both waited for an introduction. These women were strangers I had never intended to meet. Any topic might veer the wrong way.

"How did you know I was here?" I stalled, needing a diversion for time to think.

Kathy gave me a look. "Lisa."

I felt stupid for asking, knowing it would have to be my sister.

Before anything dumber came to mind, a nurse popped her head in. "You rang?"

"I need to use the bedpan," I said, relieved by the interruption.

The efficient nurse removed my lunch and drew a curtain around my bed. "Excuse us, ladies. She'll be right back."

"So, how do you know Shelly?" Aunt Kathy's voice, polite and inquiring, penetrated the quiet outside the curtain.

My heart missed a beat. This was it. The end of my relationship with my mother's family. There was no way Leslie could know how I wished she would hide my involvement in her church from this woman.

"Oh, we attend the same church," Leslie's cheery voice answered.

"Our Lady of Sorrows." My aunt's voice assumed a friendlier note.

I cringed as Leslie replied without hesitation. "Oh, no. We go to The Church of Jesus Christ of Latter-day Saints."

I collapsed inward in the shocked silence that followed.

I closed my eyes, knowing I'd lost the chance to broach the subject with my mother's family on my own terms. My aunt had heard from a stranger's lips how I'd forsaken my mother's faith. Worse yet, she'd inform my grandmother, who would never forgive me.

"Isn't this accident horrible?" Leslie attempted to recover the conversation. "I feel so bad, especially after her back injury last year."

"Of course." Aunt Kathy's tone had lost any warmth.

The nurse cleaned me up and whipped open the curtain, revealing the two women. Aunt Kathy turned to me and raised her eyebrows as Leslie stood to go.

"Well, I don't want to intrude on family time, I just wanted to let you know we were thinking of you."

I waved before the door clicked shut behind her. The walls closed in as Aunt Kathy seated herself beside me. A long silence passed as she studied my face. I couldn't meet her eyes. Instead, I looked at the cross on her necklace. *Jesus, help me now.*

She cleared her throat. "Why didn't you tell me you joined another church?"

I looked down at my hands. "I was afraid to tell anyone. I mean, of course Dad knew. I didn't want to hurt you or Grandma, though."

"This happened after your mom died?" Kathy sounded sad. I looked up at her eyes, heavy with sorrow.

"Yes. A few months ago." I swallowed. "I joined in February."

She exhaled a sigh heavy filled with assumptions. I could almost hear her putting two and two together. My mother's loss and my new connections while cut off from my mother's family had led to my defection from the Holy Roman Church.

I couldn't set her straight. If I explained my mother's visits or the feelings I had when I prayed, Aunt Kathy would assume I was a liar—or crazy. I chose to let her think whatever made the most sense to her. At least with her explanation, she might pity me.

"Why didn't you tell me?" Aunt Kathy leaned forward and put her hand on the bed. "I would have liked to know, to come or something."

I shrugged my shoulders, surprised. I had expected her to demand with holy wrath that I recant in my mother's name, not any sort of regret.

She gathered her thoughts.

"Well, what's done is done. I can explain to Grandma if you want me to," she said. "She will accept it." She sat back and rubbed her temples.

She forced a smile. "Now, tell me how you've been."

Dad had been pushing Kathy out of our lives. He'd spurned my mother's family at every opportunity. Yet, here was my aunt insisting on being part of my life despite Dad's efforts. I was grateful but afraid that the tenuous connection I had to my mother's family would be severed by the chance meeting.

I wished I could explain the connection between the faith I'd been born into and the faith I now chose. In my heart, the two ran together. My mother had raised me with reverence for an omniscient but distant God, and now she had helped me climb out of despair with a sense of God's love for me. My aunt thought I'd abandoned my mother's beliefs, but I believed Mom had led me to greater love and peace than she had known herself in life. It was her last gift to me.

Though Kathy's gentle and restrained response surprised me, I feared my grandmother's reaction. Since I couldn't explain my reasons to either woman without sounding crazy, my only choice was to wait and see.

Catholic Confirmation, 1983

"Have you thought about what name you'd like to take?" Grandma asked me, referring to the new name I would take at my upcoming Confirmation in the Roman Catholic Church.

Mom smiled at me. I had already shared my intentions with her. I nodded and bit my lip, unsure whether Grandma would approve.

Mom smiled. "Go on, Shelly. Tell her."

It was common to take the names of Saints to signify a connection to a role model, a spiritual patron who could be turned to for guidance and support. I had chosen someone I admired very much, someone I most wanted to emulate in my life, but it was an unusual choice.

I ducked my head, then blurted my grandmother's name. "Sarah."

Saint Sarah was seldom used for confirmations. Abraham's wife was primarily known for being the first female convert to the Abrahamic faith and also being childless to an old age, which made her less appealing than others, like Saint Therese or the Holy Mother Mary.

Still, a smile stretched across Sarah Catherine Findlay's face. She knew the name was a nod to her. My grandmother was Catholicism incarnate. Choosing her name as my own paid homage to the living saint who'd spent hours tutoring me on catechism and showed me every day what it meant to be a woman of God.

I had read little of the Bible, but I knew Sarah Catherine Findlay had read it all and loved God. I trusted her faith more than my own. I was asking her to be my guiding star.

Grandma embraced me.

"I am so proud of you, my girl. So proud."

For three days, every knock on the hospital room door made my heart skip a beat. I anticipated my grandmother's visit, but I didn't expect the smile on her face and bucket of the Colonel's fried chicken she held when she actually came five days later.

Grandma looked as if she'd come straight from Mass, dressed in a cream blouse tied in a bow at the neck and creased trousers. She loved fancy blouses as much as my mother had loved shoes and bags.

"Grandma!" I said, shocked and a little timid. I had not had any visitors since my aunt the week before. My dad called occasionally for updates on when I'd be getting out. While I'd been lonely, I wasn't sure if this would be a happy visit.

She put the grease-stained paper bucket down and bent over to hug me. I held on longer than usual, hoping she felt my apology for not telling her myself. Our family habit of not talking about important things made for so many silent moments. This one was one of the few that made me feel better.

She stepped back, pulled a chair closer, and pushed the chicken at me. "Eat while it's warm."

The aroma of eleven secret herbs and spices filled me with gratitude, and my tension dissipated. Despite my appearing to reject her faith, along with the chicken, Sarah Findlay had brought me unexpected grace. She was the answer to the prayer of a still-immature heart wondering once more how loss and love could coexist.

In my fear of losing her affection, I'd run from an opportunity to know it better. I believed my grandmother loved me, but until that moment, I was unaware of how much. Her love showed me that what I'd believed would be another nuclear rejection turned out to be a harmless smoke bomb.

As my fears cleared and my grandmother and I visited and laughed together, I felt closer to her than ever before. Her forgiveness and love were still guiding my path, and I realized that I was less alone than I believed.

I would later thank God for the disastrous scene with my aunt. It revealed a higher purpose in some of my pain. That hospital stay gave me my mother's family back in a way I'd thought impossible. Sometimes when life takes an unplanned turn, it's actually God altering our path in order to make our lives go in the right direction.

Chapter Twenty

Early May 1987

The sound of crying woke me midmorning. Groggy, I rose to my elbows and strained to hear the noise coming from downstairs in the condo. It was definitely not Lisa. Was it the TV? My body stiffened when I realized with great anxiety that it was my father who was upset. The last time he'd cried, my life had fallen apart.

Someone else murmured comforting words. We weren't alone! That eased my terror a little, and I listened harder. In the stillness, their conversation carried all the way across the vaulted ceilings.

"You don't understand. I love him." Dad's emotions flowed unchecked.

The second voice sounded like Dad's friends Anthony. Whoever it was, he was consoling my father. "It will be all right. You have to give him time."

In my confusion, I worried something awful had happened between my father and his brother.

In disjointed fragments, I gathered what had happened between Dad and another man the night before. "I know . . . but I basically made a fool of myself. I told Ted how attracted I . . . and he just refused. He won't . . . said he is already involved . . ."

My eyes widened when I realized this intrigue had happened as I'd slept. I fell back flat on the mattress and covered my ears with my hands.

I felt as if I'd discovered that my father had cheated on my mother, though I knew she was dead. I wondered if my mom had known. Why would she have stayed if she knew Dad hadn't wanted her at such a basic level? Questions flooded my mind, the last twenty-five years of their marriage suddenly flipped inside out. Nothing had been what it seemed at any level. I didn't know whether to be angry or hurt or sad. I think I was all three.

I didn't want to know how deep the layers of deceit went in my family. It had already fallen apart. Knowing more wouldn't change anything.

I had come home late the night before. Molly had been carrying my books inside while I navigated with crutches and my huge cast. Dad had a friend over, which was unusual. Dad's friends rarely came to visit. They normally met up at bars. In addition, this particular friend was not a drinking buddy, which made his presence even stranger.

I only knew Ted because, since the fire, the only option for me to get a haircut was tagging along with Dad to Ted's shop.

I didn't mind the man's haircuts, but his scissor skills didn't explain the man's late-night presence at our home. Dad's thick mane didn't require emergency attendance. Fortunately, I'd been too oblivious in my exhausted state to make the evident conclusions and slept well. Now, I understood why the vibe the night before had been so off. We'd interrupted Dad propositioning his friend. My father was gay.

I gave a weak cough, wanting to halt the unending flow of sordid details. Whatever kind of affair my dad had wanted to embark on, I had heard enough. Dad had assumed I was at school as usual. Otherwise, I would not have been hearing this conversation.

I heard a quiet curse. "Shelly? You up there?"

I pretended to sleep. All went silent. The men downstairs changed the subject. I heard the garage door open and close a few minutes later. A car drove away.

I wished I had gone to school. There are some things you can't unhear. This was the eighties; LGBTQ+ sympathy and understanding were not

176

elements of society in general. News coverage of AIDS had been fomenting homophobic fear for a decade. Everyone heard rumors about certain kids in school, but I'd never imagined my own father being one of those that had to hide their sexual preference for fear of retaliation.

Understanding broke through my bewilderment. It suddenly made sense why Dad hated religion and hated Mom for believing it. One of his most basic identifying features as a human, his need for love, was entangled with an attraction condemned by the Holy Roman Catholic Church. I knew he had been beaten by his father growing up and that he had gone to the Korean War an angry youth and returned a withdrawn man. Mom had blamed his drinking on the war. I wasn't so sure now.

Dad's repeated assertion that Mom had tricked him into marriage echoed in my mind. Though I didn't believe she had deceived him, he had seemed to feel trapped in their relationship. That frustration made sense now. Mom had refused to leave him, wanting to make their marriage work at any cost. Maybe his abuse had been an attempt to force her to do what he couldn't—end the charade. Maybe the drinking had been an attempt to smother his feelings.

While I now had some kind of explanation, none of it was an excuse for murder. These new insights didn't comfort me. The bottom just kept falling out from under me.

May 1987

My father's shout, loud enough to be heard from downstairs over the Bon Jovi on my radio, made my head snap up over the homework spread before me in the loft. "You're just like your ungrateful mother!"

"Why are you such a selfish jerk?" Lisa screamed back.

My twenty-pound, full-leg cast forgotten, I flew out of my chair and bounded downstairs without crutches as the sounds of a scuffle began. I reached the bottom as my sister screamed. A thud followed.

Pure adrenaline flowed as I hopped into the kitchen. Dad had pinned Lisa against the counter. He gripped her shoulders and lifted in preparation to slam her head against the gray laminate. His back was to me. Instinctively, I dropped my shoulder and charged. Wrapping my arms around his waist, I heaved—slamming him up onto the counter.

I had the element of surprise, and he was unprepared for my rear attack. I knocked the wind out of him and freed Lisa, who fell to the floor in a crouch.

I pulled her up and pushed her toward the door, but she stood her ground.

"Go! Get out of here! Leave!" I hissed. She shook her head.

I saw she was afraid to leave me alone. For years, she had kept me from the most horrific attacks on Mom. This was different. Mom's absence had made Lisa the new target. If she stayed, this would escalate.

I mouthed my argument. "He won't hurt me."

She looked at me, eyes softening, then bolted. I turned to face Dad. He had gotten to his feet and now glared at me. In spite of my brave words, I wasn't completely confident that Dad wouldn't hurt me, just sure that he'd hurt Lisa worse.

I tried to strike the sweet spot between confidence and being too defiant, hiding my fear. Tense, I waited and wondered again why the system had housed us with a murder suspect. If he had killed mom, why not us? But then, adults usually ignored me unless they wanted something. Why would the criminal justice system do anything less?

He went to the window and watched Lisa drive away. I began to head back upstairs before his crosshairs settled on me. I knew I might have a problem defending myself on one leg.

Behind me, Dad found his voice. "Why don't you leave too? Hell, I don't know why I bought you that car if you refuse to use it!"

Dad wasn't in a reasonable mood, so I didn't bother replying. I couldn't drive anywhere, not with that clutch and my cast. He came to the bottom of the stairs and glared up at me.

I tried to ignore his hulking figure beneath me. Push up, sit. Push up, sit. He cussed me out. My arms began to burn, but I didn't stop.

"I'll take that car away from your ungrateful ass!"

I stopped at the top stair, far enough away to feel safe responding. "Fine with me. I'll just take my own money and buy a new one."

"Really? What money is that?"

His sarcasm should have warned me, but I plowed on. "My college account," I said, referring to the $40,000 my mom and grandparents had stashed away for me and Lisa each.

They had intentionally put only our names on those accounts. Whenever I felt overwhelmed by the thoughts of Dad's upcoming trial and the possibility of him being imprisoned, I thought of that money. I'd get access to it at eighteen. I only had to get through graduation, and I would be able to take care of myself.

Dad laughed out loud. "It's gone. I used it to pay for this condo! Your and Lisa's accounts, both!"

I stared at him, speechless. He laughed at my face like it was the best joke he'd ever heard. With one last push, I went over the final riser with a roll. I lay out of sight, wondering if he had lied. I couldn't imagine how he'd managed to empty our funds. Then it hit me.

Neal Simpson had convinced Lisa and me to put Dad on our bank accounts when Dad needed bail money. We'd signed the papers at the bank the day after Neal loaned him bail money and sprung him. They must have included the college savings accounts on that list.

Anger settled in my belly. I wanted to punch a wall.

Had Dad thought so far in advance, or had the accounts just been accessible in a weak moment? Either way, my father had spent my future on his fourth house. At that point, he owned the condo, the cottage, the house on Rhonswood, and a remodeled colonial he'd bought the summer before to flip. I had marveled at the flow of money in Dad's retirement but never imagined it was mine!

Frustrated, I curled up in a ball. He continued to chuckle to himself but stayed downstairs. His arrow had hit the mark. There was no need to come after me. I was helpless and in his power.

How would I tell Lisa? I couldn't tell my grandmother, who already loathed my dad. She would be irate at our stupidity. I decided to keep it a secret for the time being. One problem at a time. I had a hard time completing my homework, though.

Chapter Twenty-One

July 1987

Sabrina waved from the passenger side of a huge Lariat king cab truck parked at the San Francisco airport's curb. Her brother Steele grinned from behind the wheel. I hugged Sabrina tight, then climbed in the back, relieved to have my new double-hinged brace. I couldn't believe how good it felt to get out of Michigan. With Dad's trial approaching, the press coverage had heated up and he never left home. When I walked off the plane in California, no one took a second look at my face, wondering where they'd seen me before. I was beautifully anonymous.

The best part was that Dad had paid for my ticket, anxious to have me out of his hair. Lisa had all but moved out after their fight, so it had just been me and him for weeks at home. With my cast, summer vacation had been a prison sentence until it'd been removed days before. Sabrina's invitation to California was a godsend.

Two hours past San Francisco's suburbs, Steele exited the interstate. We followed a dusty, ten-mile path to Oak Flat Ranch. High desert terrain spread to the horizon, broken into sections by barbed-wire fences snaking through hills to the south.

Steele stopped the truck at a heavy steel gate, and Sabrina hopped out to open it. He rolled the truck through it and over a cattle guard on the other side, then stopped again to wait for Sabrina to close the gate behind us. As I opened the door for her, a hot, dry wind blew into the air-conditioned cab.

A lone cow bellowed from a nearby rise, startling me.

"We have several thousand head on thirty thousand acres; that's only one of our obnoxious bulls," Steele explained.

Sabrina jumped in beside me and rolled her window down. She whooped at the horned beast, which began chasing us. I laughed in amazement at their Wild West life. Clouds of dust bloomed behind the truck as we entered a small valley.

An expansive one-story stone home with long porches came into view. A huge barn sat just to the north of the homestead, several trucks parked beside it. I had never seen anything like it, but when I smelled Mrs. Perrett's cooking again, I decided I needed a pair of cowboy boots.

"Tennessee will be fun," I said to Molly a month later. "I'm grateful your mom agreed to let me come."

Molly rolled her eyes, studying the pictures of Sabrina and me at the beach. "Yeah, but it would be so much more fun with Sabrina along." She pouted.

The Snow family planned to leave in the morning. Molly had come over to help me pack but was now in a funk about visiting her Southern cousins. I regretted describing how great visiting the California ranch had been since it had soured her mood.

I didn't care where I went, the Smoky Mountains or San Francisco, as long as I left Dad behind. I hated living alone with him. It was only a matter of time before something else happened. I'd rather not be there when it did.

Molly's blue eyes lit up suddenly. She jumped to her feet and began pacing. "If only we could . . ." She pulled on her long blonde hair.

"Could what?" I asked.

Molly stopped and faced me, hands clenched at her sides. "What if we didn't go to Tennessee?"

I finished folding a shirt and tossed it in my bag. "And do what else?" The half-crazy shine in her eyes made me nervous.

"What if we drive to California and surprise Sabrina instead?" She grinned.

I stopped packing. "You think your mom would let you?" I had a hard time imagining Leslie Snow agreeing to the last-minute change. Having six kids, Molly's mom spent a lot of time giving pep talks about being responsible and accountable. Unlike me, for example, Molly had a curfew.

"Oh, sure." Molly waved the notion away. "It's just a boring family visit. Let's call Melissa to see if she can go tonight! Then we'll have three drivers."

I smirked. Melissa was a volleyball teammate who'd harbored a huge crush on Steele Perrett before Sabrina's family had moved. If anyone could be talked into driving to California that night, it'd be Melissa.

I shrugged.

"Sure, why not?"

The speed at which Molly's plan unfolded should have given me pause, but I admit that the idea of returning to Oak Flat Ranch tempted me as well. I could almost smell the wild tarragon.

Molly ran home to get clothes to leave that night after convincing Melissa. We all met just after ten o'clock, threw our bags in my trunk, and stocked up on sugar at 7-Eleven before taking I-94 West. I assumed Molly had mentioned the change in plans to her parents, though I neglected to mention it to Dad. He wouldn't care. Being rid of me was enough.

Molly called her mom from a gas station on the outskirts of Cheyenne, Wyoming, the next afternoon. Melissa and I could see Molly's face turning red across the parking lot. She listened for a long time before hanging up.

Molly returned to the car and climbed in. I waited, keys in the ignition, to learn of her mom's response to our unexpected departure in the wrong direction.

The back seat was silent. Melissa gave me a worried look.

"Molly, you okay?" she asked.

There was a remarkably long pause. "It's a good thing my mom is a thousand miles away right now," Molly said at last. "We are both going to be in serious trouble when we get home, though."

I winced. I had forgotten what it was like to have someone who cared. I started the car, then looked at Molly in the rearview mirror.

"So, do we have to go back now?" I asked. I turned onto the business route paralleling the freeway, not sure which exit to take—west or east?

"She said she was calling Mrs. Perrett and that she needed a week to think about our punishment anyways." Molly groaned.

I took the exit heading west and gunned the gas. Shielded from Mrs. Snow's wrath by twelve hundred miles of pavement, we maxed out the Mustang until the speedometer spring broke. With the needle bobbing around somewhere over eighty-five, we accumulated speeding tickets in every state. I used Dad's "emergency" credit card for everything. I figured he owed me after emptying my bank account. Dad must have agreed because he never said a word about either the number of tickets or the locations. I didn't keep an exact total, but with credit card stubs collected from Illinois, Iowa, Nebraska, Colorado, Utah, and Nevada, it must have totaled over $800.

We made it to Oak Flat Ranch in thirty-three hours. To her credit, Mrs. Perrett handled our unplanned visit with a grace I would appreciate only as an adult. Despite our presence being a thoughtless burden that week, she welcomed us.

During that visit, she offered me a room in their sprawling ranch for my senior year if I wanted it. To say I was excited is an understatement. It was an escape hatch from hell. I wouldn't have to live with Dad during his trial. Without consulting my father, I made plans to return in a few weeks, before school started that fall. He, it would turn out, would be equally enthusiastic.

Seven days later, we drove much slower along I-80 East. Molly wasn't anxious to face her mother, and I wanted to see the famous Temple Square in Utah, so we detoured onto I-15 South into the Salt Lake Valley and found our way to the city center. We only had an hour, but it was long enough to change the way I saw my life.

I hurried ahead of the others up a circular ramp in the North Visitors' Center. At the top, Bertel Thorvaldsen's Christus towered over my head, white marble arms outstretched in invitation. A wall of windows opposite looked out over the flower beds and the rising granite spires of the Salt Lake Temple.

Molly and Melissa were wandering the exhibits downstairs, but the atmosphere of peace on the empty rotunda made me stop. I sat down on the closest bench and listened to a short recording that read the prophet Isaiah's descriptions of Christ.

I thought about how my first real experiences with His love had dove-tailed with my life falling apart. So much was changing with my father's trial starting that fall. The prospect of life getting even worse weighed me down.

I waited in the stillness for some time, pondering. I had so many opposing forces operating in my life, it was hard to keep my balance. I whispered my confession. "God, I still don't understand. If you love me, why does it have to be so hard?"

Into the stillness came a response. It wasn't a voice speaking, and it failed to answer why, but it was like my mind suddenly grasped two truths that had been hidden from my understanding until then.

My circumstances were known to God and, incredibly, had been explained to me before my present life. Knowing that I had previously agreed in some way to endure these events brought comfort and created astonishment.

The comfort came from realizing that both God and I had known how hard this would be, and even knowing the anguish, I had chosen this life because God had promised everything would be all right in the end.

The astounding part was that somewhere deep down, I had already known this. My mother had been trying to remind me.

Chapter Twenty-Two

February 1988

I sat in the Oak Flat Ranch kitchen doing homework after school one Wednesday during the last semester of my high school career. I hummed as I worked quickly through my math. I had only a few minutes to finish before Sabrina got home.

The phone rang. Steele answered it.

"It's your dad," he said with a puzzled look. He walked over to me with the receiver in his hand, the long cord stretching across the room.

Surprised, I frowned and put my pencil down. Besides a quick trip home at Christmas, which had been remarkably quiet, for months, I'd rarely spoken with my father. Lisa was the one who'd called and kept me updated on the trial. For Dad to call himself, something unbelievably bad or incredibly good had to have happened. My father being who he was, I feared the former.

"Hi, Dad. How are you?"

He cut straight to the point. "You need to come back. Neal says you have to take the stand."

I froze. I had already explained to Detective Keller everything I knew about the day of the fire. Though it was true I hadn't shared all my misgivings, I had told them everything I'd seen and heard that particular day. It had been several years, but I had nothing to add and really didn't want to go home.

"But why me?" I asked. My mind raced with excuses.

I had midterms the next week in English and math. I stood up, then sat back down, bewildered. I couldn't possibly disappear, not if I wanted to graduate.

I took a breath, ready to refuse. "I can't—"

Dad interrupted. "You have to. It's called a subpoena."

I gasped. My hand had been forced again.

"There is a flight at three Friday afternoon," he said. "I'll book you on that."

He hung up.

Sabrina, who had just walked into the kitchen, saw my fallen expression and hugged me. I lay my head on her shoulder and cried for reasons I couldn't explain. I didn't want to be cross-examined. My home life was horrible, but I hadn't witnessed what happened the day of the fire.

Not only would going be senseless, but I was sure it would also ruin my life in California. Transferring as a guest student following my late mother's tragic death was socially acceptable, but having to testify at my father's murder trial would change the narrative.

For the last six months, living at Oak Flat had lifted me out of the horrors at home. Until now, I had belonged everywhere via Sabrina. I was just a normal teenager. I hadn't needed to hide my father's drinking or avoid inviting people to my house. I hadn't walked in the door at night, wondering who was there. I hadn't been responsible for the laundry, housecleaning, or shopping. I could sleep at night and just be a seventeen-year-old girl.

The subpoena forced me to ingest the bitter truth that even moving two thousand miles away wasn't far enough to hide my past. I would have to explain my coming absence to my teachers and watch their eyes widen. Even if I refused to look at their faces, I'd hear them stammer while they sorted papers and made copies for me to take along.

When I left on Friday, Sabrina promised to cover for me with our friends, but I was willing to bet that gossip was already flying through the rural high school hallways. In all honesty, whatever wild rumors teachers or students concocted, they couldn't touch the horrendous truth. My life had been worse than anything they'd be able to imagine.

Detroit was the last place I wanted to be, but I had no choice. I boarded the plane and put my Walkman headphones on, wanting nothing less than to be invisible.

I might have disappeared altogether if I'd realized who had subpoenaed me.

Saturday, February 13, 1988

After sleeping in late at the condo, I woke and got dressed. The house was quiet, and Dad was sober. He gave me an address and the keys to his car. I drove myself to a plain office building and waited for a few moments in a small foyer before a thin woman with short, curly hair called me back to her office.

"Hello, Michelle. I'm Jane Thomas." Jane pulled out a chair at a large desk and motioned for me to sit down. She leaned against the desk and tilted her head.

We studied each other for a minute while I wondered what connection she had with Neal Simpson. This lawyer was different, lean and intense, so it was hard to imagine them working together. Neal was not fat, but he clearly enjoyed indulging. Plus, he creeped me out. I was glad it was this lady interviewing me.

She spoke first. "I have some important questions to ask. But first, I want you to know how sorry I am for your loss."

I nodded, mute. Jane turned to a filing cabinet and pulled some papers out. She referenced them as she cited the allegations against my father and quoted relevant pages of my testimony covered in her handwriting. She was thorough, but there was nothing I could add to what I'd already said.

I began to feel very irritated. Once again, an adult had manipulated my life without regard for its effect on me. This woman had ruined my life in California for little reason, sacrificing my happiness to get kudos for thoroughness with her boss. Who cared what Neal Simpson thought about anything?

Anger focused my mind, and I read the nameplate on her desk for the first time: *Jane Thomas, Assistant Prosecutor.*

The reality of my situation clicked into place with a resounding boom. This was the new prosecutor I'd read about. She wanted me to testify *against* Dad. I began to sweat. Whereas before I had answered her with monosyllables, now I evaded her questions, shrugging my shoulders or looking out the window.

A hint of frustration crept into her voice. I understood her intention to use me as a tool of justice. She would gladly wield me to decimate what was left of our family.

"Shelly, you were the last one there besides your father. We need to know anything you saw or heard. It might help us discover what happened to your mother," she explained.

I stonewalled.

"Do you understand?" Jane asked.

"I already told you everything I know." I resented her even asking. If I voluntarily delved into our family history, I would lose everything—not to mention risk my life. I had no false notions about safety if I crossed Dad. Even Lisa would hate me. Family came before self-righteous lawyers.

Jane could tell I wasn't convinced. She went to a cabinet and retrieved a large cardboard box. Coming back to the table, she lifted the lid. File folders crammed with paper copies and reports made the sides bulge. Selecting a green dossier, she spread pictures from it across the desk between us.

An enlarged photo of our living room caught my eye first. Our beige living room couches framed the top and sides of the glossy picture. The sofas appeared ruined despite the sheets my mother had always carefully tucked around them. The sodden couches had been covered in ash and debris. The sheets were askew and even torn off one end completely. My heart hurt thinking of her futile attempts to protect her beloved possessions. Nothing she could have done would have saved any of her furniture from the fire. Nothing we had done had saved her. My eyes filled with tears.

Then I saw it. In the forefront, a huge rust-colored stain spread over the dirty carpeting.

I blinked.

"I need to know. Had you ever seen that stain before?" Jane asked.

"No." My heart raced.

"Would you have noticed if it was there?" she continued.

"Yeah. I sat there waiting for Sabrina to pick me up," I said, pointing to a window barely visible in the top left corner, past one of the couches. "I walked right over that area. There wasn't any stain before I left." I leaned closer to examine the photo.

"The police took these pictures the night of the fire, but when they returned to get a sample, the entire carpet was missing." Jane paused. "Do you know what might have happened to it?"

I thought back to my first time scavenging for creamed corn in the dark. I'd noticed the carpet missing but assumed it had been destroyed in the fire or pulled out by the firefighters. I hadn't thought about it since. It would have been difficult to remove carpet and padding unseen. I couldn't recall Dad being gone.

I shook my head. "No."

It didn't seem a good time to mention the fact that I had been in the house multiple times, with a key from Dad. I silently cursed Dad for his secrets. Every time I hesitated, feeling something was off, he'd railroad me. That he had had a key to a police scene hadn't made sense to me, but I never felt I had any choice but to accept his word.

Now the pictures validated my fears, but I said nothing because I was afraid to incriminate myself along with Dad.

Jane asked more questions about my father's actions in the weeks after the fire, but I said I couldn't recall, which was mostly true. A painful haze obscured that period in my mind. Only my mother's visits remained clear, I but didn't think Jane would be interested in that.

In the face of my silence, Jane pulled a dirty stunt. She began to quote Aunt Kathy's and Grandma Findlay's statements. Neither had spared any details.

I trembled as she read their accounts of witnessing abuse or injuries Mom hadn't hidden well enough. Most I remembered and could corroborate. These secret incidents had been guarded for decades. Hearing the violent descriptions of the dysfunction at the core of our upscale but broken family read aloud by a stranger made me writhe in shame.

Jane paused midway through my grandmother's recitation of the night she babysat us, when my father had tried to strangle my mother.

"Do you remember that night? You were a child, but your grandmother said you were there."

I took a ragged breath. My grandmother's words had destroyed my ability to remain neutral. Either I denied my grieving grandmother's words or condemned my father. Whatever I said, I would lose. The time to pick a side had come.

I put my hands over my face and whispered.

"Yes. I remember."

She continued reading my grandmother's description, asking for my validation of specific events.

"Yeah, I saw that."

"I heard them and went to see, yes."

She piled evidence on the table in front of me: The second coroner's report, which identified stab marks on the collarbone of the exhumed corpse. More pictures of the bloody rug. A photo of the family room that showed a body discernible under a black cloth on the floor beside the coffee table remains. Eyewitness statements describing Dad having left the home a mere ten minutes before returning to "discover" the house ablaze. The fire investigator's report detailing accelerant splashed throughout the main floor.

A mountain of arguments for first-degree murder.

A wave of cold certainty rolled over me with each new revelation. The level of betrayal overwhelmed my doubts, finally and absolutely. I had spent months in the shell of the house seeking proof. Now I knew Mom's death wasn't a horrible accident. It was much worse, and everything I'd feared. Jane finished her proposed argument and silently made notes.

I returned to the picture of my mom's body lying in the family room, chin in my hands, elbows flanking the glossy paper. Tears fell on the tabletop. If Jane hadn't been sitting there, I would have curled into a ball and screamed. My guilt for leaving my mother with my father swallowed me whole.

Jane turned to me. As I had grown more affected by the evidence, she had become gentler. "Sorry, I have one last important question, then we can be done."

I nodded at her to continue, wiping my eyes.

"Do you recall a time when your father said to your mother, 'I'm going to kill you and burn the house down?'"

I swallowed. "Which time?"

When our discussion ended, Jane put a paper in front of me. It contained the truth I'd hidden my entire life, typed neatly in black and white. I signed on the lines she pointed to, confirming my statements.

Dad had lied repeatedly and purposefully. In my grief, I had needed to believe him in order to save my family. I'd been blinded by my own fears. My punishment came in the form of being the star witness for the prosecution.

The worst thing was, I still loved him.

Chapter Twenty-Three

That night, I didn't dare return to the condo. After driving side streets for hours, I knocked on the Snows' door. Molly opened the door and shrieked.

"Shelly!" She hugged me and pulled me inside.

Her parents greeted me and then went to bed after asking if I wanted to stay the night. I was thankful her parents didn't ask more. I needed space to think before I could answer coherently.

I had to face the fact that the people closest to me had hurt me, and I had helped hide it. I had known, deep down, for over two years that he had done it all. He had lied, murdered, manipulated, and taken everything from me, and yet I had remained silent. I had repeated his lies until I believed him.

I was so distraught I felt as if I were floating, separate from my body. I chatted with Molly while my soul screamed. The disconnect between reality and how I acted, for even a few moments with Molly, exhausted me. Eventually, I asked to borrow a toothbrush so I could go to bed.

In Molly's basement that night, my nightmares returned. I dreamed I was fifteen and at basketball practice. I remembered that Mom was alone and sprinted out the gym doors. Running through the streets, I despaired of making it home in time to stop Dad. Sprinting up the deck stairs, I saw him through the windows. He ignored my screams for him to stop as he splashed gasoline through the house. I pounded on the locked back door. He lit a match.

I awoke with a shriek.

Sunday, February 14, 1988

After a miserable day at church, hiding the devastation I felt, I opened the condo door that night and ushered my friends upstairs with a finger to my lips. Dad was watching a movie. A heavy sense of waiting hung over him. Though he couldn't have missed the four sets of feet climbing the stairs, he ignored us.

Two months earlier, at Christmas, I had spent the holidays with a perfectly respectable father. His coloring was clear and healthy. He had started walking around the complex and lost ten pounds. He looked great.

The change was so remarkable I had ventured an observation. "You look ten years younger."

He had welcomed the compliment and informed me of his graduation from an intensive in-treatment facility that fall. It had taken thirty years and a first-degree murder charge to sober him up. With presents and pie, we had celebrated a quiet Christmas, the best one since Mom's death. I had hoped it was the beginning of better days and dreamed our grand misfortune could yet be overturned.

But as I followed Molly, Melissa, and Vicki upstairs, I knew he hadn't changed enough. After seeing the pictures, I knew he didn't care about turning his life around or healing his estranged relationships. The trial had scared him sober.

I thought back to the second coroner's report, the stab marks on her bones, and my hands balled into fists. No matter how his appearance had changed, I knew the truth.

196

He was a murderer at heart.

I had a sense that inviting my friends over, knowing what I now knew, was morally wrong, but I felt trapped. I was too terrified to return home alone and too overwhelmed to share why. I rationalized that I was not putting anyone in danger if there were four of us. It was only me he wanted to silence, and having witnesses always inhibited his violence.

I turned to my friends and smiled, still unwilling to admit how much I needed to maintain appearances to myself. "Well, what should we do?"

"Tell us about Steele," Melissa said.

I launched into the latest on the Perretts. While we talked and gossiped about anything but my problems, the next morning pressed closer. I tried to ignore my growing dread. I had only hours left before any appearance of normalcy would be impossible.

Past two in the morning, the four of us lay on my king-sized bed, heads together. Between the exhaustion setting in and my circling thoughts, I could hardly pay attention to the tittering conversation.

In the last twenty-four hours, the memories of the fighting, drinking, and threats I'd previously suppressed assumed new meaning. My testimony would be the prosecutor's linchpin. Without me on the stand, my father was suspicious but not proven guilty; with my account, he became a violent man who had been threatening to do this very thing for years.

One moment, I resolved to speak the whole truth; then my courage faltered the next second. Dad's conviction meant everything changed for not only him but me. Orphaned at seventeen. Was I ready for that? Could I be fair but not too condemning at the same time? Even knowing what I knew, I didn't want to lose my family.

The conversation lapsed and, in a moment of sheer frustration at my own vacillation, my tired defenses fell. I decided to ask my friends' opinions. I cleared my throat.

"I am going to be honest. About tomorrow—I need your advice," I said.

Once everyone listened, I proceeded.

"You all know parts, but there's more to my story than you can imagine," I said. "My dad drinks. I can't ever remember a time he didn't. You all know I hate it. You haven't seen him get mean, but he does." I sighed.

How could I explain my dilemma? Could they understand how much he meant to me? How, despite the drinking and violence, I still loved him?

I described the evening at the cottage, where he choked Mom after they argued and she ran out in her underwear. I described waking up to them fighting and how Lisa pushed me out of the room. I spoke in a hush, afraid my words might carry too far. Their occasional gasps let me know they'd heard everything.

I talked and talked while folding and unfolding a candy wrapper. I avoided their eyes during the worst parts.

When I began relating details of my father's strange behavior the day of the fire, my heart leapt toward fury and mercy at once. He was so broken, and he had broken us all in turn.

". . . and so, I left," I concluded.

Exhausted, I ran out of words. I lay back on the bed, and the loft stayed silent for a few minutes. It was almost four in the morning.

Molly reached out and took my hand, squeezing it.

My resolve hung in the balance. I doubted my courage to speak.

"No matter what the outcome, in order for me to live with myself, I have to tell the truth," I said.

I hadn't meant it to sound like a question, but it did.

Molly yawned. "That *is* the only option you have."

I turned my head toward her. "But telling the truth is harder and scarier than you might think. If you were me, your first instinct would be to say nothing—not to lie or make stuff up. You would simply want to be silent."

Molly didn't argue with me. She just squeezed my hand. "You can do it, Shelly."

No one spoke after that, and the prone forms surrounding me fell asleep. I repeated Molly's words to myself. "That is the only option you have."

She was right, but Molly didn't understand the price I would pay. My alarm woke us two hours later.

February 15, 1988

I faced the judge as I raised my right hand. He swore me in, looking through his notes as he recited the words by heart.

"Do you promise to tell the truth, the whole truth, and nothing but the truth, so help you God?"

"Yes." I left a sweaty palm print on the Bible. I winced and wiped my hands on my skirt under the small podium. The witness chair, unimaginably uncomfortable, had a scratchy crack along the vinyl where my hands convulsively gripped it.

Jane Thomas approached and smiled. I didn't return it.

"Michelle, you go by Shelly, right?"

I nodded.

"Shelly, how old are you?"

"Seventeen."

"Is James Arnold Edwards your father?"

My dad sat opposite me, at the defense counsel's table. My friends sat almost immediately behind him, to my right, from where Molly smiled at me.

"Yes."

"I would like for you to recall, if you would for a moment, back in October 1985. Were you at that time living at an address on Rhonswood in Farmington Hills?"

"Yes."

Ms. Thomas pointed to a floorplan of the house one of her assistants had set on a large trifold stand.

"I would like to direct your attention to what is already marked as People's Exhibit Number 17. This has been identified as the lower floor, or the first floor, of your house there on Rhonswood. The formal living area, the study or the den area, the dining room, the laundry room, the family room, the kitchen and breakfast nook here, the screened-in porch, and then the garage on this side . . ."

Jane pointed and continued speaking as my mind, tired and torn, dropped into my own speculation. I recalled the bloody rug picture as it related to the floor plan. My best guess was that the fight had begun in the kitchen, soon after I left.

The bloody living room rug caused me to suspect he'd chased her there. Was Mom panicked before he stabbed her? Or did it happen in the family room, where her body ended up? I imagined the different scenarios based on my years of experience while Jane droned on about what was found where.

I knew how their fights started. I had witnessed thousands of them. I just hadn't been there to defuse this last one. Had they argued about Lisa's arrest or something else? Regardless, my father had murdered my mother. With that thought, my body started shaking in front of everyone.

"Now, it's my understanding that the bedrooms are upstairs. Is that correct?" the assistant prosecutor's words broke through my nightmare

I wrapped my arms around myself and held on, trying to stay present enough to answer Jane Thompson's questions.

"Yes. Upstairs."

Upstairs. I remembered smelling my mother's pillow. Her perfume filled my nose, and I saw myself lie on her pillow. The young girl beneath the covers sobbed uncontrollably in her bed.

Jane's strong voice brought me back to the hard chair. My eyes watering, I reached for a tissue from the shelf next to me. I couldn't cry about bedrooms being upstairs.

"Now, Shelly, in terms of giving us some idea of how you get upstairs, we have marked here an area that appears to be a stairway, with the word *up* on it. Are you familiar with the stairway here that goes out of the entry by the formal living room?"

"Yes." The same staircase I had descended, straining to overhear my parents' conversation.

"Now, in terms of getting to the upstairs, Shelly, how do you go from the kitchen area or the family room up to the bedrooms?"

"Through the small hallway, by the bathroom, and then down the main hallway—to the stairs by the living room," I said. Her benign questions gave me time to compose myself.

"Now, the living room—the stairway opens into the living room. Is that correct?"

"Yes."

"Now, did you use this room frequently to live in at this time, or were you more or less using the family room to live in at that time?" Jane asked.

The living room was mostly for show. My mother's fussiness made dusting dreadful. Candlesticks, small porcelain figurines, and souvenirs from around the world were wiped and put back exactly. Even in the family room, we normally kept sheets over the couch cushions. When company came, we hid the sheets in the laundry room by the basement stairs.

"We lived in the family room mostly."

The evening before the fire, Sunday night, we had sat in our customary seats in the family room. Mine was next to Dad on the couch on one side of the room, opposite the television. Perpendicular to us, Mom and Lisa sat on the other couch. Mom always sat on the end closest to Dad, the end table holding her empty ashtray between them. These had been our seats for years. I had shared popcorn with Dad.

My mind rushed to the debris I had found in the house after the fire. Her eyeglasses, the ones she had worn to help me with my geometry, were indeed under the spot where her body was found, Jane's photos had proved that two days earlier. All of a sudden, the two memories, finding the frames and watching TV the night before the fire, fused into one truth.

I blinked. The frames were in the wrong spot. *She* had lain in the wrong spot—in front of Lisa's seat. In twelve years of living in that house, she'd never sat there.

I looked over at Dad and then back at my hands. He had argued that she was watching TV when he left and had had a heart attack while smoking. He'd lied. He had always lied. He had made a tiny mistake only I could catch.

The eyeglasses' location, a small detail, was insignificant to everyone else. Even I had failed to grasp its importance until that moment. All along, it was right in front of me. Jane didn't know, but I did. Mom *never* sat there. Our habits were ingrained.

I knew with perfect certainty that she had been put there, by him.

The epiphany set my jaw with perfect timing. It was undeniable evidence that I alone knew, which linked my father to the scene. I was convinced of his guilt beyond a doubt. Without that singular proof of his lies, his history of abuse may have been too excruciating to divulge following Jane's next question.

"Did you ever see your father and mother argue?"

Here lay the fork in the road, where I either opened the door exposing the violence or focused on the fact that they weren't arguing that October day when I left. Jane waited, seemingly calm, but her steady gaze implored me to speak the truth.

My eyes closed, seeing my mother's frames covered in ashes once more. I gathered my courage and whispered.

"I . . . yes."

The judge frowned at me. "Ms. Edwards, would you please speak up and repeat yourself so that the court can hear your answer?"

I straightened in my seat and repeated, louder. "Yes, they argued sometimes."

"When you got into your home that afternoon, did you have occasion to see your father at 2:30 p.m.?"

"Yes."

"And first, where was he at the time?"

"In the kitchen, making dinner." An easy answer.

"And what, if anything, was he doing other than making dinner?"

Dad listened closely while the walls closed in. Every step down this road would have consequences for us both. I couldn't bring myself to abandon him all at once.

"I don't recall."

"Do you recall whether he was eating or drinking anything at the time?" Jane asked, prompting me.

I looked at the floor. "I think he was drinking when I came home."

"Now, do you know what he was drinking, Shelly?"

I rubbed my face and cleared my throat several times. Dad glared at me full-out. Panic set in. Tonight, we would share the same house. He had attacked Lisa for so much less than this. She loathed him but had been scared enough that she had already testified for his defense. I knew she didn't believe him. She just wanted to live.

I deflected Jane's questions, trying to decide how to be truthful but minimize my risk. I wanted to tell the truth for my mother's sake, but Dad's eyes held dark promises.

"Would you like a glass of water?"

"Yes," I whispered. A clerk ran for a glass and brought it back. I sipped.

"Okay?"

"Yes."

"Now, Shelly, do you recall what your father was drinking that afternoon when you came home?"

"Uh . . ." I shifted in my seat. If I opened this door by specifying what had been in his glass, Jane Thomas would barrel through it.

Our family would be destroyed.

Chapter Twenty-Four

Jane's question hung in the stale courtroom air.

My throat had gone dry. I looked past Dad. Behind him, Molly met my eyes and leaned forward. She gave me a small thumbs up. She understood that I desperately wanted to say nothing.

The judge grew impatient. "That calls for a yes or no answer is all. Just yes, you do recall; or no, you don't recall."

His reprimand brought a hot flush of embarrassment to my face.

"Yes, I do recall," I said, looking down at my hands. The tissue I held was nearly a clotted mass of fibers, wet and stringy. I swallowed. "He likes Manhattans. That's what he was drinking then."

Dad brought his forearms onto the table in front of him, hands clenched together. His eyes bore into me. Sick fear rose as vomit. The back of my throat stung. *Oh God, don't let him kill me.*

Prosecutor Thomas brought up Lisa's arrest, inquiring whether my dad had mentioned the incident to me.

"Yes."

She asked, "Do you recall how he appeared to feel about that incident, based on your conversation?"

"He was upset."

"Did he tell you what, if anything, he was going to do about it?"

"No."

"Now, when you say he was upset, if you could describe the intensity of emotion . . ."

"I don't know how to describe it." I sipped water, trying to evade the question.

Dad's tears had terrified me enough that I'd left the room, afraid of an explosion. My answer implicated Dad in the strongest terms but condemned me too. I had recognized his volatile state of mind but left for practice anyway.

Shame flooded my heart. Our family had rotated through this violent progression with regularity, but Lisa and I had always been able to defuse it. I had wrongly assumed we would contain that one as well.

Dad staying home, my phone call, Mom racing home early, Lisa's reluctance to leave practice . . . nothing had gone as expected. In fact, everything I'd done had made things worse. I swallowed my grief.

Jane clarified, trying to help. "Was it just annoyed, frustrated, upset, angry? In those sorts of terms."

I considered her suggestions. None were strong enough. I picked the closest.

"Very upset," I said.

A small twinge of disappointment told me I was being a coward again. A braver, better Shelly would have added "imminently violent" to Jane's list. I hushed my inner critic; otherwise, I would cry.

"So, what did you do next?"

"I went upstairs and changed my clothes."

"And when you went upstairs, did something happen upstairs that—or what did you do when you went upstairs?" Jane asked.

"I went into my parents' bedroom and did my homework in front of the TV." I stumbled a little over the last part. I'd done no homework, in fact, but I didn't feel capable of explaining why I'd spent the entire time running between living room windows and hiding upstairs. I didn't want

206

to paint out how distracted by fear I'd been. It was a small lie born of self-defense, and I felt justified by having revealed so much other truth. I didn't correct the record.

"Did you talk to anyone besides your father that afternoon?"

"Yes. I talked to my mom."

"And when did you talk to your mom?"

"I don't remember what time it was."

"Did you call her, or did she call you?"

"I called her."

"And what were you discussing with your mom that afternoon?"

"The ride situation with basketball practice—if she was still coming to get me after practice," I explained.

I had acted as if everything were normal on the phone. I felt guilty that I knew something Mom hadn't heard about yet, but I didn't want to rat on my sister. Worse, my obscure warning about Dad had only triggered her early arrival. Her death was my fault. I had regretted my silence every day of my life since.

"When you completed your conversation with your mother, did you hang up, or did someone else talk with her?"

"My Dad talked with her."

"When he was talking to your mom, was there a specific topic?"

"Lisa's being arrested."

"Could you again describe the emotion that you could hear in his voice?"

"He was still upset about what had happened."

"Shelly, did your father say anything about what was going to happen to Lisa?"

"He said that they were going to discuss it later on, after Lisa got home from practice."

"And did he say why they were going to wait until Lisa got home from practice?"

"He wanted them to wait and talk all together."

"Did he relate to your mother any ideas that he had about punishment?"

"He felt that she had already been through enough with the police."

"Now, after the conversation, what did you do?"

"I kept doing homework." I tensed at the need to repeat the white lie. I had been desperately wondering where Lisa was, but I didn't want to drag my sister into this.

"And how long did you continue doing your homework?"

"Until I heard the garage door open and knew that my mom was there. I needed to ask her a couple of questions on my geometry. And I came downstairs." I thought that tied the loose ends together nicely.

I didn't have to explain that math had been a diversion to prevent Mom from talking to Dad. My toolkit of survival tactics had called for a distraction. It hadn't worked.

"Let's talk about the bad times for a minute. Recently, before the fire in October of 1985, had there been any arguments that you overheard between your mother and your father?"

"Recently?" I repeated, trying to digest what she was asking. The fire had happened two years earlier, a lifetime ago. Their fighting had terrified me for over a decade. It was all running together by then.

The prosecutor clarified her time frame. "Well, just before her death in October of 1985?'

"Yes," I said.

She looked at me expectantly, but I offered no details.

Did she really want me to talk about their fighting here, in front of him? She clearly hadn't stopped to think about what he might do to me. I looked blankly at her and waited.

A dozen incidents leapt to mind: Mom, stripped of her nightgown, fleeing for her life through the sliding glass door of the cottage. The time Dad tried to rip her tongue out of her mouth. The times he threatened to kill us. When he choked her and screamed his intent to kill her. The fact that Lisa and I pulled him off weekly during the summer party season.

"Were there any times when they seemed to argue more frequently?"

I lowered my voice. "Yeah."

"And when was that, Shelly?"

"When my father would be drinking."

Jane didn't ask how often. I guess she didn't think that mattered. I hated summer break.

"And when he and your mother would argue, describe those arguments for me in terms of what would happen between your mom and dad?"

"Could I have another drink?" I whispered. The prosecuting attorney handed me another glass of water from a pitcher on the prosecuting attorney's table. I took a few sips, wetting my throat and giving the roiling wave of grief and fear time to recede.

"Okay." I took a breath.

"Shelly, your mother and father would have arguments—yes?"

"Yes," I mumbled. I avoided looking at Dad's face.

The judge intervened. "Ms. Edwards, you must speak up." He asked the prosecutor to speak louder so that it would encourage me to speak louder.

"Shelly, when your mom and dad would argue, would you describe what he would do?"

Did no one care that I had to go home with this man after they adjourned for the day? I felt an incredible pressing fear building with each question. Every fiber of my body wanted to run.

"He would sometimes—just say things—and yell. And sometimes—"

"Now, the types of things that he would say, would they be nice things or not so nice things?"

"Not nice things. He was angry." I admitted. Dad frowned and leaned back, arms crossed. He absorbed my every word. A small tremor ran through me.

"Would they be about the situation or about your mother in particular?"

"Both." I wanted to say all the nasty vile words he threw at her, but I couldn't. Dad stared at me, daring me to.

"Would any of these comments include your mother?"

"Yes."

The prosecutor led me through a list of pointed questions with damning implications.

"Did your father ever threaten, that you heard, to harm you or your mother or burn down the house?"

I began shaking as I carefully detailed numerous instances where Dad had threatened to kill us and burn down the house. These threats were much harder to disclose than his drinking or mood that October day. His own words were proof that he had been toying with the idea for years.

I knew I was the only one willing, or able, to give evidence of his premeditation to murder. He knew it too. Dad smoldered behind an iron-clad front. Sensing his simmering wrath, I swallowed. *He will beat me*, I thought. *He will smash my head against the wall. Then he will kill me.*

Stuck in fight-or-flight mode, with no off button, I struggled to be coherent.

I needed something to relieve the pressure of my position. Every word I uttered tore apart my father's defense. Amid my panic, Molly gave me another thumbs up. I almost cried. The absurdity of her little token of faith against the mighty fear that assaulted me might have made me laugh if I'd had time to process it. Instead, I barely managed to whisper the details Jane Thomas intended to use in convicting my father of first-degree, premeditated murder. I would stutter, start to speak, then have

210

to look past my father, again and again, for Molly's tokens of courage in order to continue.

Finally, the judge found compassion as I struggled to contain my composure. "Do you need a break?" he asked.

I could only nod. He banged his gavel. "The court will take a short recess."

He dismissed the jury so I could testify without them watching, but it was Dad I feared, not them.

Chapter Twenty-Five

The massive courtroom emptied quickly. I walked downstairs to stretch my legs, then found a drinking fountain in the hall outside the cafeteria. As I leaned over the stainless-steel bowl, letting the water run before drinking, panic set in again. What would I say to my father? How could I justify my testimony? I took a long drink, unsatisfied and still shaky.

I wiped my lips and used the bathroom before heading toward the stairs that led to the courtroom. Looking over my shoulder, I saw Dad striding my way. I froze. My pulse ramped up. He wouldn't attack here, would he?

He stopped a foot away. His face searched mine. I avoided eye contact. I looked at Neal, who stood behind him.

Not here. He wouldn't dare.

Dad placed his hands on my arms. I stiffened. He gathered me in an embrace. I couldn't remember the last time he'd hugged me. I felt trapped and expected a whispered threat as he put his lips to my ear.

"Just tell the truth. Say what you have to say."

The tension in my spine snapped. My shock abated enough to wrap my arms around his waist for a squeeze. I cried into his shoulder. His once-familiar smell of Hugo cologne and coffee held me close.

Few people paid attention to what may have been the best moment I'd ever shared with my father. His words then were the most selfless and kind he'd ever spoken. Each syllable I'd uttered incriminated him, and we both knew it.

I resumed testifying in a near-empty courtroom. Only the judge, the lawyers, and Dad watched. They taped my testimony for the jury to hear later. Jane Thompson continued to press me, seeking specific details from years of horror. Dad's display of compassion made my testimony harder. Later, I wondered if he had calculated that exact effect, but it had felt sincere at the time.

I said what needed to be said, but the brutal experience left me more exposed than I'd ever been, just when I'd never been more alone.

Later that evening, I heard the condo's garage door open. I had been waiting for his arrival, and now that the moment had come, I could barely breathe.

Looking back, I am sure people question why I returned home. To someone accustomed to safe environments, any other option would have seemed preferable—the streets even. But I had always lived with the possibility of violence. I had learned from my mother that there was no haven to be found. So I dealt with it the only way I knew how—I convinced my reinforcements, Molly and Vicki and Melissa, to stay the night again.

When Dad entered the house, the four of us were upstairs sorting pictures from the previous summer's trip to California. Trying to stay calm, I smoothed back a plastic page in my new album. Still, every muscle tensed, listening for his tread on the stairs. *Don't come up. Don't come up.*

Dad closed the door to his room downstairs. I relaxed.

Around midnight, we ran out of junk food. I figured Dad was asleep, so I tiptoed down the dark stairs, hopping over the third step from the bottom, which creaked.

I opened the fridge door, and white light spilled out over the floor. I hunted for some salsa I had opened the day before. Someone shuffled in and stopped behind me. I stood slowly, holding cold pizza in one hand and the salsa jar in the other. I closed the fridge and turned my head. Dad's silhouette leaned against the doorway three feet away. He was silent and unmoving, hands in his robe pockets. I couldn't see his face, so acting like nothing had happened, I opened the pantry door with a foot and grabbed some chips while my heart pounded in my chest.

Finally, I stood opposite him in the dark, arms full of snacks and heart full of trepidation.

"Well, I suppose you just said what you had to . . ." His unreproachful tone astonished me.

A sober and gentle father faced me in that moment. I was at a loss as to how to respond to him. My heart throbbed at his seeming attempt to bridge the gulf between us. I was touched he would try so hard for my benefit.

"I love you." I passed him with a quick kiss and fled upstairs.

He rumbled deep in his chest in an acknowledgment.

March 2, 1988

I returned from California ten days later to hear the jury announce their verdict. It had taken them forty-eight hours of deliberation to find James Arnold Edwards guilty of second-degree murder and arson. It didn't surprise me, but it was a blow. I bowed my head after the jury foreman's statement.

Grandma Findlay hadn't come, but I stood between Lisa and Aunt Kathy during the sentencing. Our family's fate lay in the hands of the honorable Judge O'Malley.

He banged his mallet and paused as the room drew an expectant breath. "In accordance with the statutes of this state and as is my responsibility as acting judge, I will now pronounce sentence."

Dad stood shackled in an orange jumpsuit. His sobbing was audible.

"For the charges of arson, seven years. For the charges of second-degree, unpremeditated murder, thirteen years imprisonment in a state facility."

Judge O'Malley's voice rang out over the murmur that had begun. "Time already spent incarcerated will be applied, and both terms will be served concurrently."

Thirteen years seemed a small penance for a murder that had been dragged out over decades. My father had taken pieces of my mother one at a time. I shook my head at the mournful hope that sprang to life as I realized I would only be thirty-one when he was released. Part of me still wanted him, wanted to be a family again someday. The short prison term disgusted my head and thrilled my heart.

Dad's wavering voice rang out unchecked in the courtroom. He took a step toward the judge, his pale face stricken.

"I did not murder my wife," my father appealed. "Please! I don't know what more to say. My daughters don't believe me."

For once, Dad was right.

The judge ignored him and dismissed the court. Everyone stood again as the judge stepped down. I stood as well. The bailiff had Dad by the arm and was leading him away. My father turned at the door to wave to Lisa and me.

"Goodbye."

Lisa and I raised our hands in silent farewell. In a moment, the chained prisoner disappeared, and I lost my father.

In all the deliberations and judicial exercises, no one had raised the idea of a guardian or court-appointed care. Lisa was legally an adult, but I wouldn't turn eighteen for another month.

I drove alone to the condo. Walking through the front door felt like being thrown out of a plane at ten thousand feet. My life had no tethers, no foundation, nothing protecting me. I missed Dad's drunken body on the couch. I wanted the refrigerator door to close with a bang while the Red Wings game blared. I needed a parent, however unfit.

I turned on every light in the house, then ate a microwaved burrito in front of the television. I fell asleep wrapped in my duvet on his couch and awoke to mild gray skies and dried sauce on the plate next to me. The VCR clock blinked 10:15 a.m.

I entered the kitchen and opened the pantry. A lone box of Frosted Flakes, half empty, sat on the top shelf. I took it to the couch, eating it straight out of the box. Mom hated that.

She was careful about many things but had vastly miscalculated the costs of staying. I wished she had left Dad years earlier when she'd asked. Her fear of losing everything had cost us exactly that—everything. That morning, I would have traded it all for even a fractured family—all three houses, the cabin, my Mustang, my loft, European vacations. Anything.

I lost almost all of it anyway. The thievery began as soon as the sentence was pronounced.

A Week Later

In California, Mrs. Perrett handed me the phone.

"Hi, Shelly. It's Diane." My aunt's voice sounded strained. Aunt Diane had been given Dad's power of attorney.

"Hi. What's up?" I leaned against the counter.

"Well, I wanted to let you know . . . Mark went out to the cottage, and it's been broken into," she said in a long breath.

It took me a second to process who Mark was. Mark wasn't technically my cousin, but I remembered her mentioning in passing that her brother's son was unemployed.

216

"Wait. What?" I straightened. "Why was Mark out there? Who broke in? What did they take?"

We had moved all our storage to the cottage when we moved into the condo. My baby pictures, basketball trophies, photo albums—any childhood mementos that survived the fire were there.

"Well, your dad said we could use it if we kept an eye on it." Diane paused. "Mark needed a place to stay, so I told him he could stay. Anyway, when he got there, it had been cleaned out."

"How?" My mind flew, cataloging all the boxes I'd helped carry into the house that were now stolen.

"The neighbors said they saw a moving truck pulled up the day after the trial with a couple of guys who emptied the place out." She huffed. "The neighbors considered calling the police but figured no criminal would be brazen enough to do it in broad daylight."

I reeled. That had been quick.

"Who would do this?" I asked, tears welling up. It had to have been someone who knew our family. Maybe one of Dad's "buddies" from up north. We would never discover who.

"I don't know, honey." Diane sighed. "Worst thing, though, is they vandalized the inside of the house too. One word, *Murderer*, in red spray paint."

Tears slipped down my cheeks.

Everything had vanished. Neal Simpson put a lien on the condo to pay his fees. Diane packed up the contents for storage and sold the condo along with Dad's three cars and the fixer-upper house. She sold everything fast and cheap, but it still must have totaled near a half million, which was a decent chunk at the time. Lisa and I received nothing from the proceeds, and I assumed at the time that Diane had funneled the funds into my dad's accounts. He'd never spoken about money with me and directed me to my aunt Diane if I wanted anything.

Luckily, my needs were minimal with the Perretts. I hoped Dad would agree to cover my university tuition since he'd stolen my money, I knew he was paying Lisa's community college fees, but I hadn't asked yet. With his early retirement, he was drawing a hefty pension and stacking it away for after his release. Prison life required little cash—enough for soap and snacks at the commissary. I figured tuition for four years shouldn't be a problem for him.

In California, I straddled two worlds, basking in the Perrett's sunshine-filled life and dealing with the drama back home. Lisa called every week with updates on how much things had sold for or what was going on. For my part, I kept shoving down the worry and fear and tried to act like a normal kid. A couple of months after the trial, I graduated. Lisa called.

"Did you know Aunt Diane and Uncle Bob are building their dream home?" She skipped her usual greeting.

"What?" My eyebrows flew up. "Did he get a new job?" They'd rarely had two nickels to rub together their entire marriage. For years, I had overheard my parents complain about how Aunt Diane envied our life and coveted our money.

Dad's words back at the rental after we'd bailed him out came back to me.

"They will come after the money now," he had said before passing out drunk.

My sister and I had privately laughed, believing his "they" to be nonspecific and paranoid.

Now, Lisa's short laugh held no humor.

"Nope. Somehow they bought a lake lot in Keego Harbor and are building a custom home. It's been like pulling teeth to get her to cough up tuition money, and then I find this out!" She sounded ready to punch someone.

How could we, at eighteen and twenty, win a financial guerilla war?

He had been prophetic. The walls of Diane and Bob's new lake-front home went up as our family's numerous assets disappeared. The only thing left of our family's was the cottage, which they used, and a huge storage unit of salvaged items from the Rhonswood house (whatever we hadn't fit into the cottage).

The single thing I managed to hang on to was the blue Mustang Dad had put in my name. I drove it to Brigham Young University that August to start college.

Chapter Twenty-Six

Fall 1988

Iam telling you, there are so many holes in my case my lawyer says I should be out by Christmas!" Dad repeated for the fifth time in as many phone calls.

I happened to know his "lawyer" was an inmate friend pursuing his Juris Doctor from behind bars. I rolled my eyes and lay back on my bed in the dorms. It was Sunday evening, and my roommate tapped her watch to signal it was time to meet our friends.

"Leave without me. I'll come in a second," I whispered with my hand over the mouthpiece. She nodded and left.

The felon on the other end was wound up. He had twenty minutes to talk, and the clock had just started ticking. Interrupting him would mean risking losing the tuition money he had promised to pay. I needed to stay in his good graces. I had to listen.

"What was that?" he said in my ear.

"Oh, nothing. Sorry, my roommate left."

"Well, like I said . . ." he continued. I knew my plans for the evening were ruined.

Dad used his phone calls to remind me of my guilt. He always reiterated my contribution to his wrongful incarceration and lectured me in false detail about my misled stupidity. There was no room for rebuttal.

Whenever the phone rang on the weekend, I paused, not knowing if it was a friend wanting to go to the ball game or to get ice cream—or my father. I always answered, and if I heard Dad's voice, an immediate sense of dread and obligation trapped me.

If I inquired about his health, he would complain how he was wasting away "inside" and explain in gory detail his inmate lawyer's progress on his appeal. That might remind him of some vague aspect I had misconstrued on the stand, or he'd share the latest made-up facts he planned to include in his appeal. I thought his argument that one in five juries had been proven to convict wrongfully sounded a bit high, but I listened until his time ran out.

"I love you," I always said in a parting shot of self-defense.

"Mmm. Okay. You too." He would hang up.

My father force-fed me his propaganda weekly. His efforts only convinced me that I didn't fit in at the private church university. I was fairly sure no other freshman took collect calls from prison on weekends. The students surrounding me came from families like the Perretts and Snows. Sure, some kids had divorced parents (a minor difficulty from my perspective). Maybe a few had lost a mother or father to illness or accident. I assumed I was the only student whose father had murdered anyone, much less their mother.

Not that I asked anyone else. If there had been another, we were lonely outliers. It was the kind of distinction one didn't flaunt in a culture of squeaky-clean believers. Adherents didn't drink coffee, much less alcohol; how would they process my father?

One Sunday, my dad's voice unexpectedly cut off, followed by a short message:

"This is Officer Jones. All inmate conversations have been terminated due to a security situation. We apologize for the inconvenience."

The phone clicked.

I spent the rest of the week distracted, wondering when Aunt Diane would send word that my father had been killed in a prison riot. My moodiness was apparent.

"Are you okay? You don't seem yourself," my roommate said.

"I'm fine. Only tired."

Tired from waking up at two o'clock in the morning racked with worry. Tired of guilt, knowing that if my father had been murdered behind bars, I would have caused both my parents' deaths.

The next Sunday, when the phone rang, I snatched it up.

"Hello?" I answered, breathless.

"Hi, it's me," he said. "You won't believe it. The guy behind me got stabbed last week."

"What?" I said, thankful my father wasn't the target.

"Did he live?"

"Yeah. He's been in the hospital all week. Crazy, huh? This place is bananas. I gotta get out of here."

Dad picked up right where he'd left off. "Did I tell you what my lawyer said?"

December 27, 1988

Grandma Findlay brought me home for Christmas. I spent the day with her, Lisa, my aunt Kathy, and her family. Afterward, my grandmother's house grew too quiet, and I decided to visit Jackson prison. I wanted more than the phone dance. I wanted to look into Dad's eyes and hear the truth. There was no reason for him to pretend anymore. He had nothing to lose.

I borrowed Aunt Kathy's car. I wondered if I was crazy for going and argued with myself the entire two-hour drive. I felt compelled to fix things and salvage a relationship with Dad, but on the other hand, I was disgusted with him. I needed his love, and I wanted to wring every detail from his lying heart. I knew having both was impossible, and that drove me bonkers.

The gray winter light was already fading as I arrived. I parked in front of a concrete building with stark landscaping. The cracked, small asphalt parking lot crumbled into gravel around the edges, and its painted lines had worn to almost the same gray as the neglected surface. It was a bleak place, as if all the color had been sucked out.

I swallowed. I hadn't seen Dad since the sentencing. I had no idea what to expect.

Exiting the car, I stepped into the ten-by-twenty lobby onto a patchy utility mat. Coarse salt and mud had ground the fibers down over time. Dust bunnies clung to the corners. Quarter lockers for visitors' keys and purses lined the south wall, opposite the sign-in desk. I showed ID to the guard and explained who I wanted to see. He left to check Dad's approved-visitors list.

I waited on a hard bench for an hour before two female guards showed me into a closet-sized room with metal detectors. There, after a rough and thorough pat down, they asked me to pull my bra away from my body and shake while they felt up my shirt to see if anything was hidden. Last, they made me turn out my waistband to prove I hadn't stashed anything there. My cheeks burned as I tucked my shirt in and put my shoes back on.

Finally, one guard opened a heavy door leading to the visiting room. Ten or twelve small plastic tables were scattered around an open meeting area. Several had small groups sitting at them. I saw my father alone in the center. Dad raised his hand in greeting but didn't rise. I took two steps before a metallic clang behind me sent a wave of panic shooting through me. I had never been locked in before.

Shouting came from farther inside the prison. Startled, I looked for the nearest exit. Nobody else reacted. Feeling stupid, I walked to his table and pulled out the chair opposite him.

"Hi, Dad."

He looked like he'd lost a few more pounds, but perhaps it was just his loose-fitting uniform. Instead of the bright orange I'd last seen him in, it was a washed-out blue with a single orange stripe down each side.

Dad patted my hand. "Thanks for visiting. No one comes. Your sister showed up once, and she lives here."

I grunted. Lisa's estrangement from Dad was ten times worse than mine. Considering the scene in the kitchen when he had tried to bash her head in, I didn't blame her.

I changed the subject. "The female guards were awful."

My cheeks reddened again, remembering their cold, gloved fingers pulling my clothes away from my skin. I looked at him. This was where I had sent him. A place of humiliation. I shook my head, feeling worse for Dad.

Dad put his elbows on the table and clasped his hands, grinning. "You think they're bad? The ones inside are sadistic." He launched into a pornographic story.

I winced. He laughed, completely changing my compassion to disgust. The moment to connect was ruined. My attention wandered to a young man nearby in a navy-blue uniform chatting with an older woman, his mother, perhaps. I furtively searched the man's face, returning to it several times. Did killing someone alter your face? I felt like you should have to look different. I inspected Dad. His face hadn't changed from what I remembered.

Maybe coming to visit hadn't been the best idea. I had no idea what I was doing.

"Dad . . ." I so desperately wanted to ask him what really happened the day Mom died. "What's it like in here? How is the food?"

"Well, it's crap, pretty much. Except Thursdays. That's taco night."

Even face-to-face, our dance was unchanged. We talked for an hour about his life in prison. He didn't ask me a single question. My courage sank under the weight of reality. The truth was off the table.

Chapter Twenty-Seven
January 1989

I opened my dorm mailbox to find a large envelope with "Jackson State Correctional Facility" stamped in the upper left corner. When I turned it over, an intricately drawn butterfly in colored pencil surprised me.

I smiled, touched. The insect almost flew off the paper. I studied it, appreciating the effort my father must have taken. He had wanted to be an artist before having a family made engineering more practical. I carefully slit the envelope top and withdrew the card from inside.

My heart stopped at the unfamiliar handwriting. The illustrator reintroduced himself. I'd met the creepy, thirty-something, also "unjustly incarcerated," friend of Dad's who'd never mentioned, either at the prison or in the note, what charges he'd been found guilty of. In cramped scribble, the disturbing man offered again to correspond.

I shuddered to think what my father might have traded my contact information for. I shoved the card and envelope into my book bag. Now I had two felons in state prison sending me letters. What must the student mail clerks think of me?

February 1989

I sorted the mail quickly. No check from my aunt Diane. My January rent and board were long overdue. February's balance hung over my head.

I frowned. To his credit, Dad had paid for college the semester before, despite my incriminating testimony. He'd never acknowledged it was his fault that I needed to ask, but his decision had been a relief.

Diane had sent checks from his accounts. She had mentioned at Christmas that she would send money for the next term soon. Now it was almost halfway through the semester, and the promised funds hadn't arrived.

Was this some new twist in the Diane drama? Lisa's conspiracy theories were a constant topic on the phone. She believed Aunt Diane had been funneling funds to her own accounts. I had to admit that the new home was compelling evidence.

Still, Diane was the only way to get money for school, so I had to stay in her good graces. With my fourth delinquent notice in hand, I dialed Diane's number.

"Hi," I said when she answered. "Sorry to bother you, but I was just wondering if you'd been able to mail that housing money yet?"

Diane was curt. "Your dad hasn't given me permission to disperse anything still. There's nothing I can do."

I was dumbfounded. It'd been two months since Christmas, and she hadn't bothered to tell me anything while knowing my bills were long overdue. I tried not to lose my patience.

"Could you ask him why? I don't understand."

"I'll ask him again," she said.

I heard nothing. After another week, I called again. No one picked up. I left messages. A couple more weeks passed.

In March, my college ID card was denied at the cafeteria and book-store. It took just a couple of days to get really hungry.

A few friends smuggled small items out of the cafeteria. They thought they were helping until I could resolve the "clerical error." Meanwhile,

I panicked. I told no one, not even Sabrina, what was really happening because I was too humiliated to explain, much less ask for help.

What could I say? *I haven't eaten a real meal for weeks and am broke. My felon dad, who stole my college funds, is refusing to send me money from prison. I have no idea why, but could you lend me a couple thousand?* I would rather go hungry than reveal my situation.

Finally, light-headed after three weeks of a few hundred calories a day, mostly stolen apples and granola bars, I called my aunt one last time. Well, actually, I called five times in a row before she answered.

"I don't know what to say," Diane snipped. "He's cutting you off, both of you. I can't give you any money."

My heart stopped. He had finally done it. I was disowned. My father had taken everything from me. No family, no savings, no hope. I hung up and dropped to my knees in my cramped dorm room.

"Please, God, change him. Don't let him do this to me."

I received Dad's last letter a week later.

Dear Michelle,

I'm sorry you didn't take heed to my request. Now there will be no more money, and that encludes [*sic*] the $300 a month I have had sent to you. Your action is a clear indication that you don't "love" me or respect any thing [*sic*] I say. I love you dearly but you have left me with no alternative than to cut you off of all financial support until I can get out of here. I need all the money I can muster so I can fight Neal and get my money back from him so I can get myself out of here. You've gotten your Aunt Diane mad at me, and now I have NO ONE out there who I can rely on to do anything for me. This all but terminates my chance of ever getting out. Thanks a lot! Get yourself a job and try being the adult you told me you where [*sic*]. I haven't any money, and Uncle Bob hasn't the money to let you live as you have been accustomed. Also, do not drive the car until you get yourself some insurance. If you injure or kill someone you can be sued and pay for the rest of your life. You can also go to jail for driving without insurance. I don't have the $8000 Allstate is asking. I had the title signed over to you so you can do what you want with it. I am in a bad situation at the present time and it doesn't look like it will improve. If any thing [*sic*] should happen to me, I want you to know that I have fired Neal because he butch [*sic*] our lives in more ways than one. I am proceeding with my case pro-per [*sic*] and my friend Joe [inmate number] is actting [*sic*] as my legal addvisor [*sic*] . Contact him if the need arises. NOT being out there I can do nothing for you. I can only wish you all the best and pray things will improve for you. Love,

Dad

I'd lost ten pounds by the time I received notice that I'd be on the streets if my debt wasn't paid by the end of the week. I looked at the stack of textbooks on the shelf above my bed, terrified I was losing my chance at a better future. Even if I knew things were supposed to work out in the end, at the moment, they weren't.

"God, I know you hear me. What should I do?"

Call Grandma Findlay.

It was a quiet thought, and I hated the idea. She had far outlived my grandfather and was in danger of outliving her nest egg. But I had four days to come up with over $1,000 and only eighty-one cents in my bank account. I hadn't even been able to do laundry lately. Grandma was the best option.

"Hello, this is Sarah."

Hearing my grandmother's voice undid me. I pressed my fist to my chin, checking my emotions. "Grandma! Hi, it's me. Uh, I am in a mess. I didn't know who else to call." A little sob escaped. "I need some money."

I bawled while she tried to comfort me. She said the money was no problem, but I knew the truth. This was a sacrifice for her.

Grandma Findlay sent enough for me to finish that semester. I was so ashamed to be a burden to her, especially as it was my fault that I'd signed over my account to Dad, that I promised myself I would never ask anyone for money again.

Knowing I was a burden was worse than any pain I could ever suffer standing on my own two feet.

April 1989

One morning, alone in my dorm room while studying for finals, I opened my desk drawer and saw my pile of Dad's letters. Resentment filled my heart. The way I saw it, my misery sprang from one source—a father who had profited from abandoning me. Loathing ate at my soul.

He himself had instructed my sister and me to contact Diane about money, insisting we not pester him. His illogical claim about us bothering Diane was a flimsy excuse. We had simply asked for what he'd promised. I had no idea what had set him off. Perhaps, Diane had taken the money out, spent it, then asked for more, claiming it was our greed that had drained his accounts. Maybe Dad had just changed his mind, remembering our supposed "betrayal." Either way, I was blindsided.

What made me angriest was that he had stolen my money, then left me penniless. If not for my grandmother's charity, I would already be homeless while he enjoyed taco Thursdays and waited twelve short years to haul his retirement hoard to Mexico. My hurt had changed to hate.

Harsh reality lodged deep in my heart. My desire for answers would remain unsatisfied no matter how long I listened to or gratified him. I would never know why my life had spiraled out of control. He'd never share what had happened in those last moments of my mother's life or his reasons for cutting me off.

I had held on to these pages of lies too long, looking for the truth that I'd already known but refused to accept. There were things I'd never know. Not ever.

With that, I bowed my head. The only truth that mattered was that my parents were lost. Nothing would bring them back. I was alone.

Chapter Twenty-Eight

April 1989

Boxes and suitcases lined the halls. I started to panic as I watched my friends' families come to take them home. I numbly watched the halls empty, knowing I'd be kicked out of the dorms in two days. I had survived that semester by not allowing myself to think beyond finals. Now, I had no plan.

My checking account held less than ten dollars, so I checked the help-wanted ads in the university paper as I watched cars leaving from my dorm window three floors up.

"I just wanted to say bye." A friend who'd stolen cafeteria food for me stood in the doorway. Tears filled my eyes as I hugged her goodbye.

"You okay?" she asked.

"Yep." I tried to smile. "Just don't know where I'll be in two days."

My friend frowned, then brightened suddenly. "Hey, my sister has an open room in her condo this summer."

She called her sister's name down the hallway. A chestnut-haired girl a couple of years older came over.

My friend gestured to me. "Do you think Shelly could stay a couple nights with you until she finds a place?"

Her sister thought for a moment. "Yeah, we have an empty room. You can be my guest for a few nights if you want. The rent is $120 a month if you want to stay long-term."

She wrote her address on a post-it note, and I melted in relief. It was a start.

After feverishly packing and submitting résumés all over town for two days, I moved into the new place. That night, I dreamt about the fire for the first time in months. Distraught, I awoke and choked back my scream, afraid to wake the other girls living there, who slept peacefully in their own rooms.

I lay back on my pillow and tried to calm down. I supposed I was the only girl awake in the valley at 2:00 a.m. reliving her mother's murder.

The sleepless minutes ticked by. I tossed and turned, wondering why my nightmares had returned. I tried to pin down what might be bothering me and realized my sense of belonging was gone. Watching my friends leave with their families while I stood alone had undone my soul.

I had no home. It wasn't only not having a plan or money; it was the reality that I was drifting with no safe harbor. I had no family waiting for me at home.

Overwhelmed by fears that I never would again feel that sense of belonging or have a family again, I sobbed. I worried that others had recognized my peculiarity and that any friendship had been born of pity. Images from the attacks, Tony's words, and my father's threats all echoed in my head.

I was not worthy of love.

After four hours of trying to fight the black feelings, I slipped out of bed and onto my knees.

"Help me, God. Help me find a way to survive."

It was all I had the courage to ask for. He blessed me with enough peace to finally fall asleep for a few hours.

The next morning, I found a job posting in the student center seeking a CAD (computer-aided drafting) intern at an architecture firm. They hired me two days later. Now I could eat, and I had enough to pay rent. I lived and worked with strangers who knew nothing of the aching at the core of my being. It was a dark and lonely start to summer.

I had been so hurt for so long. My anger at my father had become my self-defense, a way to survive—until it wasn't. There is a fine line between anger and hate. I began to realize how it was affecting me when I read these words from 1 John chapter 2: "He that saith he is in the light, and hateth his brother, is in darkness even until now."

There were times in my life when I needed to be angry, times when I wasn't when I should have been. Now, I realized, was the time I needed to let the anger that had become hate go.

I had physically found some stability, and the threatening figures were gone from my life. But my soul was stuck in resentment. I needed to forgive to move forward, but it was so hard to leave behind the compulsion to revisit my hurt.

Sometimes all I could pray for was a desire to forgive; forgiveness itself seemed too large a task. Ever so slowly, my desire to be changed grew, and I could begin to pray for the peace of forgiveness without the list of my father's sins instantly coming to mind.

In trying to forgive, I began to understand I had never known my father. Insights about different dimensions of the man I had reviled began to pull at my pity. Not until then did I begin to grieve with the kind of hot sting that heals.

His compulsive need to lash out at the world and his manipulative tactics became clearer when I allowed myself to imagine him as a shattered youth coming home from the Korean War with PTSD. He was an alcoholic's son, and my grandfather's bloody beatings had not only left him with stained underwear as a child but psychopathic tendencies and serious relationship problems. I didn't know if the hammering of battle or his abusive father had damaged him more, but something had utterly broken him.

Dad had concealed his true self—including his sexuality—from everyone. Hiding behind my mother's religiosity must have been torture. Though I had already recognized this as the probable root of his aversion to religion, it was only part of the truth: my father's life had been a hell-hole. He didn't believe in a God or love because he had never experienced either. None of this excused his behavior, but it helped make sense of the unthinkable.

My compassion for the man grew despite my disgust at his choices.

As forgiveness began to lift my soul out of the trenches of despair, I was ready to move on. Next on my agenda was figuring out how to return to school. I had done the calculations. Making eight bucks an hour for four months, I wouldn't be able to save enough for living expenses and tuition. For a month, I stewed over a FAFSA application. I knew there was no way Dad would help me, but on paper, our family had too much income for me to qualify for any help.

On paper, I still had a family.

July 1989

The financial aid adviser across the desk from me frowned, her eyebrows drawing closer together. We were in the Smoot Building two weeks before the deadline for fall semester applications. I had walked in with Dad's last letter, my purse, and a still-blank FAFSA form.

"I am sorry to hear that your parents have no intent to support your education," the woman said kindly. "But the only way to get any financial aid is for them to sign the forms. Then we can process them and most likely offer you a Stafford loan." Her smile wilted at the look on my face.

A tear of frustration escaped. I wiped at my eyes, humiliated. "I understand. But they can't fill out forms. Or at least my dad won't."

The woman handed me a tissue. "It might help if you explain to him that filling out these forms doesn't mean he has to pay anything; all it does is release his tax numbers so we can offer you a loan," she said.

I sighed. This was the moment yet another person's estimation of me changed. I needed her help, but that required more of an explanation.

"He is in state prison for murdering my mother." I attempted to sound like it was an ordinary thing. I was just another kid with normal problems. No biggie.

The woman's eyes widened, and she froze. I went on, hating the silence. "I had a college savings account that would have paid for everything." I cleared my throat. "But he cleaned it out before his trial."

I looked down at my hands. I still held the letter. I placed it on the desk.

"Here. He disowned me in this." Saying these words wrenched my heart. There lay the real evidence, showing what I had lost. My eyes filled again. I was unable to pretend this was normal anymore.

How must this woman view me, being disowned by a felon? My cheeks flamed with mortification, and tears rolled down my face. I felt compelled to justify myself a little.

"I testified against him. I think that's why, even while he receives his pension in prison, he won't send me any."

The financial adviser put her hand on the letter but didn't bother reading it. "Oh, my goodness. I am so sorry." Her voice was kind. "I think I can help you."

I looked up, grateful but embarrassed by the pity shining in her eyes.

The woman turned and pulled open a filing drawer, looking for papers as she spoke. "I think we can get you declared independent. I believe the first qualifying condition is that you can prove your parents are either incarcerated or dead."

She stopped suddenly. The room filled with awkward silence.

"Well, that would be me," I said, trying to lighten the mood. I hated being such a downer everywhere I went.

She held out the forms, and I reached for them. She didn't let go until I looked at her face.

"I rarely provide these. I am so sorry you need them," the woman told me.

Her sympathy made me feel worse. My life really was that bad. I was grateful, though, to have found a way around Dad. My adviser described the evidence I needed to submit, starting with mom's death certificate and how to obtain affidavits from Jackson prison. I also had to write a letter explaining the entire situation.

That would be humiliating, and I hated writing every word, but I had no choice. I either proved I was orphaned and unloved—or I received no aid. It was hard enough to admit to myself, let alone get together the paperwork to convince the federal government.

The walk back to my condo was bittersweet. I had possibly found a way to start school again in the fall, but to do it, I had to convince the federal government how alone I was. At least the financial-aid clerk was the only other person on campus who knew.

I would mail in my proof and wait to see if it was enough.

Early August 1989

A month later, I walked into my off-campus condo after work and stood in the unlit entry. The evening sun sank across the valley behind me.

As usual, no one was home. I didn't really know my housemates, but I had made little effort to change that. Bone-tired from working full-time at the architect internship as well as a part-time cleaning job, I preferred sleeping to being social.

That night, as music thumped through the wall we shared with the neighbors, a deep depression settled over me. It had been a long, boring day of retracing plans and cleaning toilets for my bosses. All I did was work and sleep. There was nothing else. Life seemed pointless. I turned around and left, hopping in the Mustang.

I stopped at a red light just before the mouth of Provo Canyon and noticed a laughing couple in the car next to me. My eyes stung, and the light turned green. I shifted and powered ahead into the gorge.

What was this? I had money, a place to live. I had pulled it together and was making it on my own. The emotion rose again.

Sadness. Tired of pretending, I dismissed my strong impulse to ignore the emotion, and I let my survival barriers drop. Falling through the bottom of sad, I landed face-first in grief. Then all my emotions exploded at once, as if in touching my grief I'd detonated everything. I raced up the highway while the shrapnel flew through my soul.

Devastating piercings, loneliness, abandonment, and betrayal bled unstaunched. Everything hurt. I felt a cutting sensation of loss. My trust, my innocence, my wholeness, my family, my home. It was all gone. Every shattering memory punctured me with feelings of worthlessness.

My hands tightened on the steering wheel. I sped through the bowels of the canyon. The Mustang's wheels skidded on pebbles as I steered past corners amid the steep, winding cutbacks. Pain pursued me.

The road followed the river. Shadows spread, devouring the remaining light and descending to the canyon floor. Steep walls serrated with dynamite scars climbed into the darkness overhead. I flicked the headlights on.

A sign warning of falling rocks flashed yellow in my beams. I could only wish it might be so easy. I drove ten miles into despair until I rolled to a crunching halt on the shoulder overlooking Deer Creek Reservoir.

The headlights dropped over the edge of placid fathoms. Light faded into dark. A squeal of wheels could finish this. Breath, bubbles . . . beyond the pain.

But what if I still felt this way afterward?

I closed my eyes and leaned my head against the headrest. That couldn't be right. I had had a glimpse into the next life. Mom had appeared to be happier. My hands grasped the wheel. I could end my life, but something made me question if it would end the pain.

I didn't know how to overcome being unwanted and unloved. I rested my forehead against the steering wheel and cried out to God.

"I can't do this!"

I pulled my legs up, curling into a ball of frustration. I needed my mom, but there was no pillar of light. No soft voice. My soul lay in pieces.

I wept alone as night descended and the engine ran on and on in my indecision.

Finally, near midnight, the gas gauge pointed just above empty. I had three choices: pedal to the metal and die, leave now, or balk until I could do neither and would have to walk out of the canyon alone.

Trying to ignore the voice in my ear that said I was a coward, I reversed off the shoulder. Shifting into first, I had no idea why, just when I had figured out how to live on my own, I didn't want to. If I was going to stay alive, something needed to change.

I descended from murky heights with the windows down. My hair whipped in the gentle roar of the wind, cool and sweet with the scent of high-desert foliage. I drove out of the mouth of the canyon to a stunning burst of lights over the valley floor, stretching to Utah Lake. A bright moon glittered above me as I sighed and turned off Highway 89 and headed toward the closest gas station in Orem.

It would have been a beautiful night to die.

Chapter Twenty-Nine

Late August 1989

I walked into my dark living room and switched on the lights. My roommate Amanda was seated on the couch, eyes red and surrounded by used
tissues. A few had fallen to the floor by her feet. She blinked at the light
and turned her face away, startled. Her look of embarrassment stirred my
lethargic heart.

"Are you okay?" I sat next to her, clearing some books.

Amanda looked down at her hands. "Yeah. Well . . . not really." She
wiped her eyes. "I had a really bad day today."

I put a hand on her leg. "I am sorry. I have those too." I flushed,
remembering the canyon trip.

"Yeah, but you probably don't make yourself sick."

I was silent, not sure what she meant.

She put a hand over her face. "I'm bulimic."

I had no idea.

"I've been going to counseling and was doing better." She began
bawling.

I put an arm around her. I knew how excruciating sharing secrets was.

"But today, I saw an old boyfriend." Amanda continued sobbing. "He
looked so happy without me."

I grimaced, knowing all too well that the world's tendency to continue in its happy turns while you silently died. It was an excruciating observation that highlighted how miserable your own existence was.

I had never struggled with bulimia, but I had seen the bottoms of countless Dixie cups of beer. I remembered my night on the doorstep, realizing I was turning out like my dad. Hitting your lowest point was never pretty.

I hugged her.

"I don't know if I can ever stop doing this," Amanda whispered. "I don't know what's wrong with me. I hate myself, hate that I do this . . . and I hate that I can't stop."

"It will be okay," I said, hoping I was right to echo my mom. I still wasn't sure, but what else could I say? Maybe "It will get better"? I wasn't exactly an expert on living your best life. I was deep in the trenches beside Amanda. I hoped for both our sakes that my mother knew something we didn't.

"Thanks," she said. "Sorry I'm such a mess. I have an appointment with my therapist the day after tomorrow. I'll feel better after that."

You should go to the counselor.

I recognized the prompting immediately. My heart sank. Heaven's advice was exactly what I didn't want to hear, but it was spot-on. I wasn't myself—whatever myself meant. Amanda and I talked for a long time. Afterward, I made her soup. I hadn't made a real meal for myself in weeks.

Amanda had no idea how much she helped me by being honest. For an evening, I had a reason to care again, and caring about someone else gave me the courage to care about myself.

The next day, I walked into a small basement reception area of the student center. I asked to see a woman counselor and filled out intake forms.

My responses to the new-patient questionnaire shocked me. I had to mark every positive statement or action as something I "rarely" experienced or thought. When asked about thoughts of self-harm, I had to admit the "occasional" bubble I filled in was probably optimistic. I'd never inventoried my life before, and though it shouldn't have surprised me, the exercise was enlightening.

The receptionist ushered me through a warren of rooms and into a cozy office. She left me with a middle-aged woman who had short hair and a warm smile. Closing the door and going to a small wooden desk, the older woman pulled out a notepad and sat down. I parked myself in the only other place to sit, a blue loveseat.

"Hi, Michelle. Why don't you share what prompted you to come in today?" she asked.

"Um, well," I said. "I guess, to begin, my father murdered my mother when I was fifteen and set our house on fire. He is in prison."

The counselor's smile wavered. "Oh my, that sounds traumatic."

"Yeah, you could say that, I guess," I weakly joked. "At least I don't have to live with him anymore."

The counselor nodded for me to continue. Sharing part of my burdens was easier this time and brought immediate physical relief. I rehearsed my story matter-of-factly—as if it were someone else's. At this point, I couldn't explore any emotions. There was so much going on inside, all I could identify was intense emotional pressure powerful enough to render the separate feelings indistinct. They all pushed at once.

As I continued meeting with my counselor, one feeling finally broke through the surface. Shame ran through every single emotion and bound them together into one great seething mass. Its primary role didn't surprise me. I had recognized it as my lifelong adversary in Mexico, but that didn't mean I had figured out how to defeat it.

242

I knew I needed help, though I didn't understand how talking could change anything. I only went to counseling because God had told me to. I didn't like probing questions and couldn't even admit to myself all the hateful feelings I had for myself—for leaving my mother, for testifying against my father.

Revealing my sexual assaults was out of the question. I lacked the courage to disclose those searing memories. I actively tried to forget I was a victim. I talked only about what I could bear to—what my dad had done, how my mother had suffered. Sharing with another human being some of what had happened released enough pressure to find the strength to go on. My counselor couldn't fix my life, but I felt less alone.

Summer 1990

This time, I joined the mass exodus from campus after finals. I packed my bags, hugged my friends goodbye, and hit the road. I was excited to drive the fifteen-hundred miles "home" to Aunt Kathy's house. I was excited to see the Snows, my original church family, and my sister. In counseling, I had realized I still had connections, though distant, and my heart had taken one more step toward healing by planning my return that summer.

The only downside to being home was my summer job. I discovered my boss was a known womanizer, and I was the only young woman in the office. I tried hard to avoid him, and thankfully he left me alone.

However, he turned a blind eye to harassment by male coworkers. I needed the good paycheck I was making, so I avoided attention and refused to respond to off-color remarks. I focused on my projects and kept to myself.

Near the end of that summer, my job went from tolerable to terrifying in two minutes.

I booted up my computer. I had come in early to get some uninterrupted time to finish a set of drawings. Believing I was the only one there, I sat at my desk and leaned over my blueprints from the day before. I didn't notice John until he whispered in my ear.

"You look great today."

I stiffened in surprise.

He sniffed. "You smell even better."

I scooted my chair closer to the desk, away from him. "Morning, John."

His compliments over the summer had become more and more personal.

I changed the subject. "How are your kids?"

His hands covered my shoulders. An alarm went off in my head.

I turned. "John, keep your—"

His lips pushed against mine. Shocked, I reeled back. John leered. Footsteps came our way. Someone was whistling. John hurried to his desk.

I sat stupefied, staring at his retreating form. After all my promises to myself and years of learning I had a voice, another man had ignored my obvious disinterest and forced himself on me. Again. I had done nothing to invite his attention; in fact, I had actively tried to deflect it after his first comment months ago.

I finished my drawings that day in silence, hoping my shaking hands didn't ruin them.

Later, Aunt Kathy greeted me from the kitchen where she prepared dinner.

"How was work?"

I'd already made up my mind to tell her everything. I was terrified to hide anything after Tony's escalation following my silence in Mexico.

"Um, weird and awful," I told her. "You know that guy, the one who kept making comments about how I looked?"

"Yeah?"

"He kissed me today!" I exclaimed.

"He kissed you?" Aunt Kathy stopped peeling potatoes and set everything down, rinsing off her hands and coming around the counter to sit by me.

"Isn't he married? With kids?!"

"Yep," I said. "What should I do?"

"Tell me everything," she urged.

I explained, and she thought for a minute. "What do you have left? Another week?"

I nodded.

"Well, stay away from him," she advised. "I mean far away. Never be alone with him."

I nodded. No more early mornings or late nights. I had no intention of being vulnerable again.

The next day, as soon as I walked in the door at nine, my boss came over.

"Shelly, glad you're here. I need you to help assess a job site in Lansing," he said.

"Me?" I hedged. "I'm not quite finished with those drawings."

Not having been out of the office much, I wasn't sure what he wanted me to do.

He looked at the designs lying nearly finished on my desk. "Those look great. Really, it's nothing big; just hold the grade rod steady for John. He'll do the rest."

John?

I felt nauseated and wondered if the pair of them were in cahoots.

"Any questions?"

I shook my head but had a million. There were others my boss could have sent. Had John suggested me? I felt trapped. I didn't want to make a scene but couldn't back out without disclosing the humiliating incident the day before. Afterward, I would think of possible excuses, but my brain had ceased working.

After an all-office meeting, my boss dismissed John and me to go off-site. I followed John out the door, panicking. A chill swept through me, and I shivered despite the heat, imagining the worst. I had an intimate store of details about bad men. John smiled and opened his car's passenger door for me. My hands shook. I got in.

John rounded the car and slid behind the wheel, starting the ignition. I slid away, almost perching on the door itself.

It'll be okay. Aunt Kathy knows. I repeated that solace to myself over and over, all the way to Lansing. *We will be in public the entire time.*

At the same time, my mouth ran endless questions about his wife and kids.

"Any plans with your kids this weekend?" I asked. "Going to the lake?"

I prayed. *God, don't let him hurt me.*

John gave me an exasperated look. "Not that I know of."

Why did these men always find me?

"I told my aunt about your . . . kids," I said finally, not looking at him. I'd meant to say that I had told her everything but couldn't quite rise to vocalizing the threat. "You are lucky to have such cuties."

He didn't reply.

We finished our survey without incident. When we got back late, the office parking lot was almost empty. Instead of returning to my desk to clean up, I jumped inside my Mustang and sat with the doors locked. I let my heart rate drop back to normal before driving away. I wanted to quit but stuck it out for six more days.

Aunt Kathy was my safety valve. Every day, I consoled myself that she knew, and if anything happened, she would believe me without blaming me. I congratulated myself for not hiding anything from Aunt Kathy.

At the time, I didn't even consider refusing the car ride or calling out my coworker. There was no "Me too" movement in the nineties, and I was one of the few women entering my field. In fact, I would be the first female to graduate with a manufacturing-engineering degree from my large university. We were just trying to prove we could do the work as well as the men who preyed on us.

Like the society that failed to protect me, I felt I was making progress but missed the obvious ways in which nothing had changed.

Chapter Thirty

March 1991

Back at school, I continued to plow through at a grueling pace, taking a full load of engineering classes while working full-time at the CAD job. Most of my engineering classes also required attending a weekly three-hour lab, which made fourteen hours of credit seem like over twenty. When I could, I made time for counseling, which was helping me process my feelings of guilt and responsibility for Mom's death.

The church-owned university I attended required all students to meet with their spiritual leader, regardless of denomination, at least once a year. One weekend, I left off studying to check off this requirement.

I was supposed to meet my bishop up on campus that day, and I hurried to be on time. He seemed like a kind man, but with over two hundred young adults to look after in just his congregation, building relationships with them all in a few months was impossible. Besides, I didn't like calling attention to myself. We were basically strangers.

I arrived at his office a minute early and out of breath. I knocked on the door and entered at his invitation.

We began a short but typical chat. We had both had done this before, in other offices, with other people. This was a formality. He asked about my family. I kept it brief. I always did.

I said, "I lost my mother several years ago."

The bishop leaned forward. "I am sorry to hear that. Losing your mother so young must have been difficult."

I paused. "My dad disowned me last year, so we don't have contact either."

The man's eyes grew concerned. "That is unfortunate. Was it because of your conversion?"

I nodded, not wanting to describe my burdens to another person. It wasn't exactly the reason but close enough. Explaining was worse than letting people assume they understood. I found it easier to let people draw whatever conclusions seemed appropriate to them. My past defied peoples' worst expectations. I cleared my throat.

"It's been a rough couple years. Things are better now."

The bishop continued, and we discussed the role my faith played in my life. The chat was pleasant, but I was anxious to get on with my homework and plans for the weekend. I fell quiet as the bishop filled out the required document. I slid forward to the edge of my seat, expecting an imminent goodbye.

Nodding to himself, the bishop posed one last question I had not anticipated, "Is there anything from your past that needs to be discussed?"

I quickly dismissed the substantial family trauma my therapist had been privy to. There was no need to burden this man with information about which he could do nothing.

Tell him.

I shrank in my seat at the shocking impression. I knew it referred to something I had buried deeper than murder and drinking and lies. There were memories I had never allowed myself to dwell on, much less share with anyone else up to that point in my life.

My assaults.

I'd hoped my baptism would have washed the feelings away. It hadn't. The self-disgust and angry humiliation were like polluted groundwater that kept resurfacing no matter how much time and excess dirt I piled on top.

Still, the rife smell of men pushed me under in unguarded moments.

The bishop waited. Tears formed in my eyes, and I looked down at my hands, sure the truth was written across my face. I'd had a very bad past. I could barely breathe for several moments.

Heavy silence filled the room. My hands clasped and unclasped in agony as shame surfaced in a flood of memories. My voice shook as I began.

"When I was younger . . . when I was eleven . . . we went on family vacation in Mexico . . ." I explained what Tony did, what horrors I complied with.

I couldn't look at the man across from me. "And there's more . . ."

I pressed on, relating the bar scene in England. I admitted my drinking and what I thought would be a kiss. Tears fell in torrents. I stared at my hands, the floor, anywhere but his face. I couldn't bring myself to see a stranger's eyes fill with disgust.

"Then, I saw Tony again," I wept, covering my face with my hands. Though it was the most painful part, I shared everything, including my suicidal hours on top of the hotel.

"I was so stupid. I should have known better," I whispered. My cheeks chafed from rubbing my tears away. My ears were hot, my gut icy.

I was a lie. Broken and dirty beyond what anyone had ever guessed. Worse than a murderer's daughter, a recovered drinker and druggie, a liar, and a thief who still felt bad about all those cafeteria apples and granola bars, I had been soiled long before I knew what the word *chaste* meant.

I couldn't live behind a façade any longer. Deep silence followed, into which I whispered the most wrenching part.

"And so, my baptism is not valid. I shouldn't have been able to join any church." I took a breath, choking on it.

My previously silent bishop interrupted before I could finish my apology.

"Wait just a minute."

I finally looked at his face. Tears stained his shirt and cheeks. His red eyes, flooded with compassion, bore into mine. His lips pressed together in an unexpected smile that jarred me.

"You are mistaken. You were never to blame. Not in any of this."

My world shifted, light breaking through. I gaped at him, speechless.

"You were wronged in evil ways. I am so sorry you've felt these actions were your responsibility. They were not. Please don't carry that burden a step further."

The walls of guilt utterly caved. I sobbed in relief.

My bishop had pronounced me faultless. Maybe I should stop blaming myself as well. With that thought, light burst into the caverns of my heart, and I knew:

God didn't blame me either.

Chapter Thirty-One
December 1992

Eric held my hand as the darkness of the overcast sky deepened. Steele Perrett had introduced us our senior year of high school in California. Like me, Eric had found the Perrett family's faith-filled lives intriguing. The Perretts had conspired to make us a match ever since, but it was only in the last two years of college that we'd decided they might have been right.

I'd come for the weekend to spend time with his family. His dad had urged him to take me to see "the lights." We'd driven into town together and now walked up gravel paths through ascending winter gardens scented with camellias and magnolias. Eric dug out a penny as I paused at a bubbling hillside fountain. I tossed it in with a smile.

"What'd you wish for?" He smiled down at me.

I shook my head. "Oh, no. If I tell, it won't happen."

He raised an eyebrow, and I took his arm with a soft laugh. "Come on."

We ambled in comfortable silence until we reached the summit. I gasped at the view atop the highest point in the valley.

House lights carpeted the rolling terrain that fell away from our feet and into the San Francisco Bay. In the distance, I caught glimpses of fishing-boat lights cruising in the bay between lazy fingers of mist. Nearby, the Bay Bridge lights reflected off the dark surface. Behind us, the exterior lights of an edifice cresting the hill with a golden spire created a hazy glow as a manmade waterfall cascaded down its towering granite walls. Seagull cries echoed.

I squeezed Eric's hand. "It's beautiful."

It had been a perfect weekend. I had loved being with his family. Their commitment to each other bridged any differences of religious opinion. They were such good people. Exactly the kind of family I'd wished for growing up. I smiled at their son, whom I had fallen in love with.

His serious face took me aback. Then he released my hand and got down on one knee. He flipped open a small silver box to reveal a stunning ring.

"Michelle Edwards, will you make me the happiest man alive and marry me?" His deep blue eyes went from my astonished face to the ring, which sparkled in the dim lighting. He grinned at my speechless appreciation.

"My grandmother made it."

His grandmother was a custom jeweler with fabulous taste—large and multifaceted taste. I would be the envy of every girl in Provo, maybe in Utah.

"Well?" he asked.

I laughed, realizing I hadn't answered. "Yes, yes, yes!"

He took my hand and slipped the wide inlaid band onto my finger. The sight of it filled a long-empty piece of my heart. My future was falling into place. I no longer had to worry about being without a family of my own.

We planned to marry sometime after graduating and returned to our last semester to finish one chapter of our lives before starting a new one. I had no premonition that I'd author a plot twist of my own.

March 1993

I stayed late one Monday night at the architect's office in Provo. A colleague and I were scrambling to meet a Provo City project deadline at six the next morning when he got a call from the hospital. His wife had been injured in an auto accident. I sent him racing off with my blessing. I was okay finishing alone, having worked there almost three years. I knew what needed to be done; it just took longer by myself. Even so, I beat the deadline by three hours, dropping the finished plans on the boss's desk before I headed home.

When I entered my apartment to sleep, I left the lights off, not wanting to disturb anyone. I put my purse on the counter and saw the answering machine flashing in the darkness. Eleven new messages waited. I panicked, wondering if Lisa or her eighteen-month-old daughter Ashley might have been hurt that night too. I hit the play button, suddenly not caring who it might wake.

"Hey, Shelly. It's Eric. Give me a call."

"Shelly, just trying to get ahold of you. Call me."

"Shelly, where are you?"

"I am worried. Shelly, call me."

I skipped through the rest. They were all the same. I rolled my eyes and called. If Eric had been calling all night and none of my roommates had answered to yell at him, they would sleep through this too. At almost three in the morning, Eric answered on the second ring.

"Hi, it's me." I spoke fast. "Sorry, I'm fine. I just got home from work. One of the architects had a family emergency, and we had plans due this morning. I need some sleep. I'll call you when I wake up. Bye."

"Shel—"

I cut him off and went to bed. The boy was creating drama over nothing. We could talk later. After I slept.

Someone shook my shoulder. I opened my eyes to see my roommate Jen's face near mine.

"Sorry," she whispered. "Eric's here."

I groaned and nodded. How long had I slept? I pushed myself upright and swung my feet to the floor. I saw the clock—10:40. He hadn't even given me eight hours. I hadn't had more than seven hours of sleep for weeks with work and school projects piling up. I was slightly irritated, wondering what the emergency was.

I pulled on clean sweatpants and stopped in the bathroom to pull my hair into a ponytail. Purple bags hung under my eyes. I frowned at myself in the mirror and tossed the brush into my basket. My annoyance grew with every step until I stomped into the living room.

"Shelly!" Eric stood up from the couch, arms reaching out to me.

I stopped five feet away. "Why are you here?" Concern filled his face, but I continued. "I told you, everything's fine. I needed sleep."

His arms dropped, and he looked down, hurt. Jen left us alone in the apartment, the front door clicking softly behind her. I crossed my arms. He sighed.

"I guess I should have waited longer. Sorry. It's just that you seem so distant lately. You are always working or in class. I barely see you." His head came up, and his eyes searched mine. He sighed. "I am starting to wonder if you even love me."

I pressed my hands to my eyes. Additional relationship drama was more than I could handle on my dwindling emotional reserves. "Yes, of course. I just am under so much pressure. Everything is due next week before midterms. I am behind on my project, and work has been insane."

Eric nodded, but I felt he really didn't get it. A surge of resentment gripped me as I realized how different our lives were. His parents had helped pay for his schooling, so he hadn't had to work. Of course he had free time.

"Remember, I have to do this on my own. No one helps me," I said.

Eric swayed back a step as if stung. "How can I help if you won't let me? You work harder than anyone I know, but we are supposed to be a team."

255

I considered him blankly. Just what could he do to help? Take my midterms? Write my engineering papers? Finish my projects? Even if there was something he could do, I didn't want help when I knew I could do it by myself.

He saw the refusal in my face, sighed, and started to speak, but I cut him off. I knew there was some truth to what he was saying. I had been distant, but I didn't have time to talk just then.

"I need to get through this week. I have a big project due Friday. After that, we can talk. It's not your fault. I'm just slammed."

Eric looked as if I'd just said I hated him. I realized he just wanted to spend time together and I'd just treated my fiancé like he was an annoying problem.

I was being a royal jerk. "Sorry, I know I'm grumpy. I'm tired."

I moved closer and put my hand on his arm, feeling bad. "Forgive me?"

Eric pulled me in for a hug. "I'm sorry it's so hard. Please, let me help," he said above my head.

I nodded, then stepped away. "I need to get up to campus and work on my project."

I opened the front door for him. "I'll call you Friday when I finish. Let's talk then."

"Okay." Eric kissed my cheek and gave me a last look.

"Bye."

I closed the door and leaned against it. If being engaged was this hard, what would our marriage be like??

Locked three doors deep in the bowels of the Crabtree Building Thursday evening, I hunched over a CAD machine in the senior engineering student lab and fretted. Every hour pushed up against the capstone project deadline.

My shoulders ached. I stretched and realized how badly I needed a shower. Three days in this room interrupted by only Taco Bell runs and six hours of sleep the last two nights had taken their toll. I smelled like a rotten burrito despite the cool, ventilated air blowing over my head.

My watery eyes itched. Taking a break from the screen, I sat back in my chair and let my gaze wander. I noticed a familiar form through the glass security door. Eric? I pushed back my chair and jogged across the room. The figure slipped away. I lost sight of him as other students crossed the hallway between us. There! Someone had ducked down a side stairwell.

I knew that football player profile. Eric had been spying on me! I dropped my hand from the door handle and turned back to the computers. I would deal with him later.

I played with my engagement ring Friday evening, admiring how its diamond sparkled in the florescent lighting above our table at Wendy's. I savored a few last moments of feeling that I fit in with the college couples chatting over value meals. Eric had been my ticket to normalcy. He was a good man and everything a good woman should want. I didn't understand what had gone wrong.

I let him eat before I ruined his appetite. He was almost finished with his fries.

"Eric, I have been thinking and praying," I began. I had spent the entire afternoon on my knees, confused and upset. But I'd made my decision and didn't cry now.

"I think I'm making a mistake."

Eric's eyes glistened. "What do you mean?" Hurt filled his voice. "Is this why you've been avoiding me?"

My head came up. "I haven't been avoiding you!"

He looked at me. He was right, but that was beside the point. I wanted to explain that something was wrong with this relationship, not talk about how I'd been avoiding him.

"I have been busy," I said. "That doesn't have anything to do with this."

A tear wandered down Eric's cheek. I was officially the worst person ever.

I had been running from this, from seeing his face when I told him that his kisses no longer electrified me—that the closer he wanted to hold me, the more I wanted to run. Wanting to push him away was not what love was supposed to feel like. His spying on me was the last straw. This tug-of-war and confusion wasn't what I wanted for my future.

I'd come to say words I knew would wound him.

"Eric, I'm so sorry," I said. "I have tried and tried to figure out what is making me uncomfortable. But I don't know."

"Is this why you have never set a date?" he asked. "Have you felt this way the entire time?"

I nodded, ashamed. "Not at first, but for a few months now."

"Why did you keep going along without saying anything?" he asked.

I tried to speak but started to cry instead. Finally, I whispered, "Because I love you. I want to marry you. Only, I can't shake this feeling that something isn't right."

I looked down at my hands and slipped the ring off. I placed it on the table in front of him. Eric wiped his face and stood, stuffing the ring into his back pocket. He left the restaurant without looking back.

I let him go. On reflection, it became obvious that I wasn't ready for intimacy. When Eric made efforts to grow closer during our engagement, it terrified me in ways I couldn't explain—to either myself or him. I kept him at arms-length and shut down.

Despite starting to trust God's compassion, I doubted Eric's. I wanted to share only my future, not my present or my past. I see that now as a huge red flag, but its significance escaped me at the time. Eric knew the public version of my father's incarceration for my mother's death. He had accepted not having in-laws without hesitation. But I'd refused to share how deep and far-reaching my own abuse had been.

I assumed disclosing the details of my assaults would alter our relationship. I needed Eric to see me as desirable because I viewed myself as secretly damaged goods God had pieced together. Instead of sharing the most vulnerable parts of myself, I wanted to close the door on those memories, for remembering still brought deep shame, even if I was blameless.

I watched Eric go with a sense of relief.

I'd misunderstood the very anxiety that could have opened the door to the family relationships I so desperately wanted. My compulsion to build a wall should have taught me to evaluate the façade I protected, not question the man who wanted in. But I'd never seen healthy intimacy and had no idea how to build strong relationships, even though I wanted one.

I was more comfortable being alone than being vulnerable, no matter how much I wanted to be loved.

I graduated and kept my promise to Lisa that I'd return to Detroit. My sister needed help as a single mom, and I needed to hold onto the remains of my family. Someday my dad would walk free, and I still harbored a secret hope that we'd find a way to bridge our estrangement.

The road to understanding my own life and future would begin where it started.

Chapter Thirty-Two

July 1997

The kitchen phone rang as I pushed open the door with my hip and hopped inside my Rochester, Michigan, apartment. Balancing on one leg, I emptied armfuls of wet tent gear beside the door. My bum leg was once again in a cast. Though I'd spent a fun but rainy week using plastic garbage bags to keep it dry in Traverse City, I was looking forward to a dry bed that night.

The phone rang again.

My immobilized leg ached as I jumped to the counter on one leg and stretched across to grab the ringing phone. Having recently had surgery to hopefully correct the still-stiff joint left by the trampoline accident, I was supposed to be using crutches, but I couldn't carry stuff with crutches.

Caller ID showed an unfamiliar number. I cradled the phone against my shoulder. "Hello?"

"Shelly?" I recognized my cousin Denise's voice. Diane's other daughter.

"Hi. What's up?" I hopped back to the front door and propped it open with a shoe. I had more things to get from the car.

Denise hadn't answered, and I wondered if the connection had gone bad. "Denise? Hey, you there?'

"Oh, geez. I don't know how to say this, but your dad . . ."

My stomach tensed.

"He passed away from cancer last week. He asked us to let you know when it happened. I am so sorry."

He's gone. I hadn't even known he was sick.

I stood there holding the phone, wet tent forgotten, front door wide open. I stared out at nothing.

Denise went on, filling the silence.

"Madeline is having a memorial service for him down in Missouri on the nineteenth. She wanted me to tell you. Anyways, give Madeline a call."

She hung up after an awkward pause. Horror hit first. My dad had died a week ago.

I'd gone camping while he'd slipped away.

Though I had not talked with my father in years, the last few months, I'd had an unshakable urge to make contact again. I had gone to prison on Father's Day a month earlier to try, but the guards had said Arnold Edwards was unavailable. I'd thought it was Dad refusing to see me, but now realized he'd probably been in hospice.

I hung up and sobbed for a long time, torn between anger at him for not telling me and guilt for not knowing.

Both my parents had died without saying goodbye.

Lisa took the news amazingly well. "Finally. He did something right."

That weekend, I was supposed to watch Lisa's six-year-old daughter Ashley. After they knocked on my apartment door, Ashley made a beeline for my couch, and I put in a Barney video. Lisa had only a few minutes to talk before her second shift of the day began, but she was excited.

"I want to use whatever I get from Dad as a down payment. I found a two-bedroom townhome in Southfield for $80,000." Her eyes were alight with hope. "I think that I could finally afford to move out of Gary and Linda's."

Lisa had been living with the parents of her best friend from high school for eight years. Like the Perretts had for me, Gary and Linda offered shelter to someone in dire need but for much longer. They'd acted like grandparents to Lisa's daughter, Ashley, when she had come along unexpectedly, and helped care for the precious blonde girl whenever they could. But being able to provide a home for her own daughter would give Lisa the self-respect she'd long struggled to hold on to.

"I'll help with whatever you need," I said.

Lisa smiled. "You know," she said. "I slept better this week than I have in years."

I hugged her. Dad hadn't just cut her off, he'd threatened to kill her when he got out of prison.

I felt guilty for crying over his death, but I managed not to do it in front of Lisa.

I dialed Madeline's number in Missouri. I'd met her as a child but had not interacted with her in many years as my father's family was not particularly close.

Dad had chosen his cousin Madeline to replace Diane when it had become obvious from prison that Aunt Diane had misappropriated funds. The first thing Madeline had done as executor was to move Dad's storage to Missouri to hold until his release. It was an entire semi-truck load of household and family items. Both Lisa and I had had stuff in the condo at his sentencing that we weren't able to remove right then as we were both relying on friends' kindness to house us. So Aunt Diane had boxed it all up together, his and ours, and put it in storage. Madeline had possession of everything.

Aunt Diane had been bitter about that.

"She's probably going to start selling it this week," Diane complained to Lisa and me. I thought Diane was paranoid because that's what she'd have done.

After getting the funeral details, I was desperate to know whether there was any hope of salvaging anything of my childhood. In particular, I wanted the jewelry box I'd left in my condo loft when I'd fled to California. It had held the pearls from my grandmother, my mother's wedding rings, and the bent and burned frames I'd found in the ashes. If I could get those and my varsity jacket, along with some baby pictures, that would be enough. I didn't care about the rest of Dad's stuff.

Madeline had been cordial so far, so while I hesitated to sound impolite about wanting my stuff, I went ahead and asked, "While we're there, Lisa and I wondered if we might look through Dad's storage boxes for some of our things. He had our lettermen jackets, baby albums, and things we didn't have time to move out before the trial. Stuff like that."

Madeline cleared her throat. "You need to know ahead of time that your dad wrote you and Lisa out of his will. As I have taken care of him these last few years, *he left everything to me.*"

Her emphasis dropped my jaw more than the facts. I hadn't heard anything from my father for years, so I hadn't expected much. I knew Lisa would be devastated by Dad's last cruel blow, though maybe not surprised. But neither of us had anticipated Madeline's brazen self-interest. It seemed obvious she had manipulated my father into his decision, and I later learned that the will had been altered after the cancer diagnosis, when my father would have been most vulnerable to Madeline's lies about his daughters' intentions and feelings toward him.

Now, Madeline's voice rang with condescension.

"Luckily for you, there is one smaller life insurance policy he forgot to change. I don't know how much it is, but maybe you could buy the cottage back from me."

I pressed my lips together and clenched the phone. Her audacity to dangle what should have been mine like a piece of meat before a dog flooded me with emotions. She expected me to jump at it. Instead, I took a deep breath and a few seconds to think.

Regardless of her having conned my father and cheated us out of everything, I certainly didn't expect her to assume my things were now hers. A fight before the funeral would accomplish nothing. I didn't need her to give me everything, and something would be better than nothing.

"Okay, I understand." I tried again. "I meant things that you wouldn't want. Just family mementos. Stuff that wasn't my dad's." I repeated myself. "My letterman jacket, baby photos. No one else would want it anyway."

There was a long pause. "Just those things?"

I reassured Madeline. "Of course. I don't care about the furniture, ugly death masks, or artwork. I can't fit much in my car anyway."

"A lot of that stuff is gone already."

"Already?" I repeated in disbelief. It'd only been a week since Dad's death. How had she sold it all so quickly?

Madeline seemed to backtrack a bit. "Well, I sold those African masks a couple of days ago."

"Oh, I see." I did see. I realized that Diane had been right. It took one thief to recognize another. Madeline had probably started selling things the moment she heard the cancer diagnosis. She hadn't waited one minute to start cashing in on her exploitation. Still. I wondered who she was selling the high-end items to in a rural Missouri town of four thousand people. "My dad paid over $5,000 for each of those. They were collector items."

There was a long silence.

"Hello?" I finally asked.

Madeline's irritation was palpable. "Wish I'd known that. I only got $400. Damn it."

I had a hard time feeling sorry for her. I turned the subject back to my things.

"Yeah," I said. "Anyways, we don't have much room in my car. I just wanted my stuff that got left behind and packed up by accident."

I assumed my father's will didn't legally include my things. Madeline finally seemed to come to the same conclusion.

"I guess that's fine."

I was about to hang up when she asked, "How are you girls doing?"

I fumbled for a moment at the personal question. "Since we had no idea Dad was sick, we're a bit stunned, I guess."

"Yes, well." Madeline enunciated her words with dagger-like clarity. "Your Dad didn't want you to know about the cancer. 'If they didn't want to have anything to do with me when I was alive, I don't want them to have anything to do with me now.' Those were his exact words."

I rocked back on my seat. I had tried to contact him numerous times over the years. "But he was the one who cut us off!"

"Oh, but that was only after you constantly asked for money. He told me everything." She seemed to relish my shocked silence.

I fumed at her insinuation of greed, especially in light of her stealing my inheritance. My father had only ever paid about three grand for my college, not even a tenth of what he'd stolen from my bank account—and Madeline had just stolen the rest. And I was a money grabber?

Madeline enjoyed flexing her power as Dad's confidant and fraudulent heir to his and my mother's estate. "You betrayed him. It was your testimonies that imprisoned and killed him. You both should have been imprisoned for perjury."

I gasped. "But Lisa testified for him—for the defense."

"Yeah, well, she obviously didn't help much." Madeline shot back.

I was speechless while Madeline lectured on my sister's and my moral deficiencies. At last, I tried to defend myself by describing what living with Dad was like and how we knew he had murdered Mom. After a couple of minutes, Madeline interrupted me.

"Don't bother, Shelly. Your dad already told me what you'd say."

The woman waiting on the sidewalk of the rural Missouri chapel looked vaguely familiar from my childhood memories, but Madeline made no move to greet us. She offered no condolences.

"Follow me," she said and walked ahead of us.

Madeline's friends packed two dozen pews on either side of the center aisle. Their cold stares stood out against the warm light streaming through the stained glass behind them. It might have been a beautiful scene if not for the contempt of these strangers. Madeline sat us on the front row on the left, a few feet from a gray, fabricated marbled urn that rested on an unadorned side table. Madeline was getting a cottage and six figures for a plastic urn.

She sat beside us and nodded to her pastor to begin. When it was Madeline's turn, she paid respect to my father and humiliated us. "When his poor wife died tragically in their house fire, some family members saw an opportunity to advance their own interests."

She didn't look at us, but her listeners did. "Arnie spent his last years paying for a crime he never committed."

Madeline blew her nose. "He died alone, abandoned."

I bowed my head and wept, even though their frosty stares implied I'd no right to. I loved my father, and loving him always hurt.

I picked at my meal during the funeral luncheon. Hearing my name whispered across the room made my ears flame. It stung to be so publicly denounced, but Dad's rejection—his refusal to let us say goodbye—and his lies hurt more. My grief drained any energy I might have used to refute Madeline's narrative.

I approached Madeline before Lisa and I left the restaurant.

"Thank you for arranging everything. Unfortunately, we need to leave soon. Could I get the address of the storage unit so we can get our things?"

Madeline hesitated, then looked away.

"Your father's stuff is stored in my friend's barn. They left town this morning. You won't be able to get it."

I froze, confused. "But you said . . ."

She waved to a woman leaving. "Bye, Sue. Thanks for coming." Her smile disappeared as she returned her gaze to us. "Call me later."

I looked at Lisa, and she shrugged. "Okay," I said.

She refused to answer the phone all that night or the next morning. Lisa cussed out the woman who had stolen her hope of being able to afford a new life for herself and her preschooler.

We left town with nothing.

Lisa took over driving near Indianapolis, which left me to stew about Madeline.

Madeline had not only stolen our inheritance but hated us for imagining we were entitled to any of it. I knew she didn't want my jacket or baby pictures, that they would be worthless to anyone else but me. Yet, for spite, she had refused to return them.

Perhaps she'd pawned the pearls and wedding rings for quick cash, but I ached as much for the twisted metal frames as the jewelry. I am sure the frames ended up in a Missouri dump along with my father's ashes. I would have willingly given her ten times whatever money she'd made on the jewelry just to have those frames back.

There would be so much hurt to unpack from this woman. Just as she had kept the storage boxes just past our reach, she would later quietly sell our family cottage to the listing agent for pennies on the dollar without telling us she had done so. It didn't matter really, though, because she listed it just above what Lisa and I could afford with the single life-insurance payment we'd received. She didn't care about the cottage or our things, only that we didn't get them.

I realized I would have to let it all go, that I couldn't change Madeline's spitefulness any more than I'd been able to change my father's selfishness.

To calm myself on the car ride, I turned my thoughts to Dad's last moments. I didn't even know where he had died. I pictured him alone in a hospital room, still wearing his inmate uniform. What sort of demons haunted him as death crept closer? I shuddered, certain I didn't want to know.

I doubted angels had comforted him, but then again, what did I know of God's love? I knew Dad had been a monster to me, but I couldn't say what he was to God.

God, is there any hope left for our family?

An inexplicable peace filled me. God knew where I was at that very moment, surrounded by cornfields in northern Ohio, and God had been aware of my father every second of his life. God still knew where Dad was and still reached out to him. God's love was beyond my understanding as much as my father's heart had been.

Summer 1977

At seven, I barely fit inside the basement bar cabinets. Dad and I were installing outlets on the laminate surface above me. I kept bumping my head on the door opening as I hung half out and waited for my next instructions.

Dad explained how the wiring should thread through the joists and out under it. But first, I needed to strip the ends. "Pull off the plastic coating like this." He demonstrated how to pinch the wires and remove the sheathing with a wire-stripper, leaning close enough that I remembered his aftershave years later.

Using my little fingers and the same big tool, I copied his movements, both hands gripping the tool tighter on the wire. A small give in pressure let me know I'd broken the plastic. A wisp of hair fell into my eyes. I puffed it away with a breath and pulled the wire end. There.

"Look, Daddy, I did it!"

He inspected the connection and smiled. "Good job! That's my little engineer!"

I wondered if Dad knew now that I'd followed in his footsteps as an engineer at the company he'd retired from. There had been things about him I'd admired. I just wished I'd known the real man. Though I'd realized in college that I hadn't actually known my father, now the obvious flip side hit me. He had never known me.

As I'd grown older, I'd realized my later memories of him were transactional, never intimate. Our positive transactions were of helping each other with projects or making dinner. Even then, we'd never discussed our thoughts, fears, hopes, or dreams. The negative transactions consisted of his demands and violent tantrums. He'd called me every slur he'd known, but he'd known nothing of my truth.

He'd abandoned a stranger.

Immense relief filled my soul, as well as acute sadness.

Lisa changed the radio station. She had turned the headlights on, and I considered her shadowed face in the growing dusk. Dad had no clue who his oldest daughter was either. Like me, she had loved what couldn't love in return.

My father had never met Lisa's beautiful, blonde daughter. Ashley's mother was a far better parent than her grandfather. Though Lisa was a single mom struggling to make ends meet, she was fiercely protective and gentle with her daughter. There was much my father could have learned from Lisa.

But instead, even after Lisa had testified on Dad's behalf even though he'd stolen her childhood—he had channeled only thoughtless venom into her. His final strike had set her face in a deep scowl. She couldn't retaliate against a dead man. All that was left was to hurry back to Ashley. There would be no new home, no new start in life.

Lisa caught me staring. "What are you looking at?"

"Nothing. Just thinking." I shrugged.

We drove in silence as Dad's rejection lost its sting. Dad had missed everything precious about those two—and me.

To this day, I still have no idea what Madeline did with my things or my father's ashes; all I knew was that I returned home without his ghost. That was enough.

Chapter Thirty-Three
Spring 1998

I held my cards, twisting my wrists so my roommate Julie couldn't see. "Cheater," I mumbled.

Julie made a face. "I wasn't trying to see your cards, bar whore."

I laughed and winked at my euchre partner, "Camper," who was Julie's grandfather. We had her. If Julie had spades left, she wouldn't be so flustered.

She frowned and shrugged her shoulders at her father, Timmy. The four of us sat at Camper's kitchen table on his one hundred-acre farm in Yale, Michigan.

God had blessed me with more than friendship in Julie. She was my soul sister and filled the gaps Lisa couldn't.

Lisa and I had endured hell together, that unspoken trauma our common bond. There was nothing we wouldn't do to protect or help the other sister. We were fierce allies but not confidants. We hardly ever talked about the past.

If I ever tried to broach the topic, Lisa would sink into deep depression or anger. I respected Lisa's raw reluctance to open any dialogue about what had happened, but I needed to keep processing the layers of pain that occasionally surfaced.

Meeting Julie on the Traverse City camping trip had been serendipitous. Within weeks of the funeral, she had moved into my apartment. Julie peppered me with questions and listened to everything that had unfolded with Madeline. She understood why I cried about the glasses. Lisa didn't even know they existed.

Grateful only began to describe my feelings for my new friend. The more she listened with compassion, the more I spilled as one story after another came out. Until Julie, I'd never had a friend cry with me on Dad's birthday or bake a cake for Mom's. Ever since moving in, she had dragged me along to every family dinner or game night until the Tatoris family absorbed me also. I had family holidays, birthday parties, and card games back in my life.

Now I just needed to beat her.

Camper winked at me. I winked back. The two of us were as thick as thieves now, but several months earlier, Camper had doubted my Vegas-level card instincts. After Timmy and I decimated Camper and Julie three times in a row, had he staked his claim.

"Okay, from now on, I get the new girl," Camper had said.

That evening, we had already defeated Timmy and Julie once, and Julie was cornered and desperate.

I teased her, wanting to get under her skin. "Don't worry, Julie. Next time, I'll let you see my cards. It won't matter, though."

Julie pretended not to hear.

"I see Shelly has inherited the Tatorises' affinity for winning," Camper said to Julie.

"Wonder who I got that from?" I teased. I winked at Julie.

Camper laid down his card, a queen of spades. Trump. "Me, of course. Julie's a weak link."

I grinned as Julie choked on her Coke and Timmy patted her back while trying to hide a smile.

Camper and I took the game, winning four out of the five tricks.

Julie threw her cards down. "It's not fair. I found her first."

Their long-standing argument over which of them I belonged to warmed my heart.

Camper smiled and adjusted his suspenders. "You can have her back when I die. Now, where's the ice cream?"

Grandma Tatoris appeared in the kitchen doorway. "Ice cream? What about my blueberry pie?"

Camper winced. "I meant with my pie."

Julie, Timmy, and I burst into laughter. Grandma turned back into the kitchen with a scowl.

"Just because you girls didn't like my banana-mint cake. There's no accounting for taste in this family," she said and opened the freezer door.

Camper tapped his nose with his pointer finger, and we shushed, still grinning. Grandma's infamous baking was full of love and good intentions, just not always edible. When she got creative, we'd nominate a taste-tester to save the others from indigestion.

Grandma brought out four large slices of blueberry filling encased in thick, flour-mortared crust, ice cream on the side. Julie attacked her piece with a fork.

After watching Julie's unsuccessful attempts at dismantling the shell, Camper picked his entire piece up off his plate and bit down. His dentures smooshed the unbroken crusts together, sending blueberries cascading back out the sides and onto his plate. Camper made a face and dumped what remained of the filling over his ice cream, disregarding the crust entirely.

"How did you slice these?" Julie asked.

"Hmph." Grandma left the kitchen and went into her room to read.

Timmy, Julie, and I melted into quiet fits of laughter until we cried. Sharing inside jokes and knowing family idiosyncrasies had restored a feeling of belonging to my life.

Before we left that night, I helped Camper throw kindling into his basement heater. He preferred the temperature inside the small frame home to hover around eighty degrees to ward off the deep chill in his bones. He handed me a log, then bent over his walker to reach another. Small pieces of bark and sawdust clung to his plaid shirt.

"You know," I said, "modern furnaces don't get you so dirty."

Despite needing a walker, his wide shoulders tossed the split logs with ease. Camper's full head of hair was usually hidden beneath a baseball cap as he did chores every day, splitting wood or feeding the chickens. Though he'd retired from farming, he couldn't stop moving.

But that evening, I worried about his balance as he navigated the stairs with a walker. I wasn't sure *I* could do those narrow farm-cellar stairs with a walker, much less an eighty-six-year-old man. He tilted his head and chuckled.

"But then, Mother wouldn't have as much laundry to do. She might start baking more."

He mimed trying to eat the pie. I covered my mouth, laughing again.

Camper, of course, ignored my concern and never bought a new furnace. He was a stubborn farmer forged by years of battling Mother Nature and held what he considered to be The Right Opinion on everything.

Yet, he took me under his wing with surprising tenderness. Every farm visit included him inquiring about my life and career, offering me advice about people, and encouraging my patience in dating. He assured me that men were dumb and life was too short to cry over them. I adored that obstinate old coot.

Though the aching for my own family never left my heart, the Tatoris family's love made it endurable. With them, I belonged somewhere and to someone again. I wasn't without a family anymore.

Just forever single.

January 2, 2004

Timmy called Julie from Port Huron Hospital. Camper was fading fast.

"If you want to say goodbye, you girls should hurry."

I let Julie enter the intensive care room first. Camper's body made a frail outline under the sheet. At ninety-one, his staying power had diminished every day during his three-week battle with pneumonia. He was a thin shadow of himself seven years earlier, when I'd first met him.

The quiet room almost pulsed with sorrow, but instead of the sadness tearing the Tatoris family apart, everyone sat together. Timmy and his wife, Carol, sat by Camper's side. Julie's brother Justin occupied the seat next to them. Grandma Tatoris cried in a chair by the window, and Julie went to her. Julie's sisters, Jessi and Jodi, arrived shortly after us, and we all sat with Grandma and Camper, waiting for his release from pain.

A nurse came to check Camper's vitals. She smoothed the sheets and nodded to Timmy. "It won't be much longer. Let me know if you need anything."

Timmy swallowed. He moved closer to his father and took his hand. The goodbyes began. I hung back in the raw moment. I had never told someone I loved goodbye. After two decades of mourning, I had no idea what to say. I watched as my Tatoris family showed me that even if goodbye was not what we'd planned, there were still good ways to say it.

As I listened to the others' messages of love and appreciation, of shared memories to hold close, a sweet peace filled the room unlike the shock, guilt, and anguished pleas I'd experienced with my parents' deaths. I'd never imagined death and loss as a way to bind a family tighter in love, but the Tatoris family proved it was possible. They poured out their love over their patriarch as he passed in and out of consciousness, the death rattle filling his chest.

For several hours, I was torn between crying out to God for a miraculous healing and the feeling that my time to express what the old farmer had meant to me was fast disappearing. I eventually realized that my suffering paled in comparison to his and that I needed to let him go rather than pray he'd stay.

Last of all, I moved to his side, still lost for words. Many men had thought little of me, but this old farmer had nourished my famished soul until I had secretly believed I was his favorite grandchild. He'd made me his own while under no obligation to. He'd gained nothing from it except my undying love in return. With that thought, I understood that was what I needed to tell him.

I took Camper's hand. He looked up at me with tired eyes. His hand trembled in mine, his body straining to breathe. Oxygen tubes and IVs wound about his shoulders.

I leaned near his face and kissed his cheek. He closed his eyes.

"You'll never know how much it meant that you picked me to be your euchre partner, stupid as it sounds. And how you loved me as much as your real granddaughters," I began.

I put my forehead against his. The soft connection seemed right. His feverish skin glistened with sweat.

"I love you, Camper. You did good, better than many men. You gave your whole stubborn heart to God. You can leave us. We'll be all right. I will miss you, though, and I'll miss beating everyone too." I gasped, half laughing.

He squeezed my hand. My tears fell on his cheek. I swallowed and shifted my face closer to his ear. I whispered one last request for my grandfather. "When you see my mom, will you give her a hug from me?"

Camper squeezed my hand one last time.

I kissed his cheek. "Thank you for everything."

Camper released a soft sigh, taking my goodbyes with him.

Timmy hugged his mother, who gazed down on the body of her husband of sixty-seven years. Solemn peace filled the room.

The Spirit whispered to my heart, and I wept, knowing he wasn't alone in his new home.

The next week, Timmy sent me Camper's obituary. The clipping, published in the *Yale Expositor*, detailed Albert "Camper" Tatoris's life and his love of card games and family. When I reached the list of surviving family, I was shocked to read:

"He is survived by his wife, Alfreda, and two sons: Timothy (Carol) Tatoris with five grand-daughters [*sic*] and one grandson, Jayme Stratton, Julie Tatoris, Jodi (Mark) Atkinson, Jessi Tatoris, Shelly Edwards and Justin Tatoris."

My heart leapt at the unexpected inclusion of my name. Though proof that I'd lost a grandfather, it was also official confirmation that God had given me a family again. It was Camper's last gift to me.

2006

Three hours into our session, Kathie held my arm while I repeated, "I am okay even though Dad killed Mom and burned down our house."

"Some resistance," Kathie said softly. I opened my eyes.

She checked her watch and hugged me. "Still, great work for today. Are you all right?"

I nodded wordlessly. Well into my thirties, I hadn't progressed to "I am safe" yet, but "I am okay" was the right direction. With a new kind of trauma therapy, during the past six months, Kathie had helped me begin to grasp how unlovable and unsafe I'd felt since childhood.

I had coped for decades by telling myself how I *should* feel: I should feel grateful and happy for surviving my teens. I should feel happy to have found new hope in Christ. I should feel grateful to have another family to love me.

The effort Kathie asked of me felt like the equivalent of suicide drills, just emotional. We hammered at the barriers built around my trauma with relentless focus. An exhausted peace remained with me the next few days.

I'd quit cognitive therapy in my late twenties, feeling there was nothing more to be gained from endless talking. There would just always be a shadow in my life. I just needed to endure to the end with faith.

But endurance and time hadn't vanquished the darkness. Instead, clinical depression and PTSD combined and grew to threaten my life again in my early thirties despite having what I considered a fantastic life—no one was abusing me, I owned a house, my career thrived, and I had an adoptive family by way of Julie.

I couldn't figure out what my problem was and tried my best to ignore the festering pain. I had endlessly rehearsed my history to multiple therapists. I had no more secrets. I had learned to create intimacy with people, sharing my past when appropriate. I had friends and family. I just hated being me. I was exhausted all the time. After a sixty-hour work week, all I wanted was sleep or TV. I gained weight and hated myself even more for being so weak-willed.

In desperation, I complained to Jessi, who recommended a trauma therapist she'd used named Kathie Schofield. In our first meeting, Kathie had explained why the cognitive behavioral therapy I'd done to change my thinking often proved ineffective for trauma. Over thirty years, I'd shoved my pain into my neurological system to continue surviving, and it all remained unprocessed and stuck. My frontal cortex, or thinking brain, possessed little overlap with my primal survival network—also called the nervous system. She demonstrated with uncanny detail how I'd stored memories this way.

In our neuro-emotional technique (NET) sessions, Kathie had me repeat statements such as "I am loveable" and then measured my physical biometrics and their fluctuations (or responses) at acupressure points. For each statement I recited, Kathie discerned an emotion and an age by pressing on these acupressure points. Each time she relayed one of these combinations to me, specific memories came flooding to my mind that matched her description exactly. It was uncanny.

She might have guessed I felt resentment at age seventeen, but she nailed anger at three and terror at fifteen. She did this without knowing my background at our first appointment. She simply explained the process and demonstrated again and again. No combination she uttered failed to bring a valid and vivid memory, even if long repressed. Though shaken by her accuracy, I was an instant believer.

The only way my frontal lobe could interact with these events was to relive them. Once I processed and reframed them from my more mature perspective as grown woman, they could fade to normal memories. Only then would the repressed events lose their power to drain my body with a child's gripping fear or a teen's betrayal and trauma.

Sometimes I described the memories; sometimes I couldn't. Now and again, when Kathie accessed a memory, an emotional wall would appear around my mind, blocking the release of details. When this occurred, I couldn't describe the incident, only the that a wall of horror or shame or fear had risen up.

Kathie explained that my body regarded these memories as top secret on its trauma scale and so had extra protections in place. At first, I couldn't imagine what might have been worse than what I already remembered, but I understood better when I broke through one of the walls a year later. I had been just four and five years old when I'd been abused by a young man at a local campground several summers in a row. Mexico hadn't been the first time I'd been forced to do horrible things. I cried for a long time about that discovery.

It made sense then why my entire body ached and why I struggled to get out of bed. Suppressing those memories had required increasing amounts of daily energy as the hidden trauma festered. Over time, toxic emotional storage had polluted my entire body.

Cleansing my emotional health through these sessions, combined with other trauma therapies such as EMDR (eye movement desensitization and reprocessing), was the hardest work I had ever done. Kathie and I prayed individually for God's guidance before each meeting. I needed His strength and the courage to face the mountain of abandonment and neglect, the painful silencing of my truth, and the diminishing of my worth.

Rescuing myself required that I dive beneath words into the dark recesses of memory. There, I found my younger self inert and paralyzed, drowning in terrifying moments. I remembered what it was like as a three-year-old to watch my father strangle my mother and wonder if I was next. I held that tiny version of me and cried with her. I let her know she would be okay, that Mom would be okay. I affirmed that she was safe now. I released her with the memory and its emotions. She faded into the background, still part of me but no longer poisoning me with fear.

In those moments, I came to understand God's grace as never before. I discovered I wasn't alone reliving my trauma and that neither had my younger self been abandoned in those extremities. I could sense God's sorrow for what had happened even if she hadn't been able to.

Christ's grace infused His light into each uncovered scene, helping me stay oriented and clear amidst the screaming voices and currents of misery that filled each episode. Through His power, I could walk whole out of each memory, comforted in His love. It hurt, but I came through each one safe.

If I began to sink into the memory as if present and lost myself, Kathie pulled me out with a gentle touch. She reassured me that I was there in her office and unharmed. We would pray for His peace to restore my mind and heart. It did.

Over time, my fragmented past combined to reveal a woman of strength. The pieces I had hidden, had refused to remember, became testaments of my resilience. I discovered a cementing compassion for myself instead of shame. I had been abused, silenced, and thrown away. As a result, I had believed myself worthless. When I ignored the demeaning chorus of memories and focused on one event at a time, I uncovered a precious little girl.

For once, therapy was really working. I could sleep, my body lost its aches over time, and I slowly stopped hating myself. I continued recovering small pieces of myself and shedding my insecurities. Miraculous as my therapy seemed, there were so, so many memories. After more than two years of rigorous twice-weekly visits, I wondered if it would ever end.

I asked God how long it would take to heal, concerned whether the shards of misery would ever be completely gone.

I will be beside you no matter how long it takes.

His answer was enough. Over and over, we walked into my past together.

May 2007

When Julie's Mr. Right appeared first, I struggled with despair. I was genuinely happy for her, but even at her wedding, I couldn't help but be convinced I would never find anyone to love me. Watching her drive away after the reception left a huge hole in my heart.

For weeks afterward, I holed up alone with my dogs, Puddles and Bella. Though we'd adopted them together, Julie and I had agreed that whoever got married first would lose custody of our Labrador sisters. The dogs kept waiting for Julie to come home, and I cried when they ran to the door when a car came down the street, tails wagging in expectant relief. It felt as if I'd lost another family.

Julie posted pictures of their honeymoon and new apartment on social media accounts. They looked so happy and perfect, and I admit I wallowed in self-pity. I tried to hide my envy when she called, and I asked for all the details. I was miserable and lonelier than I'd been in years.

I called one evening three months after their wedding. When Julie answered, I could tell she'd been crying. "What's wrong, Jules?"

"He hasn't talked to me for a week," Julie said. "I came home from work yesterday, and he wouldn't let me touch him. He just watches movies all night when I'm home."

Her confession threw me. How could they be at such odds? They'd appeared to be so in love! I listened to Julie as my self-pity melted into regret. Of all people, I should have known better. Appearances mean so little when it comes to happiness.

"He quit his job because he hated his boss. But then he was depressed stuck at home, so I bought him a brand-new car," she explained. "But he wasn't satisfied with a used one, so he got a brand-new one—but he traded mine in for thousands less than I owe. Everything is a mess."

I listened in stunned silence and felt sick to my stomach for being so wrapped up in jealousy, thinking she had everything I wanted when it was obvious she didn't. I knew that Julie, like my mother, would do anything to make her marriage work, which worried me.

I wanted to demand she leave him right then but wondered if that was selfish. My fears paralyzed me. I wanted to say what I should have to my mother. But if I did encourage Julie to leave, Julie might feel hurt and withdraw. Maybe she could work it all out with her husband. I didn't know what to say, so I just listened.

I hung up the phone and cried, feeling I'd failed Julie. I never said the right thing when it mattered most. I sank into depression again, worried that my family tragedy might repeat itself.

New depression stalked me, and I waited for the sky to fall again.

Leaving a grueling session at Kathie's office, my mind turned to Julie's difficulties. We'd talked again, and despite my hopes, things weren't getting better. I felt powerless with Julie far away and hurting. Lost in dark thoughts, I opened my front door and was completely unprepared for the scene that greeted me.

Spring had arrived.

After a long gray winter, bright light filled the sky. A gentle breeze carried the loamy scent of a frozen mantle warming beneath the sun's vigor. I released the door handle, and the door closed behind me with a swish. I gawked in wonder. Under blue skies, tree buds burst bright green and yellow. Singing sparrows dashed between branches, showing off. Pointed tulip stalks stretched through their blanket of dark mulch, abuzz with newly hatched flies.

Life surged with anticipation, and invisible awakened energy revolved around me. Like a bass note so loud it sets your own chest humming, Nature's joy reverberated in my heart. It was a forgotten feeling. The shocking contrast between this pleasure of existence and the dreary, miserable lens through which I regarded my life roused my soul.

Into that wonderful space of reawakening, a thought came. Nature trusted in rebirth. God held the boundaries of every season. Winter would never last forever. I turned my face to the sun and closed my eyes, smiling in the new warmth.

I was filled with a new conviction that brighter days lay ahead. The road would turn. In a moment of clarity, the Son's energy brought hope to my heart again. Julie wouldn't be lost to me. She was different from my mother. She wasn't choosing to hide her pain as my mother had. She had me and the entire Tatoris family.

Joy flowed like sunshine. The encouraging thoughts followed me to my car. There would always be seasons of pain and loss. God could carry me forward into spring and renewal as long as I released my doubts and trusted Him. My life had already improved with His help, and Julie's crisis was in those same capable hands. I had to trust Him to see her through it.

Sitting in the car, I gave it all to Christ: my fear of losing Julie, my terror of being alone forever, and my anxiety of never-ending memories. Then I rolled my windows down to hear the birds and smell the promise. Warm wind dried the tears on my cheeks.

Life waited to burst forth into so much more—if I could trust Him and hold on to hope.

Julie divorced her emotionally abusive husband and moved back in with me that summer. We had learned to trust God through different means, but our faith was centered in the same truth.

With God, there was hope for better things.

Chapter Thirty-Four

March 2010

When I was thirty-nine years, eleven months, and fifteen days old, I discovered—after years of believing the contrary—that spinsters could feel giddy with infatuation.

That was unexpected.

I was smitten with Glenn Jorgensen the moment he walked into my friends' home. My friends, Tiffany and Albert Allred, had arranged a blind dinner date. I had spent ten years learning to accept being single, and this last-minute Hail Mary pass wasn't in my game plan.

My doubts about feasible relationships at forty had caused me to consider declining Tiffany's dinner invitation, but Julie had forbidden me.

"Go. You never know what God has planned," Julie had said. "Besides, you need to find out if he has any cute single friends."

Like with Sabrina, Molly, and Julie, Tiffany and I were fast friends from the day we met. I should have known that her up-for-anything personality, tendency to go all-out on any idea, and fondness for schemes would make it all but impossible for her to stay out of my love life. Her enthusiasm to resolve my singleness was hard to refuse, even though the only thing Tiffany's friend and I seemed to have in common was our relationship status.

Singleness almost always seems a good reason for friends to set friends up but not a particularly good reason to think it'll work out

Besides being unmarried, her mystery man had lived in Japan decades before and loved seafood. I hated fish. Tiffany and her husband, Albert, had been ex-pats in Tokyo several years earlier, so it seemed the three of them had much in common. Before I'd arrived, I'd wondered how a slightly overweight single woman who'd never been to Japan and couldn't use chopsticks to save her life would fit in that evening.

When I reluctantly knocked on Tiffany's door, harboring only the teensiest bit of hope, Tiffany assured me that chopsticks were optional, and, even better, she'd made a Japanese fish soup in honor of my date. My hope was dashed.

There was no greater shock in my life than the moment Glenn walked into Tiffany's kitchen. I had to admit that maybe Tiffany was on to something. The tall, bespectacled man with sandy hair looked like a cute college professor. The geek in me was smitten.

Moreover, over dinner I discovered that Glenn and I had connections of our own. He also worked as an engineer at Ford, and his office was across the street from mine. Despite our proximity, we had never met. I was sure of that because his face was unforgettable. The handsome divorced father of four made my heart feel young again. I enjoyed his company so much I forgot that Tiffany's soup had fish in it and ate an entire bowl.

The best part? Glenn needed help remodeling his house. And I was a girl who knew how to use a hammer.

In fact, I owned two. Perfect.

April 2010

I dug a fork into my takeout box of almond chicken. Glenn shoveled noodles in with chopsticks. *Show-off,* I thought. I had spent three weeks helping gut his home after our blind date. We had hacked and hammered and hauled junk.

Famished after a long evening battling particularly stubborn green-and-white diamond ceramic tile, I had half emptied my carton before I stopped to take a drink. Glenn leaned against the kitchen cabinets, wearing torn jeans and a paint-splattered Ford engineering tee. Tile dust coated his wavy brown hair.

He gestured with his wooden sticks at the half-busted-out kitchen floor. "Let's finish this tomorrow."

My breath caught at the idea of finishing. I swallowed and nodded, smiling to cover my disappointment. I had enjoyed every moment, but it wasn't until that one that I realized I was falling hard for this man, dust, bad tile, and all.

I nodded absently at Glenn's suggestion that we try cutting smaller sections the next day and finished chewing while I thought.

It was a sobering, once-in-a-decade realization for me. Falling in love meant exposing my heart to possibilities.

Remodeling had just gotten complicated.

I returned home smelling like a lumberjack dipped in soy sauce. Lisa, who was staying with me temporarily, rounded a corner and shrank back.

"Did you go out dressed like that?" She gestured from my feet to my head with one hand, the other on her hip.

I appraised my baggy shirt over stained jeans and worn tennis shoes. I shrugged. "Yeah."

"To that guy's house?"

I nodded.

"What will he think?" Her eyes widened with shock. I saw in them her fear that I'd ruin my chances with such slouchy clothes. But Glenn had worn the same kind of castoffs, and I'd found him no less attractive. Besides, he hadn't given my outfit a second glance.

I didn't explain all that. I simply waved her protests away. "He's just a friend. He doesn't care what I wear."

Lisa raised her eyebrows and walked away. "Whatever."

It was hardest to persuade Julie that nothing was going on, for she knew me better than anyone. She noted my increasing absences despite my effort to be discreet.

One night, I came home especially late after another week of evenings remodeling Glenn's house. Though we'd finished removing the tile, Glenn had suggested that further help would be appreciated, and I had happily volunteered. That meant Julie had spent a lot of time alone that we'd previously filled doing things together.

Whether I'd kept Glenn separate from her because of my fears that any relationship would go awry at some point, or whether I wanted to safeguard my incredulous hope that things might develop into something significant like marriage, or both, regardless, I'd left Julie in the dark.

As I entered the house, Julie called out from her bedroom. The lonely tone in her voice made me feel guilty. She sat against the headboard, playing euchre on her phone. She looked up when I came in. She surveyed my splattered tee and pointed to my face.

"Painting?" she asked.

I turned to look in her dresser mirror and spied Benjamin Moore's Caliente Red smeared across my chin. I nodded, rubbing at it with a shirt sleeve.

"Is this Glenn guy even real, or did you made him up to go the movies without me?" Her words of rebuff were gentle, for which I was grateful.

I laughed. "And how am I getting this mess all over me?"

"The movie theater needed remodeling?" Julie fake guessed. I sat beside her.

"I promise to introduce you—soon."

Two Weeks Later

I finished grouting the last floor tiles on my knees and wiped the excess grout off with a wet sponge. Rising to my feet, I sighed. "All done."

I rested against the bar between the kitchen and sunken family room while Glenn rinsed off the tools and went to the garage to put them away.

He returned, and we stood in the family room, admiring our work. His home had made a huge leap into the twenty-first century. All that remained was sealing the floor.

We'd avoided the subject of us for weeks. The evenings and weekends spent renovating were clearly more than just a productive project. Now that the house was nearly done, someone had to breach the subject.

I made a weak attempt.

"You have to come over and meet Julie. She thinks you are a figment of my imagination."

"Hmmm. She does?" He leaned over the bar, daring me to respond. My heart pounded as I shifted to face him. I tilted my chin up, toward his, inches away. He paused before making a definitive statement with his lips. He tasted of mint gum and smelled of Polo cologne

"I think that proves I'm real." Glenn broke into a lopsided grin.

My cheeks warmed.

"I have been wanting to do that for a while, but I'm out of practice." He rubbed the back of his neck with his hand and flushed also.

I couldn't help myself. "Not bad. But you can try again if you think you can do better."

He proved to be quite adept.

I played John Michael Montgomery on my way home. I started humming, then sang along. Forty years old and it was as if Glenn's kisses were my first. A laugh bubbled up. I'd fantasized about romance for years, dreaming of love and intimacy.

Amid the bloom of excitement, an icy feeling in my gut reminded me I had to keep my feet on the ground.

I had told Glenn that my mom had died in a tragic house fire and my dad had been taken by cancer. I had left so much unexplained. My brows drew together for a moment before I decided that I would figure it out as I went. I turned the volume up and basked in the euphoria.

June 2010

The northern summer sun stayed up especially late in early summer, and the pink hues outside were gorgeous. Fans set in windows blew the cool night air into Glenn's family room where we sat with the lights off, the smell of new paint dissipating. Leaving Glenn here every night had grown harder.

I had made a pact with myself to share my past but then procrastinated for weeks. As the darkness settled around us, I relaxed. Glenn stroked my arm. "Tell me something. What is your favorite memory of your father? What was he like?"

It was Father's Day that weekend, and the question was natural, though Glenn had no idea how uncomfortable it made me. I saw his innocent inquiry as an opportunity to take a leap of faith.

My childhood story slowly started unraveling. I detailed my father's abuse and the aftermath of losing my mother at his hands. Explaining didn't provoke the kind of pain it had in the past, but I watched Glenn's eyes and searched for cues that he had heard enough.

"He would choke her, then make breakfast the next morning like nothing had happened . . ."

"He made me go to the burned-out shell of our house so many times . . ."

". . . Testifying for the prosecution terrified me."

Tears filled Glenn's eyes. He gently took my hand and placed it in his. He listened quietly as I went on, stroking my hand. Deep concern and compassion colored his silence.

"Perched above that reservoir, I couldn't make myself take the plunge even though I wanted to die . . ."

He wiped his eyes.

"Diane and Madeline took everything . . ."

"Lisa told me afterward that he had threatened to find her and kill her when he got out . . ."

Glenn shook his head in amazement over and over.

"I graduated and moved back to Michigan to be near what family I had left. I bought a house, met Julie, and got two puppies. And here we are." I concluded in the now-dark room.

Glenn shifted. "Come here." He pulled me close, our faces inches apart.

"I am so sorry." He stopped, pausing as pain filled his eyes. The tension in his body indicated there was more. He took a trembling breath. "The truth is, I can relate. My dad abused us, terrorized us. I swore to myself that I would never be him."

He looked down at our clasped hands. "I hate being apart from my kids. I worry that I failed them somehow, but I can honestly say I have never hit them. Never screamed like my dad. We aren't perfect, but we aren't them."

I nodded and bit my lip. My father's abuse and the fire were the easier chapters of my story to share. Glenn had reacted with compassion and perfect love, but I couldn't bring myself to reveal it all at once.

I kept praying for courage to tell the rest, waiting for a good time. You just don't casually mention being sexually assaulted, nor do you blithely explain how you've seen angels or heard dead people speak. My past had been so complicated; I hoped that after hearing it all, Glenn would still want to be part of my future.

The next weekend, Glenn and I drove to Julie's cabin for his first Tatoris family getaway. Asking him to come was akin to meeting my real parents for the first time. Things were getting serious, and pressure to clear the air was building inside me.

Finally, I blurted out, "I know I have already told you about my family, but there is something else you need to know about me."

I knew once I said these words, I couldn't recall them. I started to shake a little, and my nerve floundered momentarily. I struggled to banish the shame threatening my composure and reminded myself I'd done nothing wrong. Feeling a little panicked, I tried to breathe normally. I needed him to know this about me. I needed the wall of fear guarding my heart gone.

"Okay," Glenn said, placing his hand on my knee. He drove in silence. I sighed, relieved he couldn't do more than glance at my face, which was certainly red.

"When I was a child, I was molested by two men. Once when I was very young, and later at eleven years old. Both were family acquaintances. The abuse in my own family had taught me to hide things, so I hid my abuse as well," I began.

Glenn nodded.

"The summer before my mother's death, we went to Europe, and I was raped outside a pub. Again, I didn't tell anyone about it. I was too ashamed."

I was grateful for Glenn's silence and pressed on.

"Six months after the fire, the same man who'd molested me at eleven raped me in Mexico." Glenn made a noise of surprise but let me continue.

"I kept all of it a secret until I felt I should tell my bishop years later. He said it wasn't my fault, so I tried to forget about it, until I couldn't. I did some incredible counseling a few years ago that helped me process it all." I explained some of what I'd learned about myself.

The personal devastation and the scars were healing but still sensitive to touch. I cried a bit but never completely lost it. When I finished, Glenn remained quiet. I felt my heart thumping against my chest. He glanced at me with compassion and looked back at the road.

"What can I say but that I am so sorry?" He grabbed my hand. "I don't want to probe, but you can talk about whatever you need to talk about. I'll be okay with whatever it is."

I relaxed into the seat. He brought my hand to his lips. "I mean it. I love listening to you," he said.

Over time, I added details. I explained how, initially, I couldn't understand why I had agreed to play cards with Tony again after knowing he was dangerous. I had scolded myself for being duped twice by the same man. In therapy, I had learned my self-destructive response was typical. The concept of repetition trauma blew Glenn's mind.

I explained what it meant over dinner one night. "Being a victim of sexual assault causes a drive in the psyche to overcome that trauma. You do this by recreating scenarios, reenacting what happened the first time, with the intent to regain the power that was taken away."

I continued. "Like a broken record, the brain obsesses—playing it over and over until some sort of resolution occurs. Victims get drawn into relationships and situations where they can 'try again' but this time change the outcome from powerless to powerful. It doesn't usually work out so well," I finished with a wry smile. That was an understatement.

Glenn had never gone to therapy for his own abuse and listened for hours to the insights and healing I shared. Our discussions sometimes made Glenn angry at the people who'd hurt me, which surprised me at first. I battled self-hatred, not shadows of men. Glenn, as my knight in shining armor, wanted to protect me.

"Can you go after Tony?" he wondered. "The internet . . . we could find him."

The idea made me cringe. "Twenty years ago, I might have been tempted to look him up, to accuse him, to make him pay."

I sighed. "But now, I don't think it would help me. Not really. Therapy, time, and God's grace are what I needed . . . and still need. Not everyone in my situation may feel the same or make the same choices. But that's my conclusion after all my hard work, prayer, and thought."

Glenn didn't argue, but he didn't look fully convinced.

"Besides, think about it, Glenn. My father is dead. The guy in England, I have no idea what his name was or his age. I don't know if I would recognize him anyways. And Tony is probably in his nineties if he is alive. God will take care of him soon enough. I actually feel sorry for these men."

Glenn shook his head. "Your forgiveness is amazing."

"But it's not mine," I reminded him. "It's Christ's forgiveness, which He lends me strength to use."

Glenn laughed. "How do I get you to take credit for being extraordinary?"

I considered his face, full of frank, open admiration. If there was a time to mention seeing my deceased mother, now was it.

"Let me tell you about my conversion from Catholicism." I took a deep breath. "It's not a typical story either, and only Julie and her family have heard the entire version."

294

Glenn nodded, and I wondered how much more this man could digest. He amazed me.

October 12, 2010

We sat on a bench atop a grassy hill overlooking the lake at Stoney Creek Metro Park. Gusts of wind tugged yellow and orange leaves from their precarious holds. A glorious afternoon sun filled the crisp autumn sky with bright sunshine that warmed our hair and cheeks. A flock of geese honked as they flew overhead before gliding into the water's shallow edge. We finished our sandwiches and chips, throwing crumbs to a gander that ventured close. Our conversation lapsed. I lay my head on Glenn's shoulder, and he put his arm around my shoulders.

With the twenty-fifth anniversary of my mother's death two days away, she was on my mind. Mom would have liked Glenn. He had accepted without question my account of her loving guidance after the fire. I had never met another man quite like him. I did not doubt he had been brought to me at just the right time.

"Shelly, you are incredible. I can't believe how much I love you," he said.

I smiled. I had waited so long for those sentiments, and now I had the ability to love freely in return. "I love you too."

Glenn slid off the bench and dropped one knee to the ground. My eyes widened. My heart thumped with anticipation as he fumbled in his pocket.

Glenn opened his hand to reveal a navy velvet box with a princess diamond solitaire sparkling inside. "Shelly, I am in awe of the woman you are . . . and the miracle of our meeting. I can't help but feel we were always meant to be. I want to be with you forever. Will you marry me?" He lifted the ring toward me.

Grinning, I hugged him. "Yes, of course!"

Glenn stood and slipped the gorgeous diamond on my ring finger. I held my left hand out, admiring the sight, and laughed in astonishment. Me, engaged! Going on my toes, I kissed my love. Then I began to cry. My prayers had been answered at long last. I would have my own family. *Excited* merely started to describe what was in my soul. *Joyful. Found. Healed. Redeemed. Hope everlasting.*

Overwhelming gratitude for God's loving gifts sang within my heart. Embracing Glenn on that hilltop, I looked back on my valley of sorrow with a new appreciation for the long journey. At this summit of happiness, the sunlight having driven the shadows underground, the panorama of my life inspired me. God had helped me surmount every threatening trial, kept my feet from slipping off stony paths, and saved me from falling into bottomless pits of shadow and self-annihilation. I had made it to my happily ever after no matter what came next.

Chapter Thirty-Five

Christmas Eve, December 2010

My soon-to-be family had gathered for the first time. Glenn's oldest child, Brian, who worked as a microbiologist in Utah, read a short Christmas story. He most resembled his father, studious and handsome. Jenna, his third child and oldest girl, sat listening beside Brian. She had completed her first semester studying photography at my alma matter, BYU. She ran her fingers, adorned with beautiful handmade rings, through her long blonde hair. She possessed a polished sense of style that reminded me of my mother.

On the opposite couch, Jeffrey, older than Jenna, placed his chin in his hands, elbows on his knees. We'd met at his naval graduation the summer before. Tall like his brother but restless with energy, he reminded me of my younger self. I smiled, and Jeff flashed me one in return. Next to him sat Alyssa, the youngest. Still in middle school, she split her time between Glenn and her mother. I had met Alyssa first, attending her dance recitals and getting to know her on Glenn's custodial weekends.

I marveled at the kids' varied personalities and talents. These four children, ready-made to love, filled me with gratitude.

Brian finished reading. A sudden nervous pang struck me. Though I had not planned on unloading my heavy history on these kids so soon, Glenn had asked me to share my background while they were all together at Christmas. I'd fretted for a week. Now my moment had come.

I looked at Glenn.

Glenn cleared his throat. "I want you all to hear Shelly's story. I hope you will appreciate what I see in her." He nodded at me.

I took a shaky breath, then began to summarize my early life. The attentive young adults didn't interrupt. Some of their faces registered shock; others became thoughtful. I related how I'd met their father and expressed my gratitude for his compassion and love. They all nodded, knowing the kind of man he was.

"So, that's me." I shrugged self-consciously. What these four children thought mattered very much to me.

I'd abandoned any hope of being a mother several years earlier, and now the opportunity to be a stepmother to four strangers was both terrifying and awe-inspiring. I worried what they thought of my story. I continued past the awkwardness, hoping what I shared next would resonate with them.

I wanted to offer them what my mother had given me: hope for the dark times.

"My life is proof that no matter what happens, no matter how bad things get, it is okay! Not only okay, but exactly as it should be, even if your trials aren't what you would have picked." I gave them a warm smile. "After all, we do not know what is best, but God does. We must trust Him, let go of our fear, and know He will make it okay in the end."

I looked at Glenn. He gave me an encouraging smile. I leaned forward, looking at each face. I already loved these children.

"Difficulties aren't a curse—they are blessings to lead you to God. Everything good in my life has come from finding God in my trials. It was through those times that I learned who He was and what His help could do."

Tears came to my eyes. "So, when it gets hard, remember what my mother said. 'You are loved. Everything will be okay.'"

I rubbed my hands together, suddenly nervous. Had I sounded like an idiot? "That's it, I guess."

Glenn pulled me into a hug, and all the kids piled on the love seat with us. We cried and laughed all at once. I couldn't imagine better gifts than those five people.

It was a perfect first Christmas.

Valentine's Day, February 2011

Glenn told me to be at his house at six sharp, but as I pulled up right on time, the dark house windows made it look unoccupied. The only lights on were the porch lights. I furrowed my brow and turned off the car engine. Further inspection revealed a note taped to the front door and fluttering in the wind.

"Come in and meet me in the basement."

Standing on the windy porch, I looked down at my sweater and skirt and wondered if I was overdressed. We had just finished remodeling the basement, venturing to do the plumbing ourselves. That may have been a mistake. I envisioned us in waders hauling soggy drywall. I rolled my eyes and sighed, guessing that I might be in for a long night. When had life ever gone as I'd planned?

I retrieved my small gift bag of cologne and chocolate for Glenn from the car before opening the unlocked house door. A puff of warm air enveloped me as I stepped into Glenn's dark living room. A candle burned on the coffee table. In its flickering light, a single red rose lay on an envelope. "Open First" had been scrawled on the front. Surprised, I opened the card.

I love you a thousand ways, but tonight I will only share the first dozen. You may or may not know this, but I am head over heels in love with a beautiful woman who rescued my soul. When you came into my life, I had given up on finding love. My divorce shattered me, and

I thought nothing would ever be right again. Then, there you were. The first thing I fell in love with was your way of seeing to the heart of the problem. Whether it was tearing out tile or healing me. You have a gift for fixing things.

Another candle, rose, and note waited on the piano. I spied yet another glowing arrangement in the hallway and found there was a trail of candles leading through the house. Each had a beautiful rose and note to read by candlelight.

Glenn's thoughtful gestures and the time he'd taken to express his love gave my heart an unaccustomed sense of being cherished above all others. I had never read with such relish, almost running from one note to the next until I held a dozen roses and cards.

Music played in the basement. My heart and hands full, I descended the stairs. At the bottom, Glenn met me with another bouquet of perfect roses. He kissed me.

"You scared me," I spluttered. "I thought the basement had flooded or something."

"What? Why?" Glenn kissed my forehead.

"Well, the house was dark—" I left off, finally noticing a table laid out in crystal and china behind him. The smell of steak and potatoes hit me.

"Wow, you did all this for me?" I touched the hot, homemade rolls. "This is gorgeous! Thank you, Glenn."

I'd never had anyone do something so lovely for me in my life.

I handed him my gift bag and began to cry.

Chapter Thirty-Six

June 11, 2011

I admired my dress in the gilded three-way mirror. The beaded gown hugged all the right places and flowed to the floor. I was alone with Julie, who buttoned my train while everyone took their places for the ceremony. A shiver of anticipation went from head to toe.

Julie laughed. "Nervous?"

"No, excited."

Family and friends had flown in from all over the country. The night before, everyone had gathered at my house to meet Glenn and the kids. All the different chapters of my life had merged, creating an almost out-of-body experience for me.

I introduced Melissa to Glenn while Sabrina whispered teasing comments in my ear about wedding nights. Molly and I recalled the awkward hospital incident involving her mom while my aunt stood across the room talking with Jenna. Molly, Sabrina, and I gave Melissa a hard time about her teenage crush on Steele. I laughed until my side hurt. Sabrina exclaimed over teenage Ashley, then showed Lisa pictures of Sabrina's own kids. They commiserated about teenager drama. Meanwhile, Glenn's boys refilled their plates, and Julie manned the grill. My life had come full circle.

In His grace, God had sent these people to love me and hold me up when I couldn't stand on my own. Their love, Glenn's love, was more than I imagined deserving. I still was learning to accept it.

Now, moments before my marriage, Julie checked my hair for loose pins. The white dress had intricate crystal beadwork on the bodice, and Julie had adjusted the long train so that it fell flat in symmetric folds.

I looked in the mirror one last time before leaving my decades of loneliness behind forever. An older bride than I had once anticipated met my eyes. Deepening crow's feet framed her eyes, and a heaviness settled around her hips. I was no longer young, thin, and strong. Life had changed me. And yet, how could I be upset? Love had found me.

Julie met my eyes in the mirror. "Shelly, you are stunning!"

I gave her a tight squeeze. "Love you, Jules." I remembered how I'd felt at her wedding five years earlier and knew that this would be a bittersweet day for her. I appreciated her support more than she could know.

She sniffed. "Let's go before I ruin your dress!"

We walked arm in arm to where Glenn waited. Crystal chandeliers reflected endlessly in the mirrors lining the walls. But more stunning than the elegant chapel was the array of faces filling the creamy velvet chairs. Molly, Sabrina, and Melissa smiled at me, Molly giving me a thumbs up from their spot together in the middle. My Tatoris family beamed at me.

Julie took a seat up front by Tiffany, whose meddling ways had led to all this. Tiffany turned to give me an appraising look, then smirked at Glenn and cocked an eyebrow. It was lost on my fiancé, who only gawked at my appearance. I laughed to myself, remembering her husband Albert's whisper after church the previous Sunday.

"Thanks to you two," he'd said in a low tone, "I'll have to endure her bragging and endless match-making from now on. She thinks it's her calling in life!"

As always, these friends had arrived at exactly the right moments. I had been truly blessed and surrounded by angels.

After the short ceremony, Glenn and I kissed for the first time as husband and wife.

Hearing us introduced to our friends and family that way thrilled me, for I had come so far and battled so long for that moment. For the first time in decades, I had a family of my own again.

I thought of my mother and her mother, who had passed eighteen years earlier, believing they were there to witness my marriage also. I had grown to think of the two of them as often present, just over my shoulder and out of view. If that was the case, then certainly God would allow them a peek at the happy culmination of their efforts to love and keep me safe.

I wanted them to see I was okay and that Glenn loved me as much as Grandpa had loved Grandma Sarah. I wanted them to know I was safe at last.

Late 1970s to Early 1982–About Age 8 to 12

Grandma Findlay walked a fine line. She knew things weren't right in our home but refrained from becoming involved. As an adult, I can only guess she feared that either my mother would cut her off or that her interference would make things worse for us all.

Instead, Grandma invited me to tea parties.

On the appointed day, she decorated the front room, drawing two chairs up to a small walnut sofa table. She covered the table in an embroidered cloth from "the home country" and arranged place settings using china teacups and matching plates painted with blue pastoral scenes.

She reminded me to place my napkin in my lap while I chose treats from the hammered silver platter set before me. There was no limit on cookies, and she served my tea the way I liked it—weak, with plenty of milk and sugar.

I happily stuffed myself, ruining my dinner, while Grandma talked about life. She often spoke of my future relationships with boys. At the time, I found boys disgusting creatures, but Grandma spoke with such urgency that I watched her with wide eyes while I chewed.

As an adult, I wondered if she had believed my mother's fate to be her own failure as a mother. It was only a guess, but I knew the burden of guilt and might have done the same in her shoes.

Though I then had a good many years before I'd have to worry about such things as dating and marriage, Grandma was explicit in her advice on men.

"Shelly, my girl, marry a man who respects you—someone who treats you with love."

When she was most impassioned, Grandma would lean close until our eyes were level. I knew to nod solemnly, and I once stole another cookie without breaking eye contact while she gave the same impassioned lecture.

"Don't let him yell at you," she would admonish, wagging her finger at the window as if my father stood just outside. "Promise me you'll choose someone like your grandfather—kind, gentle, good."

I swallowed the dry crumbs and nodded with as much gravity as a ten-year-old could. She made me promise, just as I had already done multiple times, to avoid bad boys, no matter how charming. I could barely imagine middle school, much less marriage, at the time. It had been an easy vow to make.

"I promise I won't let anyone hurt me."

It'd been so much harder to keep.

Grandma's core belief in happy endings had left an impression. Somehow, despite my overwhelming evidence to the contrary, I had continued believing.

That day's events would have restored her wide smile, gone missing after my mother's death. Gratitude for my grandmother's wisdom swelled. Her foresight had sheltered a small piece of hope for decades.

Afterward, our friends and family gathered outside in a beautiful garden. Lisa was the first to reach me and squeezed hard. My beautiful niece Ashley followed her mother. Ashley's blonde hair had darkened, but she hadn't lost her big hazel eyes and had inherited her grandmother's flair for beautiful things. She looked gorgeous. I hugged Ashley.

I didn't know God's plan for my sister, but I knew Ashley was part of it. Being a mother had given Lisa a reason to live through periods as dark as any I had known. My sister put a hand to my cheek, as my mother had often done. The familiar gesture brought tears to our eyes. She said nothing, but I understood her unspoken sentiments.

I had summited mountains of forgiveness and healing Lisa had yet to climb, and we both knew where our journeys had started. I loved her for showing up to celebrate my victory.

My mother's sister was next in line. Aunt Kathy grabbed my face with both hands and softly kissed my cheek. "You look beautiful. Your mother would be so proud."

I grinned. Aunt Kathy's smile faltered, twisting into a soft cry. "Your mother must be happy for the first time since her death."

I embraced my aunt and whispered in her ear. "I know she is happy. I just hope she gets to celebrate tonight too."

Aunt Kathy didn't question how I knew, but my words seemed to comfort her.

Our reception lasted far into the morning, leaving me wrung out from joy and full of steak and cake. The still-dark skyline at 4:00 a.m. didn't dampen my spirits a bit as Glenn and I drove to the airport to leave for the Dominican Republic. Though I couldn't yet see the dawning day, I had no doubt that my happily ever after was on the horizon. Life was forever changed.

Chapter Thirty-Seven

October 18, 2011

The pain refused to release its grip on my abdomen. Pushing my IV drip aside, I seized my phone from the bedside table, its neon glow casting dark shadows across my darkened University of Michigan hospital room. The clock on it read after two in the morning on a Tuesday.

On Monday, I'd undergone a procedure to correct my sphincter-of-Oddi dysfunction. Doctors had diagnosed it two months after my honeymoon in an emergency-room visit, and the simple surgery's intent was to correct what they explained was a muscle dysfunction at the end of my bile duct, which had a tendency to constrict and thus inflame my liver and pancreas with backed-up bile and digestive juices.

By three o'clock that Tuesday morning, another stabbing pain in my lower back made me push the nurses' call button.

My door opened, bright light spilling into my room from the hall. The young nurse who'd given me my pills at 10:00 p.m. appeared in the doorway.

"Yes?"

"My back is killing me. Can I have something else? I can't sleep."

She flipped the light on and checked my chart. "I can give you some extra-strength acetaminophen. You aren't able to take anything stronger for three more hours."

Another flash of agony made me groan. She studied my face and decided to get a doctor.

The doctor on call checked my vitals. My pulse was high. He ordered the nurse to give me more morphine, then frowned and scribbled a note in my chart.

"This isn't usually needed. I'll consult with your surgeon tomorrow, er . . ." he said and checked his watch. "Make that later today."

I was supposed to be discharged twenty-four hours after surgery. But every minute that passed left me feeling worse.

October 19, 2011

Glenn entered my hospital room on Wednesday, and his smile immediately faded to concern. I was still curled on my side, IVs attached. Instead of a recovering wife with bags packed, nothing had changed.

"Not going home today either?" he asked.

I shook my head and tried smiling at my husband of four months. He pulled a chair up to the bed and kissed my head. I grunted. My room reeked of antiseptic, but I knew my flushed skin smelled bitter, not to mention the body odor of fever sweats. My mouth tasted like iron, and I was constantly thirsty.

The surgical incision from Monday was an angry red under the yellow iodine stain and taped stitches. My abdomen had begun to swell, distended by what doctors speculated that morning could be pancreatitis. A new IV bag containing stronger antibiotics hung by my head. Yesterday had been bad, but today was agonizing.

Glenn found my free hand and held it. "How bad is it?"

I made a face. Shallow puffs of pain left little air for conversing. He bent closer. "On a scale of one to ten?"

I winced and blew out. "Nine."

He furrowed his eyebrows. "Can't they give you something?"

I shrugged, too exhausted from two days of pain to explain. I knew the doctors suspected I had a narcotic dependency. Mounting doses of opioids with negligible effects had given way to raised eyebrows and whispered consultations in the hall. I understood their concern but lacked the strength to explain the real reason.

Kathie had explained it to me years before. Living with high levels of trauma for decades had engaged my brain in the constant production of chemicals to help me disassociate from my life. Those natural, defensive responses had deadened my receptors' abilities to respond to even the strongest painkillers, and any real discomfort required a morphine dosage that might make a typical patient stop breathing. Drugs like oxycodone had a minimal impact. Of course, that made me look like an addict.

The same thing had happened when I'd undergone knee replacement surgery in my thirties. The doctors had reacted then like now and ramped my dosage up slowly. Afraid to stop my heart, they'd left me breathless with pain.

"They will . . . only . . . give me . . . so much . . . so fast."

Glenn sighed. I studied his face. A sprinkling of freckles stood out against his pale skin.

Everything had started falling apart when Glenn fell sick on our honeymoon.

June 19, 2011

The Carnival cruise ship left Port Canaveral, white foam churning in its wake. After seven days, we'd left our Dominican Republic resort and flown to catch our Bahamas cruise. After a lengthy check-in, we headed to the ship's surf-and-turf bar, then watched a Broadway revue show.

Tired, we returned to our cabin. I went out onto our small balcony and admired the night sky as Glenn turned on the television to relax. In minutes, Glenn bolted to the bathroom. I winced at the sounds of Montezuma's revenge coming from the small commode.

"Turn on the fan!" I called.

Glenn only grunted. My poor husband must have consumed bad water at the resort. He stayed close to the toilet for most of the next day and finally concluded that regular toilet paper possessed disturbingly abrasive qualities. When we found an eight-dollar pack of twenty wipes onboard, Glenn cradled his treasure.

Unfortunately, Glenn flushed them away like toilet paper all night. Sometime past midnight, he watched in horror as the foul water's level in the small john rose unabated. He flung open the door, holding his unzipped pants up.

"Get a plumber!" he yelled before diving for our ice bucket.

Glenn bailed water from the toilet into the sink. Meanwhile, the concierge put me on hold for thirty minutes—until they finally roused the sleeping plumber.

I hung up and came into the bathroom doorway.

"I am never using ice buckets again," I said, wrinkling my nose.

He raised his eyebrows. "Is someone coming?"

I shrugged. "They said five minutes."

The plumber arrived fifteen minutes later, pillow lines still on his face. When he saw Glenn bailing, he sprinted back into the hallway and uncovered a wall panel. In seconds, the water hissed off.

Glenn sighed and put the bucket down. I gave him hand sanitizer from my purse.

Outside our room, the plumber banged on the pipes and swore loudly. I hoped our neighbors had stayed out later than us. Glenn opened the door a crack and saw the plumber fishing out the ratty, discolored wipes. Glenn gently closed the door.

"He is going to ream me about those wipes."

A few minutes later, the plumber knocked. Glenn squared his shoulders and opened the door.

"Everything is fixed, sir. Would you please tell your wife not to flush pads down the toilet?" the irritated plumber said.

Glenn's shoulders relaxed. "Will do. Thanks for coming out so late." He closed the door and turned to me with a guilty look.

I crossed my arms and glared. "Really?!"

I smiled at the memory of his apology. Glenn touched my cheek. "What can possibly make you smile?"

I breathed in and out. "You."

Speaking caused agony to knife through my abdomen. I curled up tighter. My pain had begun four days after the plumbing fiasco, when Glenn felt better.

June 23, 2011

I put my fork down. The remaining rib-eye steak was perfectly pink, but my stomach knotted. The huge ship's rolling was imperceptible, but I suddenly felt sick.

Glenn noticed my expression. "Are you okay?"

"I don't feel well at all." I sipped my virgin piña colada, hoping
my intuition was wrong. The timing was unbelievable.

Glenn frowned. *"Do you think you caught my bug?"*

*I shrugged, hoping he was right and that was all it was. A wave
of nausea struck. I gagged but swallowed the contents of my stomach
back down.*

"I think I'll go lie down for a bit," I said.

*Glenn offered to come, but I insisted he finish his meal. Wretched,
I went to our room. After emptying the contents of my stomach into the
toilet, I hit the wall with my hand.*

Hello, pain, my old friend.

October 20, 2011

A bright stream of sunlight fell across my bed. It hurt my eyes. I had
made Glenn go home the night before, so I was alone. I called a nurse to pull
the curtain. A blurry form slid the drape closed with an efficient rasp, cutting
off the searing light. I hadn't slept well for three days. I'd dozed, but the pain
prevented me from getting more than a few minutes of sleep at a time.

I was aware it was Thursday morning, but my head felt funny. Everything seemed fuzzy and sharp all at once. I remember the nurse's face beside
mine, listening. She returned with a man in a white coat. He pressed his
cold stethoscope against my chest and listened.

"Does your chest hurt?" he asked.

I hugged myself to contain the shaking caused by each breath "Everything . . . hurts."

An X-ray revealed a partially collapsed lung—pneumonia. A nurse
wrapped an oxygen tube under my nose and over my ears. She started
another drip and clipped on a pulse oximeter.

I became aware of my husband sometime that evening. He paced, head down.

"Glenn." My murmur was barely audible, but his head snapped up. Our eyes met, and in two strides, he was beside me.

He sat on the edge of the bed and gently stroked my matted hair. I lost consciousness again.

October 21, 2013

For me, what happened Friday remains more impressions than distinct memories. Glenn says that is a mercy. He watched me writhe in bed that morning while doctors lifted the covers and prodded the incision on my abdomen, which grew more distended by the hour. They listened to my labored breathing.

What I knew then was that though I had wanted to die several times in my life, I desperately wanted to live. I do remember how hard breathing was. Breathing had become a kind of prayer, a desperate plea for life. I couldn't quite slip into the comfort of unconsciousness, for a gasping need to breathe kept choking me back to reality.

By Friday afternoon, the doctors had finally administered enough narcotics to numb the pain, and though I still struggled for air, my mind gratefully wandered into another sphere.

Julie called my room that afternoon. Glenn talked to her. She later described him as calm and nonchalant.

"Shelly? Yeah, she is doing okay," he'd said. He didn't want to confess that he'd never been so scared in his life. I had gone from writhing in pain to lying as if I were dead. I hadn't spoken for twenty-four hours, and the doctors had no idea what had gone so horribly wrong, but my organs were beginning to approach the line at which the medical world defined them as failing.

Julie's scream that evening woke me.

She ran out to the hallway, her purse still on her arm.

"Nurse! Nurse! What is going on in there?!"

Voices responded. Julie's language got more colorful. "Damn it, get in there!"

I closed my eyes again. It was the first time I'd been fully conscious that day, and I remember wondering why she was so upset because there was nothing to make such a fuss over. I was just exhausted.

"Somebody has to do something!" Julie's voice reverberated down the corridor.

I heard a scuffle and opened my eyes to see a nurse push Julie back into the room. My friend hurried to my bed and put a hand on my shoulder. I looked at her face and tried to smile, but I was too tired to say or do anything. Glenn tried to calm the frantic Tatoris woman beside him.

"She can finally sleep today."

Julie was on the edge of losing it. "Look at her. Glenn, she looks like the Michelin Tire Man! That's not an improvement!"

The nurse crossed her arms. "I know the swelling can appear shocking. I'm sorry. We are doing our best to make her comfortable until we can diagnose what's causing the issue."

Julie faced the nurse, hands on her hips.

"That's not good enough. Put her on something, antibiotics or antivirals, anything. Everything. Can't you see she is too sick to wait?"

Glenn stepped closer, nodding. The nurse hesitated. The room might have been silent if it weren't for the beep of my heart monitor, the oxygen tank whirring, and my gasping.

The nurse looked at my IVs, pulse oximeter, and oxygen tubes. She nodded. "I will see what I can do."

Exhaustion pulled me out of the conversation, and I shut my eyes and went back to my unconscious meandering with a sense of guilt. The expressions on Julie's and Glenn's faces were so heartbreaking I wanted to explain why I'd waited so long to confess that my cruise ship discomfort had never left.

I wished I could have admitted how much I'd wanted my fairy-tale ending and described why, when I knew I'd been cheated of it, I feared telling Glenn that he'd married a ticking time bomb.

I should have trusted in God's plan, but all I wanted was more time with Glenn. We deserved more than nine days of happiness. I'd thought the least I could do was pretend everything was fine and spare him the grief of knowing it was going to end sooner than we imagined.

I'd been scared and desperate enough to lie again.

June 2008

My stomach began cramping so severely after lunch that, for a few moments, I couldn't move. I finally snuck out of the office and to my car, hunched over. I'd only made it three miles on the Southfield freeway before I had to pull over and park. I jerked my seat back and pulled my knees up. Any rational thought was blocked by the agony, so I called Julie instead of 911.

Julie insisted I go to the hospital.

"It's probably going to relax soon. Maybe it's just gas." I refused and hung up.

At thirty-eight, I still hated to make a spectacle of myself. Julie kept calling me until, finally, after a lengthy phone conversation that included threats, she left work to take me to the emergency room.

315

Over the few hours waiting in ER, the pain lessened. An ultrasound showed my gallbladder was slightly inflamed. I had surgery to remove it the next day.

Ten weeks later, in August, I was in the ER with the same pain. They couldn't blame my gallbladder and could find nothing to explain the crippling agony which had once again subsided after several hours. I spent the next five months visiting specialists and became a frustrated, regular ER patient. Doctors remained stumped.

I'd noticed that the attacks always struck after eating and tried cutting out dairy and gluten, to no avail. Another episode began after eating eggs and a banana for breakfast one morning in January of 2009. This time, when I went to the hospital, they found an obstruction in my bowels in an X-ray and ordered a CT scan. My pain diminished in the four hours it took me to get under the machine.

The only visible anomaly was an inflamed intestine. They kept me overnight, and a GI specialist performed a lower GI scan with liquid barium. I called three days later for the results.

"We didn't see anything unusual. We can only guess that you might be experiencing an intermittent twisting of the bowels," the doctor reported.

I sighed. "And so . . ."

"We need to catch it in action, or we can't make any firm diagnosis. At the first sign of discomfort next time, come in. We'll do another scan."

I thanked him and hung up.

I didn't have to wait long. The next day, Julie drove me back to the ER while I grimaced at the familiar knotting in my stomach that soon had me panting and light-headed.

"They should have frequent-patient punch cards for people like you," she joked.

I rolled my eyes and motioned for her to pull to the side of the road so I could vomit. When I finished, she handed me a McDonald's napkin from the glove box.

This time, the ER scan was fast. Barium left from the day before highlighted my appendix folded beneath my left breast instead of over my right hip. My intestine had indeed folded over on itself and twisted until the area had swollen enough to potentially cause a rupture. The next day, the chief of trauma surgery at Beaumont removed the first two feet of my large intestine.

In my recovery room, I awoke to him clasping his hands together with enthusiasm. "You are only the third patient in my forty years of practicing to survive long enough for this specific condition to be corrected. We call it Cecale bascule. In most cases, this rare condition is found during an autopsy."

I was happy to have obliged him with a live specimen.

The surgeon rocked back on his heels, smiling wide.

"You are lucky to be alive, Ms. Edwards. We removed this section yesterday," the surgeon explained, pointing to pictures taken during surgery. "Your connective tissue, which holds your intestines to the abdominal wall, is abnormally long and flexible. This probably developed while you were an infant. We can only guess why it started randomly flipping at this point. I'm sorry to tell you that though I've removed the section that we caught twisting yesterday, we unfortunately know that once it starts, it tends to repeat itself."

The surgeon's lips pressed together, and he peered at me over his glasses.

The pain hadn't recurred for years.

On our honeymoon, I'd snorkeled and parasailed on cruise excursions, waiting to die but smiling. I worried about throwing up in my mask and inhaling the vomit. I had excused myself from swimming with dolphins by claiming I had a migraine. Glenn had been sympathetic but clueless.

It took three months for me to have the courage to admit one morning before work that I hadn't been feeling well even though I was clammy and afraid I'd faint. Glenn took me to the doctor. When their verdict was a sphincter-of-Oddi issue, I was relieved to have a different diagnosis that was repairable.

I'd thought there was no point in mentioning anything else, and we scheduled the surgery.

That evening, even on new IV antibiotics and heavy Motrin, my fever topped 103 degrees. The staff panicked. Doctors called for tests. Nurses adjusted my monitors and checked my vitals again—by hand.

My original scheduled stay had been one day. Five days later, with my state worsening by the hour, death suddenly seemed a real possibility as I watched the activity surrounding me and the apprehension in Glenn's eyes. When Glenn left that evening to rest for a few hours, I sank under the weight of the fear that had stalked me for months.

I dwelt on Camper's last suffering moments, wondering what death felt like. Would Camper come for me? Or Mom? I wanted out of the pain, but I wept at the thought of losing my beautiful dream, of leaving Glenn. My terror pulsed uncharted. Intensive-care units are filled with incredible machines that monitor every discernible physical measurement, except emotion.

My hysterics set off monitors. Nurses turned up the flow of oxygen and antibiotics, rechecking my pulse every few minutes, confounded by the sudden decline. My heart raced, and my oxygen ran dangerously low until a perceptive nurse put her hand on my arm and stroked my hair.

"You are going to be okay. Everything is going to be all right."

318

Her words and kind touch finally calmed me enough for my numbers to stabilize.

October 23, 2011

Saturday morning, Glenn and Julie sat beside my bed. Hushed voices swirled around me. The constant throb of nearly unendurable pain had rendered me speechless for several days. I could only nod in response to a few questions before my raging temperature pushed me into unconsciousness, so I have no recollection of the entire weekend or of my frightened husband praying over me late Sunday night. I was slipping away, and no one knew what to do.

October 25, 2011

Seven days after I had been admitted for an overnight procedure, the infection had spread down my legs in angry red streaks. The antibiotics were failing, and my entire body was swollen with fluids. I was unresponsive, delirious.

Glenn told me later that he watched doctors running in and out, huddling in small groups. With options running out, they asked him if they could cut me open again that Monday on the chance they might discover something helpful.

Julie sat with Glenn in the waiting room at the University of Michigan's surgical wing. They prayed silently, separately. They watched the door together.

A grim-faced doctor assisting the surgeon in OR 4 came out to update them. "She is stabilizing and incredibly lucky. We removed an orange-sized abscess from her abdominal tissue. Unfortunately, the infection spread to the surrounding tissues, including her stomach. We had to remove all the affected tissue."

The doctor looked at Julie.

"You saved your friend's life. If we hadn't started her on stronger antibiotics Friday, she wouldn't have made it past yesterday. We barely got to it in time."

Julie Tatoris would never let Glenn Jorgensen live that down, but at the time, they were too relieved to debate who'd saved my life.

November 2, 2011

After another fifteen days in the hospital, I was prepped to go home. My surgical incision remained open to allow my abdomen to drain. A wound vacuum was taped to it. They'd prescribed opiates, antibiotics, and rest.

When Glenn arrived. I held up the wound vac's plastic cord.

"I pimped my ride." I rolled my eyes.

He grinned. I was grateful to have another day with him. I hoped this was finally the end of my trials and troubles. What more could life throw at me than almost dying?

Life never ceased to amaze me with its creative ways to cause suffering.

November 6, 2011

I woke up feeling awful Sunday morning. I tried to tough it out, but by lunchtime, Glenn had loaded me into the car to take me back to the ER. Ten minutes into the drive, we hit heavy traffic, and I was certain this was it. I was going to die. I didn't want to die in the car with Glenn. Not in front of my husband.

Somehow, I survived the hour-long drive. Nurses lifted me out of the car onto a stretcher. It took fourteen hours to discover the source of the swelling and pain. They first examined the small outtake bag attached to my wound vac. It appeared to be draining the expected amounts of fluids from the abdominal tissue affected by the surgery.

After an X-ray indicated massive stomach swelling, they used ultrasound to discover that what was left of my stomach hadn't been emptying properly into my intestines since the surgery to remove the infection. Though they had done a bypass and fashioned me a new pouch for food, I still needed my stomach and its digestive juices to eat. Much of its wall tissue had had to be removed to prevent my death. Unfortunately, swelling and scarring in the remaining tissues had blocked my pyloric sphincter from releasing any digested juices from my stomach. Another sphincter issue.

I was flabbergasted to learn that all the digestive juices and bile my stomach and bile ducts had produced since the surgery to fix that Oddi-sphincter dysfunction had been trapped inside my stomach because of the abscess and its surgical removal until it was a toxic stew ready to rupture and spread infection through my body again. Fixing one issue had created another.

Not bothering to knock me out, the doctor pushed the ultrasound machine aside and shouted orders. I watched the ER nurse pull a length of tubing for the surgeon. He removed the wound vac and exposed my stomach. After a shot of local anesthetic, he cut into my abdomen and inserted a tube into my distended stomach.

The nurse turned her head and gagged. The vile aroma of metabolizing microbes hit me next. I retched in response while the staunch nurse held the tube in place. Brown fluid snaked through the tube, quickly filling a three-liter bottle on the floor. It was disgusting. My mortification grew until I registered my pain plummeting. Embarrassment changed to relief.

Another full liter drained into a new bag hanging beneath the gurney as they wheeled me away to my recovery room.

I left the hospital seven days later with an additional tube to drain my infected stomach beside the familiar wound vac hanging under my shirt. When I got home, I frowned at my reflection in the bathroom mirror. I resembled Frankenstein's monster with my incisions left open to drain and all the tubes and bruising. Whatever Glenn had expected when he'd married me, I was certain this wasn't it.

A home-care nurse came to change my dressings three times a week. Glenn helped empty my bags daily. I would have felt humiliated if I'd had the energy to. Unable to digest food well with a bypass done but no digestive juices aiding the process, I became very weak and hungry. Not to mention the severe cramping.

Over the next six weeks, I kept returning to the hospital to see whether my stomach had begun draining on its own. It never did. Doctors scheduled another surgery.

Chapter Thirty-Eight

Christmas, December 2011

The blood-pressure cuff hissed as it filled and released. The machines bumping up to my bed beeped occasionally. It was our first Christmas Eve as a married couple, and we spent it apart—me recovering in the hospital after surgery to remove my stomach and Glenn at home with the kids.

I had told Glenn to go home, so I didn't blame him for my being alone. He only had the kids for Christmas Eve, and I didn't want to ruin it by making them spend it with me in the hospital. Brian and Alyssa had visited me the day before with Glenn, and I'd see Jenna and Jeff later.

Imagining them all together tortured me in my quiet room. Since October, Glenn and I had spent weeks sleeping apart. Our honeymoon seemed a distant speck in the rearview mirror of six months of hell—three months of fearing I'd die soon and three months of almost doing that. I finally had a family but could not be with them.

Despite my passionate invitation to trust in God exactly a year earlier, I wept in self-pity for the lovely dream that had fallen apart almost at the start.

Christmas morning, Glenn returned to the hospital well rested and in good spirits from spending time with the kids. I, on the other hand, was angry and refused to eat the special holiday breakfast of offensive-smelling bariatric shake they offered.

I gave him a front-row seat to the emotional carnage I'd been hiding for months.

"This sucks. All I ever wanted was a family, and now that I have one, I can't be a wife or mother because of all this." By the end of my tirade, I was almost screaming.

I had had my fill of awful things in my life. I wanted the good part I was owed.

Glenn was quiet, his happy Christmas spirit gone. I realized I was ruining his morning as much as mine. I sobbed.

"I'm sorry." Glenn hugged me before I could finish apologizing. "Don't worry. I will never leave you."

I pulled back. "Who said anything about you leaving me?" I narrowed my eyes. "Why would you even bring that up?"

Glenn took a step back and raised his hands, pleading. "I didn't mean anything; just what I said."

I gave him a frosty and disbelieving look. He rubbed his face in consternation.

"I was trying to make you feel better. When things got rough with Susan and she threatened to leave, it made things worse. I wanted you to know that I'd never do that. Threaten to leave or actually . . . leave." His face grew more scarlet with each word.

I cried, then laughed, frankly forgiving him for being so awkwardly lovable.

I went home once again with no promises from the doctors. Just pills. The waiting began again, this time for relief.

January 2012

Six months after my honeymoon, I entered the kitchen, keys in hand. I had just returned from yet another checkup that morning. I felt nauseated, as always, but that day the nausea made me especially irritable. My cell phone rang. It was my aunt Kathy.

"Are you up for a visit? I'm running errands nearby and thought of you."

I set the keys on the table and looked around. Glenn had cleaned the house that weekend, so it looked presentable. I spent most of my time lying on the couch, watching television.

"Sure." I sighed. "Come on over."

I hung up and sat down on the couch to wait. I laid my head back and closed my eyes. My doctor visit had not gone well.

Four surgeries later, the nausea and pain that had started on my honeymoon was actually worse.

The first surgery to fix my sphincter-of Oddi dysfunction had failed to cure it. Rather, it had almost killed me. The second surgery had saved my life but prolonged the nausea by eliminating much of my stomach tissue and the immediate first part of my small intestine—the organs that entail the critical first processes of digestion. The third surgery was to stop my surgically altered stomach from rupturing due to scar tissue from the second surgery preventing it from draining. The fourth surgery, to completely remove my still nondraining stomach, should have resolved the nausea—according to doctors. Well, it hadn't.

What I ate dumped directly into my intestines without the normal accompanying acids and biotics to aid in breaking down the large chunks of material. What remained of my gut was never happy. Ever.

That morning, my specialist had explained his diagnosis.

"Dumping syndrome is an unfortunate condition that, as you have discovered, causes nausea after every meal. We think scarring from previous abdominal surgeries has resulted in multiple adhesions, or scar tissue, that are contributing to your constant discomfort. Then there is also, unfortunately, your intermittent flipping of bowels. That won't ever be resolved."

He concluded with news I didn't want to hear. "We don't have a cure for either the pain or nausea, but we can try to manage your symptoms."

In other words, this was my new life—unrelenting pain and nausea with episodes of being bedridden after every meal. *Thank you, universe, for proving me wrong. This could be worse than dying.*

The doctor refilled the prescriptions that I already was taking—up to six times a day—antinausea pills and enough opiates to knock a horse out. It barely touched my discomfort. I was angry.

When Aunt Kathy arrived, I unloaded on her.

"I will be like this for the rest of my life. This is a damn messed-up way to begin a marriage, much less live in one. I barely got a week with Glenn. How can he want me? Who would want me like this?" I stopped and covered my face with my hands.

I had just acknowledged my real fear.

I was terrified that Glenn would feel stuck with me. Maybe after decades of a happy marriage, a man could resign himself to the prospect of decades of care. Glenn had only had nine days.

"I have become dependent on a man who doesn't deserve any of this. My life has always been a mess. I'd thought things had changed, but now my mess will ruin his life." I began to sob.

I loved Glenn but knew I was a drain in every way—on his money, his time, his emotions. I felt worthless when he came home every night to find me still in bed, no dinner made. I couldn't even offer engaging conversation.

326

Aunt Kathy put her arms around me. "Yes, it is horrible," she said, patting my back, "but as things go, it could be much worse."

I stiffened, unsure if she understood what I had just said. I was going to be an invalid forever.

She took a breath. "Let me explain. I don't think you ever heard about the first time we knew things weren't right between your parents."

May 1961

Six months after marrying dark-haired Marlene at Saint Mary's Church, James Arnold 'Arnie' Edwards burst onto the concrete exterior landing of their second-floor flat. He dragged his naked wife behind him, gripping her long, wavy tresses.

Their shouting, no longer muffled behind cinderblock walls, echoed in the small alley as he dragged her down the metal staircase. Her pleas and his obscenities rang with each step. The desperate young woman changed tactics at the bottom and dropped, dead weight.

Arnie growled and released her hair to slap her face. She whimpered. Despite Marlene being almost as tall as the stocky ex-naval officer, she had recently learned he was violently strong when drunk. He grabbed her waist and flung her over a shoulder, then carried her, kicking and screaming, out of the alley and over the small grassy curb. Stopping, he deposited her in the gutter with a grunt.

"That's where you belong, you lying whore!" He swore and staggered back up the alley. He climbed the stairs. The apartment door slammed.

She lay momentarily stunned, then rose. Her arms crossed in a vain attempt to conceal the truth of her humiliation.

Kathy's words brought the scene to life. I shivered, imagining the familiar chill of May morning air in Detroit, damp and earthy. I heard Dad's voice and smelled his breath. I saw the pain in Mom's eyes. Though I had not been born yet, I recognized everything in that scene as the forerunner of every subsequent act. The couple performed their inherited roles: the son of an abusive drunk, the daughter of a devoted wife who believed God could change anything—including my father.

Their perfection at staying in character and their constant fear of appearing flawed had had only one possible ending.

Aunt Kathy continued.

Trembling, Marlene tapped on a nearby row-house door. A stooped widow cracked the door ajar. Her lips tightened at the young woman's native state. Suspicious, she scanned the street behind the girl. At last coming to Marlene's face, her eyes softened in recognition of the chatty newlywed.

"Marlene? For heaven's sake, what's going on?" she demanded and opened the door wider.

"May I use your phone, please?" Marlene asked, avoiding eye contact as she slipped inside. The pensioner pointed to the kitchen wall.

"There, honey. Wait a minute, let me get you something." She shuffled upstairs and returned to drape a housecoat over Marlene's bare shoulders. Grateful, Marlene dialed the only person she could stand to let see her.

"Hello, Findlay residence. Russell speaking." Grandpa Russell answered.

"Daddy . . . I—" Marlene hadn't thought this far. Whatever she said would have consequences.

Marlene had inherited a strong dose of Scottish pride from her mother, so admitting that she'd made a poor choice in marrying Arnie would humiliate her. She weighed her dignity against the humiliation on the street. Did it matter that Arnie occasionally proved to be more of an angry drunk than a loving husband? That his punches landed in soft places? He was a good provider, and everyone liked him. They'd gotten along so well otherwise.

"Marlene? Honey, what's wrong? Marlene!"

The worry in her father's baritone choked her throat. She knew he would come to her aid any way she asked. What did she want?

"It's just that Arnie and I, we got in a fight," she began. Was it her fault, or was it his? She found she wasn't sure. Perhaps she had provoked him more than she thought.

Sarah Findlay's voice could be heard in the background. "Russ, what is going on? Is Marlene okay?!"

"Marlene?" Russ's tone demanded a response.

Marlene's younger sister, Kathy, sat in the living room beside her father, watching her parents' frightened faces. She could just hear her sister's voice when she responded.

"I am fine, Dad. I need you to bring me clothes. Arnie and I had a misunderstanding. He locked me out."

"What?! What did he do? Where are you?"

Gripping the phone tightly, Marlene described the neighbor's house and assured her parents she was safe. She waited awkwardly with a cup of coffee at the kitchen table.

Aunt Kathy described her parents rushing off and my mother's subdued manner at home later that day. I digested the anguish reverberating through the decades from Mom's decision that day—familiar yet new in that context. This was my origin story.

"I had no idea it had started so soon," I said.

"I know what you are dealing with is horrible, but would you want to trade places?" Aunt Kathy smiled with tight lips and said no more on the subject.

She'd made her point.

When Glenn came home, I told him he was the best thing that ever happened to me. He smiled and did the dishes.

I had been in a free fall before Kathy's visit.

Now, I clutched at anything—small branches, tufts of faith, to find the courage to halt that descent. I turned to God once more, and my mind seized upon a familiar passage of scripture. I'd read it before, but not with such desperation. Pushing away the layers of despondency that had immobilized my hope, I found it again:

> Blessed are the poor in spirit: for theirs is the kingdom of heaven.
>
> Blessed are they that mourn: for they shall be comforted.
>
> Blessed are the meek: for they shall inherit the earth.
>
> Blessed are they which do hunger and thirst after righteousness: for they shall be filled.
>
> Blessed are the merciful: for they shall obtain mercy.
>
> Blessed are the pure in heart: for they shall see God. (Matthew 5:3–8, KJV)

God Himself had promised to balance the scales, but he'd never given a timeline for when that reprieve would come. He only promised it would.

There were worse things than being nauseated for the rest of my life. Worse things than twisted bowels. And there was still hope, just not a delivery date, for relief.

Chapter Thirty-Nine

February 13, 2012

Glenn was late coming home, but I had company and didn't mind. Julie had dropped by after work to visit Bella and me. While Julie had initially gotten the dogs after my marriage—per our long-standing agreement—Puddles' illness and subsequent passing in late January had changed things. Bella was an old grieving dog now, and my being on medical leave made my house the better option. In reality, I needed Bella's company as much as she needed mine. Julie knew we were both mourning a shift in our realities and had suggested the arrangement even though it meant she went home to an empty house each night.

I was sitting on the family room couch watching Julie play with Bella when I heard the garage door open. I turned to greet my husband when the entry door opened but got a mouthful of rose petals instead. A red bouquet had appeared over the back of the couch.

"Oh!" Startled, I jerked my head back and looked up at Glenn.

"Here." Glenn dropped them into my lap.

I picked up the roses and raised my eyebrows at Glenn. "What are these for?"

"Happy Valentine's Day!" He shrugged off his coat and headed into the kitchen.

I looked down at the cellophane-wrapped blossoms, confused since the holiday was the next day.

"Thought I'd beat the line at the florist by going tonight." His head disappeared into the fridge. "Where are those Mexican leftovers?"

A hot flush of irritation bloomed in my chest. "On the top, behind the salad."

I put the roses on the couch beside me and mentally replayed the scene from Valentine's Day the year before. Dinner in the basement, a dozen cards, and two dozen flowers.

"Let me put those in water for you," Julie offered.

She jumped up to find a vase, then helped Glenn reheat dinner for them. I used monosyllables for the rest of the evening. Julie left shortly after dinner. I went to bed early, and Glenn stayed in the family room, watching TV.

I had a hard time falling asleep. I had spent a week shopping online for the perfect gift for my husband, but it seemed Glenn didn't want to wait in line for ten minutes at the florist. I wondered if it was my invalid status that had changed things so quickly.

I had thought real love and marriage would be different.

Daylight brightened my perspective and brought a sense of remorse for my harsh feelings the night before. Glenn's roses were a bright spot in the empty kitchen. I took a seat at the table, admiring them. Bella trotted over and sat beside me.

"Morning, girl." I rubbed her head. She licked my hand.

I had been too critical of Glenn. He was economical and precise. I could forgive him for being too practical this once.

I ate a banana and drank some Diet Coke with my pills.

An hour later, I wiped banana-tinged bile from my lips with a tissue. I flushed the toilet. The nausea medication wouldn't help if I couldn't keep it down. Climbing in bed, I pulled the quilt over me. Only dreams brought escape, so I pursued sleeping with dedication.

I slept through lunch and woke up hungry. I was always starving because I had to balance tiny meals with the dread of pain. Still, I decided to skip eating since it was Valentine's Day, and I had plans I didn't want to risk missing out on. Before dressing for dinner, I swallowed more meds with more Diet Coke—a little caffeine for energy.

I applied makeup and straightened my hair. The longer I spent in front of the mirror, the more the reflection looked like me. I hadn't been anywhere, not even to church, since October. I couldn't pretend anymore and pull off a happy face. My therapist, Kathie, assured me that my inability to fake happiness was, in fact, a good thing, but it made life harder to explain.

Most people seemed uncomfortable if I didn't pretend, so I'd stayed away from everyone but family.

I outlined my lips in muted red and filled the color in with a matching tube. I blotted the excess and smiled, imagining Glenn's surprise. I looked nice despite the mess inside.

I hurried into our bedroom to set out candles and tidy up.

"Shelly? I'm here!" Glenn's voice carried from the front hall.

Rushing to the closet, I pulled out a small white gift bag and some new Amazon purchases. *What did chronically sick patients do before Amazon Prime? Catalogs?*

"I'm coming!" I answered.

I placed navy silk boxers on his pillow and laid a black satin teddy on mine. I hurried to meet him, closing the door behind me.

"Ready!" I kissed him in the hallway.

"Oh, wow," he murmured.

I held out the small white bag. "For you."

Glenn opened the cologne and read the painstakingly composed card. It wasn't twelve cards, but I had put my whole heart into it. His eyes shone.

"Thank you." He paused.

I clasped my hands, waiting for my gift. He took a step toward the door.

"Shall we go?" he asked.

I nodded after a moment.

At Andiamo Italia, I picked at the portabella mushroom appetizers as we waited for our lasagna and chicken marsala. Glenn asked what I had done that day.

"Not much. I mostly slept." I looked down at the table and played with the napkin in my lap. I had forgiven Glenn for his efficient flower delivery, but my anticipation of a special night slowly dissolved as it became obvious he had not prepared anything else. We talked of meaningless things, like the house and the hockey game Glenn had watched.

When my chicken came, I cut into it with silent spite. Even a cheesy dollar-store card could have saved my dinner.

When Glenn pulled into the garage that night, I jumped out of the car. "Just a minute."

I ran into the bedroom and locked the door. I stuffed the teddy and boxer shorts into a drawer before I changed into pajamas and brushed my teeth. I took off my makeup and wiped away the tears.

Glenn knocked. "You want to watch something?"

"Sure," I pretended nothing was wrong. "*Law and Order SVU* is on channel four."

The next morning, I called Julie. "He didn't do anything special last night. Not even a card. Do you think he doesn't love me anymore?" I choked on the words.

"What? No," Julie chided. "This is classic clueless-man syndrome. Tell him how you feel."

"Really? Because I don't want to fight. I just thought it'd be different."

Julie repeated herself. "Trust me. Men are sometimes oblivious."

"I'm scared this is how it's going to be from now on."

"Only if you don't say anything." Julie made me promise to tell Glenn how I'd felt that evening.

"I'll stay far away." She laughed.

I scowled.

I rehearsed my speech while waiting for Glenn. The same hopelessness I'd been wrestling all winter had returned. Doubts about Glenn's feelings snuck into my heart. Exposed organs and a wound vac had the power to destroy any man's attraction to me. Glenn must feel trapped like my father had, cheated of his expectations. I had turned out to be a real disappointment. I wiped a tear away.

Right at his usual time, Glenn came humming in. I drew a breath.

"Hey, we need to talk," I said. I crossed my arms to steel myself.

He stopped humming and froze.

"Are you all right?" he asked. I saw something familiar in his eyes. Fear.

My resentment shattered. I recognized an emotion I had produced in those blue eyes over and over these last few months. I had caused him so much anxiety. I sighed.

"No, I'm fine. Nothing like that. It's just that after last year, I had such high hopes. It didn't have to be so over the top, but a card would have been nice."

Glenn looked at me blankly.

I continued. "I know it's not like we had much of a honeymoon phase." I snorted, thinking back over the brutal half year. "But I wanted to make yesterday different—because of that, especially." Angry tears escaped. Last night had been so underwhelming, so blasé, so much like the way my life had become.

His eyes widened in confusion. "Shelly, what are you saying?"

I finally spat it out. "Why didn't you do anything special for Valentine's Day?"

Understanding hit my husband. He sat down with a sigh.

"I had no idea it meant so much to you," he said. He ran his hand over his face. "Susan and I never made a big deal of Valentine's."

"How did that work out?" I regretted the words as soon as I spoke.

Glenn's face fell at the cheap shot. His divorce had sent him into deep depression. I blew out a shaky breath.

I took his hand. "Sorry. It's just that I already had twenty years of horrible Valentine's Days. I don't want even one more."

He sighed. "I see. I am so sorry for not making Valentine's Day more special."

I dropped my shoulders, relieved he wasn't angry.

He pulled me into him and kissed me. "How can I make it up to you?"

I thought for a minute. "Wait here. I have an idea." I went to find the boxers.

Chapter Forty

March 10, 2013

My boss, Bill, shuffled the papers in front of him and cleared his throat. "So, what costs do you already have in the price model for the F-Series headlamps?"

I had finally returned to work after a year's leave of absence. Every day, I battled to appear normal. Nothing had changed; I lived with constant pain and nausea.

"We already have a costed BOM from purchasing," I shifted in my seat. The cramp in my side spread toward my navel. I tried to relax. The cramping intensified, and I leaned back in my chair to stretch my side while I talked.

"Except we are still waiting for an official quote on the LED projector lens."

We went on, listing parts. A sheen of perspiration broke out on my forehead.

This attack was bad. *I shouldn't have eaten those crackers at lunch and stuck to my Coke.* I tried to eat as little as possible at work to minimize the attacks, but I'd felt so weak that day. Damn.

Bill looked at me. "Are you okay?"

I had been hunching forward, hiding my face. I looked up, embarrassed.

"No," I admitted. "I think I need to go to the hospital."

He dropped his pen and came around to help me stand. My breathing shallowed. My swelling stomach began to feel uncomfortably tight against my waistband.

He watched as I shuffled out of the room. "Should I call an ambulance?"

I looked back over my shoulder at him. "No, don't worry. I'll call Glenn."

I used the wall to get back to my desk and picked up the phone. My fingers hovered above the keypad. Maybe it'd go away on its own. As if in response, my stomach clenched tighter. I dialed.

"I need you to come," I said when Glenn answered.

Glenn's tone instantly changed from professional to panicked. "What's going on?"

At the University of Michigan Hospital, the usual scene played out. The medical staff pumped me with pain meds, took X-rays, and came to no conclusion. They scheduled a follow-up appointment with my GI specialist—the same one who had assured me the October before that having a simple procedure would solve my problems.

My frustration mounted as once again I had to recite my entire medical history. I tore through the list with memorized accuracy, flinging diagnoses and dates at the attending physician as fast as he could write them down. I was sick and tired of explaining how sick and tired I was of this pain.

"Now I don't have a functioning stomach, and the intestines I have left won't stop ruining my life!"

The ER doctor stared at me openmouthed. Then his eyes lit up.

"I am going to write up a letter for your next ER triage doctor. That should help clear some hurdles."

He asked a nurse to type up his notes on hospital letterhead. She returned and handed an official-looking piece of paper to me with a smile.

"Use it the next time you go to the ER."

The letter outlined my medical history. It suggested I be admitted with urgency considering the dire implications of further complications. The letter failed to change anything. I tried it once without success. I waited on a gurney for four hours until the pain had disappeared before I could get a CT scan. I was still alive, thankfully, but not because of the useless letterhead.

It had finally clicked: this wasn't going away. I grasped at last that the doctors' objective was no longer a cure but just to prevent death, if possible.

I was on my own to figure this out.

I applied for medical leave and tried to stay alive. Instead of going to the ER, which had proved pointless, I prayed through each two-to-four-hour attack. I searched for alternatives to ease the agony of eating. I sucked on candy, letting it slowly melt in my mouth. That led to my hair thinning and my brain becoming too foggy to make the connection between a hard candy diet and my anemic state. Plus, I had gained thirty pounds on my sugar diet and medications. That made me cry.

Glenn put his foot down. "You have to eat more."

I forced myself to consume a cup of food at meals. That was all I could swallow before debilitating pain drove me to the couch or bed. I fought to keep it down, to let my body absorb what little it could.

After an obsessive internet investigation into therapeutic remedies and my GI specialist's approval, I purchased a $300 case of partially digested feeding-tube formula. I hoped I'd found the magic bullet! Partially digested nutrients could give my diet the head start my body could no longer provide.

When the case arrived, I did a little dance. Bella barked in excitement.

"Here we go, girl!" I said. "The magic elixir is here!"

I read the back of the first can I pried out. It said no refrigeration was needed and to shake well. I shook the small can in my hand with vigor, then used a can-punch bottle opener to press two holes in the lid and poured it into a tall glass. The liquid running out reminded me of melted vanilla ice cream. Holding it up to the light, I noticed a gray hue that gave me pause. I sniffed it. There wasn't much of a smell. *Bottoms up.*

I threw my head back and swallowed. *Ugh.* Too late, I realized there had been no reason for the company to taste test with feeding-tube patients.

I gagged and ran for the toilet, cursing myself for being the only person in the world stupid enough to put that stuff in my mouth. It was the only time I was happy to be nauseated. I donated what remained to the hospital after being refused a refund due to one opened can.

I tried every medical suggestion and followed every thread of hope. I endured four shots a day for the nausea, tried the FODMAPS diet and gave up "fermentable" carbohydrates, wore a pain patch, and swallowed a dozen pills a day. Dilaudid for the pain, Zofran for the nausea, and Compazine six times a day, also for nausea. My pain specialist even suggested it might all be in my head and sent me off with a prescription for volunteer work.

Nothing worked.

After two years, I was rankled by the idea of giving up, though I could find no new options. Regardless, this was supposed to be my happily ever after, and I still had fight left in me.

Chapter Forty-One

September 2013

I read the letter several times, distrusting my comprehension because of my dyslexia. I lowered the paper into my lap and stared at the ceiling. The Ford HR form letter notified me that I'd been terminated from my job. Ever since I'd left my meeting with Bill six months earlier, I had hidden a secret hope that something might change. My time had run out while I waited for the miracle.

Bill hadn't even been brave enough to call. I threw the paper across the room. It flitted over the coffee table and gently landed on top of Bella, who raised her head and looked at me before settling back in to doze.

I had been an engineer for almost twenty years. Despite everything else in my life, I'd excelled in school and at my jobs. My performance reviews were exemplary. Even sick, I knew I could whip out the calculus. Being fired sucker punched me. Angry tears fell as I dialed Glenn's number.

"Hello, this is Glenn Jorgensen. I am away from my desk . . ."

I looked at the phone in dismay. I hung up and wandered the house. What kind of future existed being sick? Everything was falling apart again.

At least on medical leave, though I hadn't cooked or cleaned, my salary had contributed. Now, I would lose my company car and be completely dependent on my caregiver husband, who was still paying child support. I quickly did the math and knew we'd have to make some serious lifestyle alterations.

Not since I'd asked my grandma Findlay for help had I felt so helpless, so worthless. Until that moment, I'd kept my vow to never burden another human being.

With that letter, the faith, gratitude, and trust I'd been trying to rebuild felt like a farce. It seemed whatever I tried, however long I hoped, the outcome was always my failure.

I paced all afternoon, distraught. Bella trotted with me, trying to bring me toys to distract me. I finally lay on the sofa, nauseated and crying. Bella curled up beside me and licked my cheeks. When Glenn came home, she whined at him.

"Girls!" he said, alarmed. "What's wrong?"

I wailed. "I got a letter. They fired me—in a letter!"

"You were fired?" Glenn repeated slowly.

I nodded.

He sighed in relief. "Is that all?"

"How will we make it?" I cried, too overwhelmed to appreciate his calmness. I only worried that he hadn't time to think through what this would mean for us, for him.

Glenn took my face in his hands and kissed my forehead. He looked into my eyes.

"We will be okay," he said.

I shook my head in his hands. "But now I'm not helping with anything. I am only a burden."

Ashamed, I pulled back and put my hands to my face. I sobbed in pain and wild fear, sure he couldn't want me now. I had nothing to give in return for the suffering I brought. I sensed Glenn sit down on the coffee table facing me. He took my hands gently, uncovering my eyes. He waited until I met his gaze before speaking.

"Understand this. You aren't a burden. Shelly, I need you to love me. That is enough, and you can do that."

He pulled me into a long hug. My shoulders shook, hardly able to process what he'd said. All I knew was that he held me, and for the moment, that was what I needed.

After a late evening of figuring out how we'd make it on a budget, I knelt beside my bed and prayed for comfort. A long-forgotten scene played through my mind. The timing was, of course, not coincidental.

It was essential.

1980

Mom lay on the bed surrounded by snacks, a glass of water, some books, my colored pencils, a notebook, and a heart I had colored for her.

"Do you need anything else?" I asked.

She smiled and shook her head. "No, I think you thought of everything."

I hated leaving her. When Dad had received the unexpected call from Providence Hospital that Mom had arrived in critical condition and was undergoing surgery right then, I'd feared the worst.

I had fervently prayed not to be left behind with Dad. I had promised God that if my mom lived—if she came home—I'd help any way I could.

Doctors marveled that she'd driven from work to the ER with a ruptured colon. She had almost died on the operating table, and they'd worried she might go septic. Somehow, she pulled through that night and the next. Then she was "through the worst," and I could breathe at night again.

The day she came home, weak but alive, I was ecstatic. I ran errands and slept on the floor by her at night, afraid she might die when I wasn't watching. Her recovery took weeks, but I had to go back to school after three days.

I ran off the bus every afternoon, anxious to ascertain that she still waited in bed. I did the dishes and helped Lisa make spaghetti. I think we had it four times in two weeks. I didn't care. If Mom was okay, I would cook and clean forever.

The more I thought about it, the more astounded I was. Not only had I never associated my health struggles with a genetic tendency inherited from my mother, but she'd continued to provide critical lessons still. Thirty-five years earlier, God had prepared the way for me to understand how I could face what was happening to me right then.

With vivid recall, I remembered how I loved my mother during her long recovery. Her presence was as vital to me as a recovering patient as it had been when she'd made dinner and worked full time. Either way, she gave me something no one else could—her love. What she did was less important than how she loved me, how she listened when I came home from school and asked about my day. I knew I mattered to her as much as she mattered to me. Caring for her wasn't a burden. I was grateful to have her there.

On my knees in my room, disabled and unexpectedly unemployed, I suddenly saw both perspectives at once. Yes, my illness made me incapable of benefiting Ford Motor Company's bottom line, but my worth to Glenn was infinite. I hadn't lost my opportunity to love and be loved. I had only lost a career I'd let define my self-worth for far too long. My job had protected me from feeling vulnerable, but it was only in having that crutch taken away that I discovered all the blessings of being vulnerable. I was wanted despite my weakness. I was needed, and not for what I could do but for who I was. What greater blessing could I have asked for than to be loved on such terms?

Despite my medical disasters, I had a family even if the circumstances were not what I expected. Even sick, I could care for them in unique and necessary ways. Glenn needed encouragement and appreciation. My step-kids needed a stepmom who was compassionate and understanding. No one could take my place. Maybe love could be enough.

When I turned to God's word to study love, I found it was more than enough. Love was everything:

Though I speak with the tongues of men and of angels, and have not charity, I am become as sounding brass, or a tinkling cymbal.

And though I have the gift of prophecy, and understand all mysteries, and all knowledge; and though I have all faith, so that I could remove mountains, and have not charity, I am nothing.

And though I bestow all my goods to feed the poor, and though I give my body to be burned, and have not charity, it profiteth me nothing.

And now abideth faith, hope, charity, these three; but the greatest of these is charity. (1 Corinthians 13:1–8).

I had learned to have faith in God despite the pain of life. I had learned to hope in the face of devastation. Now I was learning what it meant to receive love when I had the least to give. It meant dedicating my heart and purpose to them, just as Christ and my mother had.

I began to consider being fired as a blessing. I stopped focusing on what I couldn't do and what I lacked or wasn't. Instead, I got creative with how to love.

I connected with the kids via social media and chatted with them on the phone if they didn't seem too busy. I found inspiring quotes and scriptures that moved me and shared them with my family. I went to their big events, even if it meant not eating that day, and I smiled and cheered.

I started writing my memories down and going to therapy groups that supported women recovering from trauma. I sent cards on friends' birthdays.

But mostly, I poured love into my marriage. I smiled at Glenn again and told him how wonderful he was. I sat and chopped things for dinner while he cooked. I listened to his frustrations and dreams and encouraged him on his bad days. Sometimes, on my better days, I even did a load of laundry or cooked a simple meal. It wasn't much, but I did everything with love.

Caring for others didn't relieve my symptoms, but it made me present to the people surrounding me, and it helped me find purpose and hope. I emerged from the hole of darkness my diagnoses and termination had thrown me into with renewed faith in a loving God who had prepared me for this decades before. He would continue to guide me through every day.

If I was going to be sick until the day I died, it was okay. Love had given me my life back.

September 13, 2014
San Diego, California

Another big wedding. My stepson Jeff and his bride Tatiana's marriage went off without a hitch. After the reception line, Glenn filled his plate and came to sit beside me. I stole a few bites of his dinner to take the edge off my hunger and enjoyed people-watching. I preferred mild starvation to missing the festivities.

I giggled when Tatiana pulled her single mother onto the floor for the "daddy-daughter" dance. The two Latina women transformed their dance into a show, expressive and dramatic. Their joy as they twirled each other was contagious. When Tatiana dipped her mother during the final chorus, I clapped with everyone else.

"Aren't they the cutest?" I gushed to Glenn.

Jeff's expression caught my eye. His face beamed with pride watching the two women. Even though Jeff's biological mother had chosen to be absent, he showed no hint of self-pity. I wondered if Jeff might ask Glenn to dance next. It was a nice, if untraditional, gesture to honor their supportive parents.

Tall, blonde Jeff stood as a new song began. He raised his arm, pointing toward me. Glenn grinned and gave me a nudge.

"Go."

I flushed, forgetting my nausea. "Me?"

Jeff took my hand. I rose and looked around at the sea of smiling faces that suddenly blurred. A flood of emotions ruined my mascara. I had no other family than the one with Glenn, but I knew it wasn't so black and white for the kids. They had another mom and stepdad. Jeff's gesture meant more than he knew. He chose me when he didn't have to. It was an unexpected and humbling gift.

I thought I might understand a little of what he felt in his mother's absence, as I had endured my share of parental rejection. I knew I couldn't fix what was broken between them, nor could I replace her, but I could try to make this moment the best possible for him.

As we danced, I told him how proud I was of him and what he had accomplished. I praised his choice to marry Tatiana and to give his heart to God. I thanked him for accepting me so willingly and let him know how much he meant to me.

Dancing with Jeff healed a little piece of my soul.

November 19, 2016

It wasn't long after my marriage to Glenn that all my stepchildren were grown and living on their own and Glenn and I eagerly awaited the opportunity to greet grandchildren. We were overjoyed to learn Tatiana was expecting not long after her marriage to Jeff.

Since I had missed everything about having babies with marrying late in life, I excitedly awaited the delivery of our first granddaughter. I wanted to be there every moment I could. Though Jeff and Tatiana hadn't waited long to make us proud grandparents, baby Annabella truly surprised everyone with her rush to arrive.

Her premature delivery caused some alarm. We all worried about tiny Anabella possibly being deaf or vision-impaired. After much prayer and waiting, the doctors pronounced her healthy and unaffected. She went home after a month in the NICU.

Though all ended well, thirteen months later, Tatiana had cause to fret once more.

Only thirty-five weeks along in her second pregnancy, strong, irregular contractions had started that morning. The pains reminded her of Anabella's birth a year earlier. She felt impressed to call the doctor. Out of an abundance of caution, her doctor directed her to go straight to the nearest San Diego hospital for a stress test.

After dropping Anabella at her mother's home before heading to the hospital, Tatiana called Jeff in Florida. He was doing additional Navy search-and-rescue training and had planned to be home in five weeks for the due date.

Jeff called us in a panic to explain what was happening and asked us to pray. We complied, pleading for God to be with Tatiana, the baby, and the doctors. Jeff miraculously found a flight and was in the air a couple of hours later.

That phone call shook me in new ways. I had learned to give my own losses to God, but I worried what my children's losses might do to them and me. The stakes seemed so much higher. I prayed almost without ceasing all that afternoon and evening.

At the hospital, a contraction came while a nurse hooked a fetal monitor to Tatiana's belly. The nurse stopped tightening the Velcro straps in order to feel Tatiana's bulging belly. She frowned in thought, then finished tightening the sensor belt.

When another contraction started a few minutes later, the nurse again put her hands against Tatiana's sides, gently pushing. She gave Tatiana a reassuring smile.

"I'll be right back," the nurse said and ran out the door. Alone in the room, Tatiana worried. She had noticed something strange that last time too. The left side of her uterus contracted rigidly while the right side remained soft.

The nurse returned with a doctor at her heels. He introduced himself and examined her during the next contraction. He calmly began directing the nurse and called for more help.

"Have you noticed any hemorrhaging?" he asked Tatiana between contractions. She shook her head no.

"Good. That's good. Only half of your uterus is contracting, and that can cause a placental rupture. It is dangerous for both your baby and you. Do you understand?" he questioned.

Tatiana nodded.

A nurse came in. "They are prepping surgical number two. We can take her up."

Adeline Marie Jorgensen was born weighing five pounds four ounces. Though four ounces less than her sister at birth, she measured just as long at twenty-one inches. Jeff arrived an hour later.

After holding his daughter and making sure Tatiana was comfortable, Jeff called to let us know we were grandparents again. Glenn and I jumped up and down, laughing like fools. I collapsed on the couch with relief.

Another granddaughter! Her safe arrival was another reminder that with God, there were no coincidences. He had guided everyone—Tatiana, the nurses, and the doctors. Even the airline staff in Florida had found a way to help a distraught father. There was a plan and purpose for every life, including my sweet new Adeline's.

Worried my illness might burden her rather than help, I waited to visit until Tatiana had recovered. Her mother came for the first few weeks, helping her daughter when she needed it most.

I spent the time choosing gifts for our precious grandbabies, my anticipation growing. As soon as Tatiana's strength returned and her mother left, Glenn and I came to rock the babies.

Holding tiny Adeline and reading books to little Anabella, I could almost imagine what it would have been like to have my own babies. But then again, through my own miracle, these were my own. These beautiful babies were mine to hold and cherish. Having granddaughters sent me over the moon.

I couldn't help Tatiana clean and make dinner, but Glenn ordered takeout, and I cooed at Adeline, letting Anabella have precious mommy time. When Adeline needed to nurse, we switched, and I read stories to Anabella. Afterward, we all napped. I couldn't do much, but it was okay. I loved my family with everything I had.

My soul healed while my body fell apart. I was tired, malnourished, and nauseated every day. I had intermittent episodes of crippling pain, but I understood my role for the first time in my life. God was so good to me.

Chapter Forty-Two

March 2, 2018

As my chronic illness stretched me thin, I sought strength and energy from sources outside myself. I volunteered in small ways, attending support groups for trauma survivors when possible and spent daily time in contemplation.

In childhood, my brain had assumed a pattern of constant vigil, always circling, always bouncing from one input to another. This obsessive surveillance made meditation nearly impossible at first. Instead of a peaceful sense of being, I inventoried sounds: the clock ticking, Bella lapping water from her bowl, the neighbor mowing his grass, the faucet dripping, cars passing the window. When I tried to block noises out, worries about the kids and Glenn took over.

I battled to learn to stop, be still, and let go. At the start, ten minutes of meditation exhausted me. Like trying to keep a puppy sitting, my mind ached to run in circles. Now, after years, it was easier to keep myself in one moment and not dashing to a past or future one. It wasn't an unconscious nap; it was very conscious letting go.

Meditation was the way I centered myself by not letting my mind run forward and become overwhelmed with viewing the endless days of pain before me but remaining in the moment with just that breath. One breath at a time, I accepted my life with serenity.

One morning, I found that those moments also allowed me to connect to the fountain of grace in ways I had thought long shut to me.

That day, Glenn had already left for work. I lay on my bed, eyes closed. Clearing my mind, I named a blessing with each breath. My gratitude practice enabled me to find the courage to force myself out of bed each day. It affirmed my faith in God's plan and timing.

As usual by then, peace accompanied my recital. I paused to let God's Spirit guide my reflection. Stilling my mind, I emptied it. My emotions needed space to move into; they were easily crowded out by anything else no matter how small.

Lingering emotional numbness, a symptom of childhood trauma, bothered me more and more, and I worried it impacted my relationships. It was as if my emotional receptors were worn out. I knew I loved, but I wanted others to be able to sense it too. My emotional detachment had helped me lie to protect myself for so long, but now it masked the truth when I didn't want it to.

My narrow range of emotions fell short of what I yearned to express to my family. I wanted to connect deeply with those around me. I wanted my true emotions back. I needed them all, the good and the bad, to color my relationships and express what was in my heart. That morning, I prayed for the gift of discernment to help me hold on to the small fluttering of emotion I was reclaiming.

God, help me connect to the truth. I want to feel what I need to. Take my numbness. Let me discern through Thy grace what my true emotions are.

Mom entered the room. My eyes opened, and her unseen presence filled me with unabashed joy. I wasn't surprised when I heard her voice, but her words shocked me.

"The time has come. You need to ask for a blessing of healing. You can be significantly healed if you prepare as I explain."

My nausea and pain ceased as my mother spoke, and in my amazement, I struggled to keep pace with her list of instructions. She directed me to fast in addition to praying and to increase my efforts to dedicate my life to God.

"Study scriptures about the gifts of the Spirit and ask specifically for them in your prayers, just as you have done by asking for the gift of discernment."

My mind reeled as my mother pointed me to Bible passages about healing that I knew she had never studied in this life, like the words of Paul in Acts: "And it came to pass, that the father of Publius lay sick of a fever and of a bloody flux: to whom Paul entered in, and prayed, and laid his hands on him, and healed him" (Acts 28:8).

I was dumbstruck as she explained how the Apostles of old had healed others by the laying on of hands and suggested the same could be done for me.

She also warned me that choosing who to include in this blessing of healing would be of vital importance. They needed to have confidence that God could work miracles. Together, our combined faith could bring the relief I had waited seven years to find.

My mother ended her admonition and left. The radiating pain in my side returned with a sharp ache.

I rolled over and sat up. I searched for a piece of paper to record everything I could recall, her exact words already fading from memory. With pencil and notebook, I captured her counsel as best I could. My hand shook, racing to get it all down before the nausea forced me to the bathroom. After dry heaving, I called Glenn.

"You won't believe it," I said without introduction. "I have to read you what my mother just told me."

In the middle of reading the words, I broke down. I had suffered for years. Accepting my condition hadn't made it any easier. The return of hope for healing rendered me incapable of communicating. Glenn waited for me to pull myself together.

"If the only healing I get is just a release from this ambient-level nausea," I said, "then that would be more than I ever hoped for. Even if I got sick after eating, I would still have hours without nausea. Imagine that!"

Over the following weeks, Glenn and I discussed my mother's directions. I debated who to ask to join in our blessing. One man immediately came to mind: Kevin Jones Giddins, an old friend who had experienced many trials of his own as a Black man, had always held a special place in my heart.

Kevin and his wife, Lita, had befriended me as a young single woman in their church congregation, and an instant kinship had arisen between us. Though we had experienced different kinds of betrayal and suffering, we recognized in each other the signs of grace and fortitude God grants heavily tried souls. At times, all three of us had felt like we were unseen and unheard by those around us. Lost in pain. Only with a very few friends like them did I have enough courage to share my past. Kevin and Lita had listened with pure compassion. They were wise souls who remained mentors for as long as our paths joined.

But Kevin and Lita had moved almost two thousand miles west, so I dismissed the thought as impractical. Surely there were many others of great faith surrounding me in Michigan. I listed as many as I could think of. I kept poring over the scribbled names. They were wonderful men, but none of their names settled in my heart. Instead, Kevin's never left.

I decided my first impression had been correct and called Kevin. When he answered, I asked him to get Lita on speakerphone.

I explained my extended medical drama, which I'd only mentioned in passing in Christmas cards. They already knew about my mother's death but not about her visits. Now I felt impressed to share everything.

"I had an experience recently that I don't know how to explain," I began. "Maybe I'll start with another one that happened at my first basketball game following my mother's death."

They listened with rapt attention. Lita exclaimed at various points. When I shared my mother's latest visit and assurances, Lita's voice filled with awe. "You're serious? What a promise!"

Kevin remained quiet.

I addressed him. "Kevin, you were the first person I thought to ask. I doubted that impression because you're so far away, but I have prayed and prayed. My feelings are constant. Will you help Glenn give me a blessing of healing?"

A long moment passed.

"I'm flattered that you would ask me," he replied, "but I need to know for myself if this is something God wants me to do. I don't doubt your experience. I just need confirmation that I am the right person."

The next Sunday, Glenn and I fasted with Lita and Kevin. I lay in bed all day, praying Kevin would receive peace about it.

I ended my fast with a small bowl of ramen and then sat on the couch trying not to move, willing my meal to stay down. After an hour and a half, when I could breathe easier, I called Kevin.

He chuckled. "Well, God has surprises yet in store. I am at your service."

I let out a sigh of relief. "I am flying to you. When can we come?"

Chapter Forty-Three

April 26, 2018

Our plane circled high above a mountainous valley in preparation to land. I gave Glenn a weak smile. "Almost there." I was exhausted, having fasted since the day before to prepare. Now that we were almost there, I was anxious to get off the plane.

I was only forty-eight but felt I looked twenty years older, stooped and slow. As we waited by the luggage carousel, I felt faint and had to sit right on the ground while Glenn piled our bags next to me. I didn't want to show up at Kevin and Lita's only to faint in the midst of my miracle, so I suggested we find a restaurant to eat at before reaching their home that evening.

It was late afternoon when we left the airport. Glenn glanced over as he drove the rental car. His jaw tensed, and he looked back to the road.

"What's wrong?" I asked, noting the change in his mood.

"What if I can't?"

"Can't what?" I drew my eyebrows together.

"What if I don't say the right thing? What if my faith isn't enough?" Glenn gripped the steering wheel with white knuckles.

I touched his arm.

"It's going to be okay," I said. "My mother directed me to do this. She came for a reason."

We found a Mexican joint, and I ordered a Diet Coke and a burrito. When they came, I took my pills with the caffeine. Glenn ate while I picked at my food. I reached my limit after consuming half of the burrito and waited for him to finish, head in my hands. A long while passed before I noticed his plate had been cleared.

I looked up to find his eyes heavy with concern.

"Shelly," Glenn began again. "We've prayed for healing for seven years." His eyes filled with tears. "Nothing's ever changed." His hand trembled on mine. "I am so worried. Look at you. You can barely eat ten bites in one sitting before you're doubled over with pain. I don't know what else I can say that will be any different."

"Oh, Glenn." I put my head down again atop my arm on the table, dizzy with pain and nausea. We sat for a few minutes in silence, my clenched form beside his defeated one.

When my thoughts cleared, I assured him, "God knows what He needs you to say. You don't need to know. Not yet."

Glenn didn't move. I saw familiar emotions behind his eyes. Defeat, dejection, resignation. I wasn't the only one who had suffered for seven years. Glenn had lost so much too.

I put my hand on his arm. "Maybe it wasn't time two years ago, or seven years ago. I don't know. All I know is that I can be healed if God wills. I believe He wills it now. Look at you and me. How can we doubt that, even if good things don't always come when you first ask, God is a giver of good gifts?"

Two hours after I finished eating, Glenn helped me stand up from the booth. I was so sick I could hardly walk. He drove us south as worry weighed heavy on his brow.

Lita greeted me with a hug and smile, but her eyes betrayed her shock at my condition. We didn't waste much time chatting. I was uncomfortable, and we had arrived later than planned. Kevin anointed my head with oil. Glenn straightened beside me and placed his warm hands on my head. Kevin placed his hands on Glenn's.

Glenn spoke without pause even though not an hour before he'd despaired at what more he could say. As he began, power ignited beneath their hands and slowly burned down my whole body. Fire had once destroyed my life, but I could feel this spiritual fire cleansing and healing me.

Glenn prayed for health and strength beyond that which I had even sought. He pled for the windows of heaven to open and for vitality to return to my body and clarity to my mind. He encouraged my faith in miracles, acknowledging my traumatic past and the effects still lingering in my body.

My heart throbbed with every word. An incredible aura of peace and warmth filled the room. Lita wept softly.

Glenn finished. Everyone took a deep breath.

I stood and faced Glenn. The doubt and despair in his eyes had vanished. Instead, they shone, expectant.

I nodded. "I don't feel sick." I looked at Kevin. "I don't feel sick!" I clapped my hands and let out a small squeal.

Kevin sank into a chair. Lita jumped up to hug me.

We all cried while we laughed. Kevin shook his head, rubbing his face.

"It was unreal. I knew what Glenn was going to say before he said it. Every word."

Lita looked at me with wide eyes. "A miracle."

I nodded, stunned. I put a hand to my stomach. The mesh and scars remained there, tight beneath my hand. But I had no pain, no nausea. I grinned.

Lita crossed the room to her husband. They embraced.

Glenn pulled me close. "Your mother knew."

Glenn and I held hands as we drove to our hotel, the mountaintops glowing under a bright moon as the valley settled into darkness. Along the streets near the freeway, neon signs had come to life. Seeing a small café, I suddenly wanted to test my new limits.

"Pull over here," I said, pointing to the restaurant.

Glenn laughed and obliged. "You are full of faith."

Inside, I spied a raspberry pastry drizzled with frosting in the dessert case. It looked delicious. Above all things, sweets had sent me into a rigid state. I pointed to it. Glenn raised his eyebrows but ordered it.

Seated, I took small bites, pausing after each one to smile in amazement. I licked my fingers. I wanted to lick the plate but refrained. I felt full for the first time in seven years.

Glenn's chuckle filled the booth. "Another?"

I shook my head no but slept well that night.

The next morning, I skipped my meds. I piled biscuits and gravy on my plate. I couldn't finish, but again, I felt fine. Over the next several weeks, the miracle sank in.

My new normal is, well, almost normal. My digestive system still has limits, such as an aversion to dairy, but if I respect those limits, usually I don't get super sick. Depending on what and how much I eat, I'll experience a slight nausea that subsides in five to twenty minutes. But I no longer live with constant pain or nausea. None. I am almost completely off my medications. I continue to take a couple of pills for nausea, which I am not even sure I still need, and vitamins, which I am sure I do.

The remaining vestige of my seven-year ordeal is constant fatigue. My incomplete digestive system still doesn't process food correctly, so vitamins aren't absorbed well. It's hard to wake early and move all day. Though I am not well enough to return to my career, my quality of life has drastically improved in ways I'd only dreamed possible. I am healed, body and soul. Every day, I experience more deeply the miracle that is my life—my beautiful ashes.

Chapter Forty-Four

May 26, 2019

The priest closed his small book. Smiling, Father Joe put his hand atop the two clasped in front of him. My youngest stepdaughter, Alyssa, raised her chin and looked into her groom's eyes a foot above hers. She looked beautiful in her white chiffon dress. Her blonde waves tumbled past her shoulders. Jameson, dark in his Marine Corps dress blues, squared his shoulders and looked back at the clergyman.

Military men were becoming a thing in our family. First Jeff and now my son-in-law. I smiled and felt a twinge of sadness for my father. He would have respected his grandsons. I still hoped God had plans for my father's future, as He had for my mother. My faith in miracles was absolute. Why would the afterlife not include them?

Behind the trio in front, the late-afternoon sun reflected off Lake Walden's rippling surface. The sunshine itself was a small miracle. The rain had stopped just in time for us to wipe dry the white chairs facing the white pergola on Walden's shore. The still-soaked sod warmed in the spring sunshine and might have made it humid save for the cool breeze that had pushed the clouds past and now ruffled Alyssa's train.

Father Joe cleared his throat. "Since Alyssa and Jameson have given themselves to each other through vows before God and these witnesses and have declared the same by joining hands and exchanging rings, I now pronounce them man and wife. What God hath joined together, let no one put asunder."

A chorus of approval rose as Jameson swept his bride off her feet, leaned her back, and tenderly kissed her. I whistled.

My youngest, a bride.

A decade ago, those words had been unthinkable. How much had changed. Glenn and I walked arm in arm to the pavilion behind us to celebrate with our precious family.

Dinner was served under the white canopy, and the sun flared a brilliant pink before sinking into the horizon. When the cake was cut, rope lights lit the revelers' contented faces and the real fun began with music.

After the bride and groom had their first dance, Alyssa turned to Glenn. He rose as the opening chords of "My Sweet Lady" began. Glenn had crooned his best John Denver imitation to a fussy Alyssa in her cradle. Now we all cried watching him sing to her one last time as they circled the floor.

The DJ turned the mood with some favorites accompanied by the frogs in the reeds along the shore. For a while, I watched, finishing my smothered chicken, green beans, and potatoes. I enjoyed having food back in my life and had the thighs to prove it.

Everyone had returned to Detroit for the big event, which made it a rare occasion. Jeff and Tatiana had brought the girls from San Diego. Jenna and her boyfriend, Brian, had flown in from California, taking a break from traveling the world with her camera for Airbnb. Our own Brian Jorgensen had finished his PhD in molecular biology at the University of Nevada, Reno, just two weeks before. And, of course, the bride. Alyssa had just graduated with her degree in kinesiology from Michigan State. All our kids were in good places. I was proud of them.

I felt a tug at my sleeve. Anabella, my three-year-old granddaughter, looked expectantly up at me. A young mirror of her mother, her sweet, dark eyes contradicted the playful smile and lighter hair that were all Jeff's doing.

"Come on, Grandma. Let's dance!"

I stood. Tatiana approached with two-year-old Adeline. We danced together while Jeff documented the festivities from behind an HD camera. At first, I swung arms with Anabella and Adeline by turns, then they wanted to be twirled for Daddy's lens. I lost myself amid our giggling, and before I knew it, a crowd had formed around the four of us. The girls commanded the spotlight, but I bopped along right next to them.

Glenn pushed his way through the mob to join us. Alyssa and Jameson took turns with the girls then, letting Glenn and me dance together. I laughed at the two of us cutting it up, not caring how absurd we looked. A slow melody began, and our granddaughters rushed Glenn.

"Grandpa, me first!" Anabella insisted.

"Me, me!" cried the smallest.

He tried holding them both, but Anabella pouted, unwilling to share Grandpa with her sister. I offered my hands to brown-haired Adeline, who reminded me so much of myself.

"Can I dance with you?"

Her toddler fingers grasped mine as we spun. Beside us, Glenn showed Anabella where to put her hands, his tall form bent for her short arms to reach. Beyond them, Jeff took the opportunity to pull Tatiana into an embrace. Jenna and her boyfriend, Alyssa and Jameson, and our son Brian, who had found a willing partner, all joined the dancing.

Adeline and I skipped in circles, surrounded by those my heart had been given to love. These wonderful human beings had taught me that I had value just in loving them, and they were helping me learn how to express that love and share my truth through writing my story.

"Gan-a, faster!" Adeline's brown eyes met mine.

"Is this what you wanted?" I picked her up and spun us around. She giggled in delight. I joined in, rejoicing over everything God had given me in that moment. I wanted every page of this story.

I wouldn't wish a single gorgeous scene away.

A Final Note

It remains beyond my understanding why God blesses me so abundantly. Although my mother's words carried me through the smoking ruins of my early life, a scripture from 1 John carries me now: "We love Him, because He first loved us."

Along the way, I questioned God's faithfulness and lost my own. Hopelessness assaulted me while I crouched under a frozen pine tree, when I lay torn apart in a fallow field, and as I peered down from a Mexican rooftop. But despite my anger at Him, God redirected Sabrina's family to Detroit, allowed my mother to enlighten my darkest hours, and provided friends and a new family to love me when my own couldn't. God's presence guided every step, from my first stumbling prayer in the loft to Glenn's words of abiding love. Most importantly, God allowed me to lose everything in fiery trials so He could restore my soul from the ashes. He healed my body to make sharing His love easier. I cannot help but adore Him. He loved me first.

My final wish is that my message reaches the bruised and heavy hearts of my fellow survivors:

You are loved, and everything will be okay.
Even ashes can be made beautiful.

Pictures

My mother's family in August 1955 (Uncle Tom, Mom, Grandpa,
Aunt Kathy, and Grandma)

My parents' wedding picture from November 26, 1960

Lisa and me in front of the house on Rhonswood in 1974

Me in 1974

Mom in Mexico in 1982, my shoulder to her left

Mom's last Christmas at Grandma Findlay's house in 1984

My mother, Marlene, eight days before the fire, at a family party on October 6, 1985.
I originally received this from my grandma Findlay that first Christmas after the fire.

My Mustang in front of Molly's house the summer of 1987

Sabrina (on top), Molly, me, and Melissa (left to right)
Taken in the Oak Flat Ranch family room on our ill-conceived trip out west in August 1987.

373

Lita, me and Kevin, sometime in the early 2000s

Bella, me, Julie, and Puddles at my house in July of 2008

374

Camper and Grandma Tatoris, my unofficial grandparents

My Tatoris family (Timmy pictured in inset): (front) Carol, me, Jayme, Jodi, and (back) Julie, Jessi, Justin

Glenn and me
A match made in heaven

Sabrina, Molly, me, and Melissa the night before my wedding

Uncle Ray, Lisa, me, Ashley, and Aunt Kathy at my wedding

Me and Glenn, June 11, 2011

Glenn and me with our family at Alyssa's wedding, May 2019
(left to right: Brian Jacobson, Jenna, Brian, Glenn, Alyssa, Jameson, me, Adeline,
Tatiana, Jeff, and Anabella)

Acknowledgments

A special thanks to Rebecca Shurtleff for helping me transform bullet points into a beautiful flowing story despite having a baby and moving across the world. Thank you for dedicating years of time and for your family's sacrifices that enabled you to help me put what was in my head and heart on paper.

To my husband, Glenn, thank you for encouraging me to share my story with the world. I will be forever grateful for your strength and unfailing love through all the tough times and reliving the painful memories. I love you more than words can say. I am grateful I get to spend forever with you!

For my best friend, Julie, who became a sister to me and included me in her family. I've never felt alone since we met twenty-five years ago. We spent many evenings together, poring over the manuscript with my raw emotions on display. Thank you for helping me navigate this trail, which often felt too overwhelming. You mean the world to me.

All my love to Lisa for being my great protector while growing up. I would not have survived without your sacrifice. I am so grateful for your presence in my life. I know God gave us each other.

Thanks also goes to Ashley Mundell for making me an aunt and being an amazing person. You have always been a shining light in my life. I love you to the moon and back.

Aunt Kathy and Uncle Ray, thank you so much for the love and support that you have been my entire life! I always knew you were there for me and that made a world of difference. I love you more than all the tea in China ... as Grandma used to say to me!

To Kathie Schofield, thank you for sharing your spiritual gifts in counseling, which enabled me to put my soul back together enough to live my life and write this book. I cannot express adequately my gratitude for the many hours that we sat in your office adding my emotions in to complete the first real draft. You helped bring the color back into my world.

Amy Benson gave her editing help and friendship freely. You helped more than you know. You are the best.

I also need to thank Carol Perrett, Leslie Snow, Carol Tatoris, and Carroll Zajdel for being surrogate mothers and supporting me. I love you all and am confident my mother is eternally grateful as well.

I cannot leave out Sabrina Walbrecht, Molly Dayton, Melissa Nielson, Carolyn Grusnick, Tara Childs, and Vicki Petrides for being cherished friends (more sisters than friends) who lived this story with me. I love you for the thousands of memories we created together and for your help remembering the details.

Jodi Atkinson and Jessi Tatoris-Rogers, how can I thank you for adopting me as your sister, along with Julie, Justin, and Jayme—and making me a Tatoris at heart?! Thank you for reading draft after draft. Thank you even more for the decades of family vacations and dinners that included me. I love you more than the apple fritters from Voyager Inn in Batchawana Bay, Canada.

Brian Jorgensen, Jeff Jorgensen, Tatiana Jorgensen, Jenna Jorgensen, Brian Jacobson, Alyssa Donahue, and Jameson Donahue welcomed me as their stepmom and gave their input for making our family better and, also, the book. Each of you is a crucial piece of my "happily ever after." You made my dream of being a mom come true. Words fail me.

Albert and Tiffany Allred have my undying gratitude for introducing me to Glenn and for their friendship, if not the fish soup. You guys are the best Yentas a single gal could wish for.

Kevin Jones-Giddins and Lita Little-Giddins inspired me to record my divine experiences. Thank you for your miraculous contribution to my life and this book.

Nobody can write without a community. Thank you to Kieth Merrill, Gabby Blair, Silvia Allred, Elise Babbel Hahl, RoseAnn Benson, and Barry Rellaford for reading and giving me such wonderful reviews.

Last but not least, thanks to the Eschler Editing team—Angela, AJ, Melissa, Shanda, Sandi, Michele, Lindsay, Chris, and Desiree, with editors Maddie and Brittany—for the expertise you brought to this entire endeavor.

Note to the Reader

Thank you so much for taking the time to read *Beautiful Ashes*. If you've enjoyed my story, it would mean a great deal to me if you could leave a review wherever fine books are sold online—and, of course, spread the word!

Thank you so much for taking the time to read *Beautiful Ashes*. I hope sharing my story inspires you to climb life's mountains with peace, purpose, and resilience. You can find additional resources for overcoming adversity at beautifulashesmemoir.com. While there, you can also sign up for my newsletter and find links to my social media, @beautifulashesmemoir. I love hearing from readers. If you want to share your story, ask questions, or inquire about event speaking, please email me at beautifulashesmemoir@gmail.com or via my website.

About the Author

Shelly attended Brigham Young University in Provo, Utah, where she was the first female to graduate with a degree in manufacturing engineering. After graduation, she moved back to her home state of Michigan and landed her dream job as a manufacturing engineer and began her twenty-plus-year career with Ford Motor Company. A few years into her engineering career, she decided to go back to school to get her MBA.

Shelly has spent over thirty years serving within her church congregation and community. She has always enjoyed serving others and has held volunteer responsibilities in her church and community. Shelly also enjoys woodworking and has amassed the workshop of her dreams. She loves being outside in the fresh air, trail riding in her ATV and boating and jet-skiing the Great Lakes.

Shelly is happily married to her husband of ten-plus years, Glenn. She is a stepmother, grandmother of two, and adored aunt of many!

Printed in the USA
CPSIA information can be obtained
at www.ICGtesting.com
LVHW010526041023
760024LV00004B/163